SOUTH ASIA: POLITY, LITERACY AND CONFLICT RESOLUTION

SOUTH ASIA: POLITY, LITERACY AND CONFLICT RESOLUTION

(In 3 Volumes)

Volume 1
(Politics of South Asia)

Editor

Aditya Pandey

ISHA

ISHA BOOKS

Delhi-110033

South Asia: Polity, Literacy and Conflict Resolution
(Politics of South Asia)

Rs. 2500 (Set)
Rs. 835 (Each Volume)

ISBN : 81-8205-211-4 (Set)
ISBN : 81-8205-303-X (Vol. 1)

Published in 2005 in India by
Isha Books
D-43, Prithviraj Road,
Adarsh Nagar, Delhi - 110033
e-mail : ishabooks@hotmail.com

Laser Typesetting at : Global Printers, New Delhi
Printed at : Chawla Offset Press, Delhi

Contents

Preface

South Asia is a sub-region of Asia, comprising the modern states of Bangladesh, Bhutan, India, Maldives, Nepal, Pakistan and Sri Lanka. It ranks among the world's most densely-populated regions in the world. Despite rapid economic growth during the 1990s, the nations in the region have among the lowest per capita incomes in the world. The adult literacy rate in South Asia is 48 percent which is the lowest in the world. The region is fast emerging as the poorest, the most illiterate, the most malnourished, the least gender sensitive, indeed the most deprived region in the world.

South Asia is the land of great ethnic, religious, cultural and linguistic diversity. A well-defined physical region, South Asia's cultural, economic and political identity has been shaped over millennia by a complex combination of external influences at the regional and global scales, and internal dynamics between a variety of cultural and political groups. Political development of South Asian countries are a changing combination of authoritarian and democratic components of polity in transition after Independence. Their combination varies country-wise and changes in the course of socio-economic development which gradually leads to the reduction of the authoritarian component and to the growth and entrenchment of the democratic one. When the nations of South Asia won their independence from the British almost 50 years ago, they were at once united and divided by claims of identity. Unfortunately, the common bonds seem to have been forgotten amidst the current strife along religious and ethnic lines. India, Kashmir, and Sri Lanka or only a few of the most disturbing examples. The conflict between India and Pakistan has a long history, but recently this conflict has become even more alarming due to the increasingly destructive weapons that both sides possess, including short-range nuclear arms.

The region faces substantial challenges as regards economic development, environmental protection, democratic governance, internal and inter-state conflicts, with the added dimension of nuclear capability, and new security issues such as international terrorism. The scale of the problems, the amount of people affected, as well as the potential spill-over effect to the rest of the world, make it imperative both for the South Asian countries and the international community to address these issues. The South Asian challenges are inter-related and mutually reinforcing, and must be addressed in an integrated manner. Despite all these barriers to its sustainable development, South Asia is in a period of transition as it strives to implement effective economic, political, social, and legal structures to support sustained growth. Besides state governments, international, national and regional organisations are working for human development and peace in this region.

The present publication in three volumes provides an in-depth analysis of the political, socio-economic, educational and security situation and ongoing patterns of social change in South Asia. The first volume *Politics of South Asia* deals with the political situation of the region including critical issues such as geopolitics, caste politics, communal violence, status of minorities, women's participation in politics and regional cooperation, etc. The second volume *Literacy and Development in South Asia* describes the educational status and human development in the region. The major topics discussed are: education and socioeconomic development; strategy for education development; education for human development; environmental education; women literacy; functional literacy; role continuing education and human resource development. The third volume *Conflicts in South Asia* discusses issues such as multi-level security challenges; nuclear conflicts; trends in politicisation and militarisation; women and conflicts; terrorism; interstate conflicts ; human rights violations and democratic peace etc. This work will be a highly valuable reference tool for scholars, policy planners, students and teachers and researchers. It is intended to afford readers the opportunity to become intimately familiar with the key aspects which determine the sustainable development and bright future of South Asia.

Editor

1

Introduction

South Asia is the land of great ethnic, religious, cultural and linguistic diversity. Political development of South Asian countries are a changing combination of authoritarian and democratic components of polity in transition after Independence. Their combination varies country-wise and changes in the course of socio-economic development which gradually leads to the reduction of the authoritarian component and to the growth and entrenchment of the democratic one. It can be viewed as the first and the major regularity of the process of democratization in South Asia as well as in many other developing countries and even in some major developed countries after World War II and currently in succession states of the former Soviet Union including Russia but save one state which is in fact under a kind of totalitarian regime.

The authoritarian component is conditioned fist and foremost by the absence of a d competitive multiparty system capable to provide a stable governance and economic development which in this case can be provided by the authoritarian component of the system, be it one-party dominance in essentially democratic political set-up, as in India, or even by the prevailing authoritarian military regime or civilian rule under military control, as in Pakistan. In a South Asian country no regime can dispense with measures for economic development and even a military or military controlled rule cannot dispense with some democratic forms while striving to limit them and prevent their growth.

The democratic component becomes increasingly indispensable for objectively required for transitional society approaching developed one which is a changing society and as such it requires orderly changes of governmental policies and consequently of orderly changes of political leadership as well as the achievement of a balance of conflicting and opposite interests. Hence it can be said that the progress of developing society requires a political system that contain both authoritarian and democratic components at the initial critical stage of democratization. The process of democratization is far from unilinear. It suffered set-backs and interruptions by spells of increased authoritarianism. While eventually resulting from socio-economic development democracy is achieved through political struggle.

In the fifty years of post-colonial existence there has been a weakening of social and political cohesion and the societies are progressively moving towards a violent socio-political order. The relationship between the State and civil society is exemplified by violence, exhibiting a lack of faith in the normative mode of political bargaining. Increasingly, ethnic groups and social classes are negotiating with the State in the idiom of violence as a means of articulating their demands. The rise of this phenomena is largely an outcome of the socio-political and economic processes

Colonial rule in the subcontinent was not subjected to so much of violence as is the case today with the post-colonial states. Though colonial history in the subcontinent was marked by uprisings, rebellions and mutinies, they were a localized and short-lived phenomenon or a response to specific issues. Probably the 1857 mutiny, often characterized as the first national war of independence, had a wider dimension and included various 'nationalist' forces in an armed uprising against the colonial power. India's subsequent history of freedom struggle is replete with sporadic acts of violence with the intent of terrorizing the colonial rulers to relinquish power.

However, these events were largely limited to geographical regions like Punjab and Bengal. Although the nationalist leaders who believed that the colonial powers could be forced to give up power were very popular, they failed to build a mass base. Since there was no common programme of action, attempts to coordinate activities of various revolutionary nationalists also did not succeed. Moreover, this belief was subsumed under a much more dominant ideology of non-violence and pacifism propounded by Mahatma Gandhi.

Notwithstanding these uprisings, the British were able to consolidate their political and military hold by the latter part of the 19th century. However, after the Second World War, they could no longer sustain this control and transferred political power to the indigenous bureaucratic and bourgeois class. Thus in South Asia, India and Pakistan (with a common pre-independence history) and Sri Lanka gained independence without any militant or armed struggle, unlike certain other Asian and African countries. In fact, Sri Lanka was granted independence without even a semblance of a national movement.

The indigenous rulers were not able to exercise the same political and military control as the British did. Soon after independence, most South Asian states were faced with various kinds of domestic conflicts. Some conflicts were resolved and some lost momentum, but some took the shape of insurgent movements, which predominantly made use of violence to articulate their demands. Sporadic outbursts of violence by peasants, tribesmen, religious groups or guerrilla movements took place. Communist-led peasant insurgency was initiated shortly before and after independence in North Bengal known as the Tebhaga uprising, and in Telengana, in the former princely state of Hyderabad, during the uncertainties of the transition of power. These were, however, localized actions, confined largely to particular tribal or low caste groups or to a narrow range of peasant classes.

Over the years, violence arising from ethnicity and sub-nationalism have become the main challenge to the creation of a national identity in these states and has dominated the political space. Post-colonial history is replete with violent movements arising from the demands of secession by the Bengalis, Baluchis, Nagas, Mizos, Assamese, Sikhs, Kashmiris and Tamils. Peasant insurgencies charged by ideological fervour have been far more infrequent and of lesser intensity.

Violence as a subject of political inquiry has been a complex issue. The treatment has been mainly normative. Even within the realm of politics, analysts invariably take recourse to socio-psychological, cultural and anthropological explanations to understand the phenomena. This problem is much more pertinent in the case of South Asia. Despite the increasing use of violence, whether in the assertion of an identity or for the purposes of structural change, as a dominant mode of political action in the subcontinent, enough attention does not seem to have been given to this problem.

Being post-colonial States, South Asian States are still trying to adjust to new political institutions and socio-economic structures. In a situation of scarce resources the State becomes the principal means of access to and control of resources. In such societies politicized social groups arrive at the view that their everyday struggles for livelihood have to be fought not only in the market and within civil society but also in the arena of the control of the state. The state and its resources thus become objects of considerable political attention. Its only when the politicized social groups fail to manoeuvre, negotiate and bargain within the political space that they resort to violence.

Thus, the process of identity formation and assertion are enmeshed in secular economic interests. The demands for political autonomy to fulfil developmental aspirations are, therefore, being articulated in the language of ethnicity. While most separatist violence in South Asia is based on the assertion of a distinctive identity, the question that needs to be addressed is whether the underlying causes were economic exploitation, economic neglect, and relative deprivation.

While the development process has engendered violence, in a paradoxical way violence in turn tends to be dysfunctional in the development process and retard the pace of economic growth. This happens in two ways. Firstly, by a deliberate strategy of economic disruption followed by the insurgents. This strategy involves damaging State and private property, disrupting the public sector economy, and disorganizing public transport and other essential services and militarily targeting development projects which might erode the support base of the insurgents. Secondly, the State is compelled to divert limited resources to counter the challenge posed by the insurgents. The environment created due to the use of violence on the other hand acts as a major constraint on the growth of the economy to enlarge the economic cake for further sharing and redistribution. This process further retards socio-economic development. Thus in a cyclical way one process generates the other.

British colonial rule being essentially authoritarian introduced particularly at its later stage certain limited and avowedly elitist representative institutions and rule of law that were among pre-requisites for subsequent democratization along with its indigenous historical pre-requisites which emerged both in pre-colonial times and especially in colonial period primarily through the rise and growth of organized freedom movement. However Partition in 1947 largely, albeit not wholly, resulting from colonial policy of 'divide and rule' prevented equal realization of already existing pre-requisites for democratization in the entire subcontinent and consequently led to essential differences between political conditions in its two major newly independent states.

Independent India inherited most of the benefits that ensued from a limited modernization (the present author calls it 'elitist modernization' in its social dimension) as well as most of the benefits ensued from the rise of organized freedom movement led by a national association turning political party, the Indian National Congress under Mahatma Gandhi. Gandhian non-violence meant in fact modern actions of democratic protest conducted by his own specific methods and given his own ideological interpretation. A certain unity of numerous (in absolute terms) and highly diverse middle classes and a broad mass following achieved mostly under Gandhian leadership as well as a widespread organization throughout the country enabled the INC to proceed as the dominant party after Independence. Along with the centralized bureaucratic structure, 'the steel frame' political dominance of the INC provided for stable governance and largely for political stability in essentially democratic set-up and that too in critical conditions of early years of independent national development of a vast and most diverse country.

Pakistan comprising certain relatively less developed areas of the subcontinent lacked above positive factors. It lacked the traditional centre of governance as well as the major industrial centers of former colonial India. The Muslim League was weak in areas that formed Pakistan. It could not play the role of the dominant party and soon become actually defunct while small and tiny political formations were mushrooming. As if this situation by itself was not enough for authoritarian regime to rise the two " wings" of the then Pakistan could not be held together otherwise but by authoritarian rule and that too by precisely the military one which took over after the defeat of the Muslim League in the elections in East Pakistan in 1954.

The continued tangle with a stronger India especially in conditions of cold war stimulated further militarization of governance and the entrenchment of the military in the polity so that when direct military rule alternated with civilian one the latter remained under control of the military. Nevertheless certain elements of democratization were emerging and conceded in the course of time. One-party dominance of the INC continued for about forty years, as was largely the case of dominant parties in certain big developed countries, namely in the FRG it continued for nearly 20 years, and in Italy and Japan for some 40 years after World War II obvious differences between India and these countries notwithstanding.

Meanwhile particularly in India one-party dominance was a major authoritarian component of essentially democratic political system. It limited competitiveness in political process and led to the rise of concentrated personal power of the prime minister even of dynastic nature in what has been called prime minister system in a parliamentary republic. On the other hand socioeconomic development stimulated by reformist policies of the INC government and engendered the rise of opposition parties essentially free in India and ultimately capable to present a viable alternative to the dominant INC initially at the level of states and later at the national level.

The rise of opposition parties capable to present an alternative to the dominant party means the emergence of what the present author calls a system of alternative parties which is both similar to regular two-party system in its political role and different from in composition. The two main contenders for power are coalitions of several (even numerous) parties formed around the two major parties. Obviously, the emergence of system of alternative parties as well as coalition politics inseparable from it are regularities (the second and third) of democratization particularly characteristic for India and in some way or other for the rest of South Asian countries. The emergence of alternative parties out of plethora of small and tiny parties that mushroomed after Independence resulted from what can be called regional development of opposition parties. It is particularly characteristic for India vast and highly diverse ethnically and otherwise.

Under one-party dominance of the INC an opposition party, whether recognized as a 'national party' having some following in several states or as a'state party' with a certain following in one state, could acquire a substantial electoral strength merely in a few state or in one state only. Consequently the emergent alternative parties were different in different states. It made a great obstacle to the rise of an alternative party at the national level. The obstacle was eventually overcome but not otherwise as through coalition politics. Even in the states the emergent alternative parties could effectively compete with INC in the elections to state legislative assemblies as a rule only in coalitions with smaller parties.

Meanwhile coalition politics were resorted to by the opposition just when the first signs of the weakening of Congress mass influence appeared mostly in the 1960s, but opposition parties influential enough to be alternative had not yet risen even at the state level although there were already some rare exceptions. In India one can discern two successive types of coalitions, which reflected the development of competitive multiparty system. In a number of Indian states where the INC was defeated in 1967 assembly elections state governments were formed by several different and disparate opposition parties none of which was big enough to claim any leading role. The author called them 'coreless coalitions'. The state governments formed by such coalitions proved utterly unstable.

The Janata Party which came to power at the Centre in 1977 winning the Lok Sabha elections was in fact a coreless coalition and was short-lived. Afterwards, in the 1980s in several states coalitions of opposition parties were formed around bigger parties which rose by that time in the respective states as alternative ones. The coalitions of this type were called by the author 'core-based' coalitions. They formed reasonably stable governments in the states and so was the BJP-led coalition government at the Centre in 1999 - 2004. The fate of the present INC-led government remains to be seen.

The popular vote for both the INC and the BJP themselves in 1999 - 2004 is far from impressive and it even somewhat decreased: for the INC now at the head of the wining coalition-from 28.3% in 1999 to 26.7% in 2004, and for the BJP at the head of now losing coalition - from 23.8% to 22.2%. In 1999 the BJP-led coalition of which 15 parties got represented in the Lok Sabha won parliamentary majority albeit not big - about 55% of seats, whereas now the INC-led coalition won only some 40% of seats shared by 11 parties and in fact formed a minority government. Be that as it may, one-party dominance has been replaced by a system of alternative parties one of which is the INC itself but only as an alternative party.

Whatever course India's political development may further take the restoration of one-party dominance is obviously excluded. Along with some decrease of popular vote for the INC and the BJP the vote for the national parties taken together also decreased - from 67.1% in 1999 to 63.1% in 2004 whereas the vote for state parties increased - from 26.9% to 28.8%.The vote for smaller and tiny parties ('registered ') increased still less - from 3.2% to 4.0% while the independents polled a little more - 4.2% as against 2.7% polled by them in 1999. These changes are not very significant. The national parties have nearly two thirds of popular vote, of them the INC and the BJP together - 48.9%, the other four national parties - 14.2%. The majority with the national parties in parliament is still much greater than their share of popular vote. The state parties are mostly as avowed protagonists of unity and integrity of India as are the national parties.

The sense of the unity of the country is deep rooted in popular consciousness and has not been shaken individual separatist attacks. An essentially democratic political set-up has been a major factor for India's unity and integrity along with economic planning and regulation, the administrative 'steel frame' and last but far not least one-party dominance of the INC at the critical stage. The present coalition structure of government at the Centre is likely to promote federalism as the twin of political democracy. The development and consolidation of federalism proceeding now in India is one more, the fourth, regularity of democratization.

The emergence of a system of alternative parties together with coalition politics reflecting the trend towards a fully competitive multiparty system is interconnected with the decrease of differences between major contending parties on the main issues and principles of organization of society and its development (as shown by a content analysis of election manifestos done by the present author). In fact it means the prevailing acceptance of the main principals of democracy. In other words it is the transition from confrontation to competition being the fifth regularity of democratization. This transition largely conditioned the very emergence of alternative parties along with the development of coalition polities from coreless to core-based coalitions. It proceeded mainly after the climax of reformist policies of building a mixed economy and of agrarian reforms pursued by the INC government and intensified on the threshold of the 1960s and 1970s.

More or less similar radicalization of governmental policies in response to rising popular struggles particularly of the widening sections of the middle classes from below and of industrial labour and the awakening rural poor took place in all South Asian countries. The climax of reformist policies was accompanied by acute political confrontation and struggles including the rise of left and right extremism in a kind of revolutionary crisis, which in India led to emergency in1975-76 and to a much graver spell of authoritarianism in Pakistan in the new independent state Bangladesh. Thereafter economic liberalization was gradually introduced on a certain consensus, in India very gradually.

As has been noted since long, in transitional societies including those in European countries at the early stage of their modernization, the rising new economic, social and political relationships while lacking their own adequate forms and structures penetrate the existing traditional ones and adopt them to new requirements. The dual role of the caste and the rise of caste-based parties in present India is the clearest case in point. On the one hand caste system being an all-pervasive network of essentially self-governing social organizations resembling in a way civil society, has played a role of an indigenous pre-requisite of democratization, as has been noted by various observers albeit in different wordings. On the other hand this strictly hierarchical system embodies and preserves traditional social inequality and depression of the poor.

As a result of socioeconomic development since Independence but first and foremost of competitive general elections and formation of elected local self-government bodies (their deficiencies notwithstanding), the traditionally downtrodden are increasingly turning assertive in overcoming the age-long depression. The major efforts for their liberation were started by Mahatma Gandhi and his followers in the Congress and subsequently taken up by the left parties and democratic organizations defending the rights and interests of the poor who also rely on their caste cohesion for the purpose. Particularly in the areas where the Left are strong, the rural poor still suffering from the privation, now would not allow maltreatment any more, as they say. Often they are still illiterate but not "politically illiterate", as the late Iqbal Narain portrayed the present Indian rural poor. Thus political democracy has facilitated the arduous cause of liberation from social depression. But the still more arduous liberation from poverty of a big mass of people remains a major issue of both socio-economic and political development in India as in the rest of South Asia.

In Pakistan and till the 1990s in Bangladesh military rule alternated with civilian rule so that the time of existence of both the states was near equally divided between military and civilian rule, but the latter was under military control the military retaining their independent establishment ready to take over. Yet in the last analysis the acquiescence to political parties and holding elections, even if manipulated or rigged, tended to undermine authoritarian rule. Characteristically, a military ruler turned president strived to combine his executive powers with a dominant president-led or pro-president party in an elected legislature. However such a party whether led by a general- turned president or by the prime minister in a civilian rule under military control proved unable to get a broad following and to become actually dominant party for more than some time. Yet some of them survived beyond the rule of their patron to become one of the weighty parties in developing multiparty system.

Under a civilian rule in Pakistan in 1988-1999 the party led by the prime minister resembled a dominant party but only in one province albeit in the biggest one. It had to coalesce with two regional parties being itself like a regional party rather than the all-country one. In the decade political parties and the role of the press and local self-government grew. This change materially counted in a situation after the next military coup in 1999. The elections to the National Assembly in 2002 were contested by two alliances of several parties echoing in a way parliamentary elections in India in the same year. The winning alliance led by the party of the general-turned president, the PML (Q) won one fifth of the seats in the national assembly even a little less than what was won (nearly one fourth) by the BJP at the head of the winning alliance in the Lok Sabha elections in 1999.

The National Assembly in Pakistan elected in 1999 was described as "hung" and so was Lok Sabha in India but earlier in the 1990s. Whatever may be further goings-on in Pakistan a certain growth of party politics there has been obvious. Interestingly, India under her republican system had until recently the dominant party like some developed countries mentioned elsewhere above had after World War II. Meanwhile in Pakistan the president from top brass would establish his own party as the dominant one to win elections in addition to his prevailing powers (in Bangladesh one such party was formed in 1978 six months before the elections which it won).Rather similarly in Russia the prevailing constitutional powers of the president were supplemented in 2000 by pro-president dominant party which was formed also some months before the elections and also won a massive majority in 2004 elections to the Duma. Something of the kind was there in Pakistan and Bangladesh but much earlier and much has changed since then.

In Bangladesh soon after the liberation in 1971 the party that led freedom struggle, the BAL first became the dominant party under its leader who inil tiated radical reforms aimed at building a state dominated mixed economy. In 1975 the dominance of the BAL was transformed into one-party rule like that in a totalitarian regime but it was overthrown in the same year by an army coup followed by four coups in 1975-1981. Under the regime of a general as the president (1982-1990) who also led his party, the JP as the dominant one, opposition parties grew and so was the case in Pakistan in the same period and for that matter in India too where however the process (the growth of opposition parties) started much earlier and was rather steady.

In Bangladesh a mass movement for democracy launched by the opposition in urban areas led to termination of authoritarian rule. In 1991 presidential republic was transformed into parliamentary one. The decisive role was played by educated middle classes - mostly employees, professionals, students as well as smaller entrepreneurs and industrial labour. As their Indian counterparts they have had marked traditions of mass actions (hartals, strikes ets), which stemmed from colonial times but were fostered in the struggles for Bengali identity when Bangladesh was a "wing" of Pakistaaan.

Like many different countries after the downfall of authoritarian or totalitarian regime Bangladesh witnessed the explosive multiplication of political parties numbering some 80 in the three parliamentary elections held in 1990s.

Incidentally, this was the case in India too, first in the early years of independence and later, so to say in the second time, in the 1990s when one party dominance of the INC was withering away. In Bangladesh a situation similar in this respect appears likely to be resolved by the rise of a system of alternative parties also like in India. If this being the case, it reflects the progress of democratization at all-South Asia scale. An essential progress of democratization achieved in Bangladesh, a Muslim country is particularly indicative.

In the three elections held in Bangladesh in the 1990s the main contenders were the two major parties, the BNP and the BML coalescing with several smaller parties in 'core-based' coalitions and alternating in office. However although the elections were held under care-taker governments to provide for fair and free elections (by itself an impressive innovation) the election results were challenged by the losing party and its allies, which resulted in what was called "hartal rule". Something similar was occurring in India (bandhs etc) but mostly in the 1960s and the issues there were mostly economic rather than those of violation of electoral process. "Hartal rule" reflected a current lack of acceptance of democratic electoral practice that nevertheless paves its way.

Sri Lanka, a much smaller but more developed country in terms of per capita indices than the above three countries, has had a kind of two party system and coalition politics since the 1950s in a parliamentary republic. However an acute political confrontation resulting from a certain radicalization of reformism of the SLFP government formed in a coalition with two left parties in 1970, entailed the introduction of presidential system after the electoral victory of another major party the UNP in 1972. This presidential system in a French style engendered a cohabitation of the two major parties. Essentially democratic political setup has been preserved in Sri Lanka in spite of a leftist rebellion in the early 1970s and in spite of a much deeper and protracted armed ethnic conflict which only now appears to approach its resolution.

Various differences between South Asian countries notwithstanding their political development has revealed certain common trends and "waves" similar in content and simultaneously rising and that too not only within South Asia but also in many other countries and thus having a certain global scale. In the late 1960s and the early 1970 the climax of social economic reformism and upsurge of political struggle like that in a revolution in all South Asian countries marked the fist major period of their independent national development which can be viewed as the revolutionary period or stage. Of the four top reformist leaders of South Asian countries three, Mujibur Rahman, Zulfikar Ali Bhutto and Indira Gandhi lost their lives and one, Sirimavo Bandaranaike was disqualified for some time.

From the late 1970s and early 1980s South Asian courtiers entered a new stage marked by a gradually rising wave of political democratization. Its results are yet to be consolidated and advanced. The major obstacle is communalism that plagued politics before and after Independence. Now it has markedly evolved into fundamentalism challenging the basic principles of democracy and breeding terrorist killers. Yet fundamentalism, whether hinduist or islamist or any other is far from being a prevailing trend in South Asian countries but undoubtedly it presents a murderous danger. The effective antidote is yet to be produced by continued soco-economic and political development as well as by national and international security efforts.

2

Women's Political Participation

South Asia can be observed a common trend of attempts to institutionalise women's participation in politics by legal and affirmative measures, which then get manifested in actions taken by the State or political parties. In this chapter we can see the political participation of women in the countries of the region, both historically and contemporaneously, with a particular focus on the formal participation of women in politics, both as voters and as elected members.

South Asian nations share certain predominant features: centralised governments; socio-economic inequalities based on class, gender and caste; and nationalistic divisive claims on grounds of ethnicity, language and religion. India and Sri Lanka have remained democracies for the past 50 years, while Bangladesh and Pakistan have been swinging between democracy, militarism and autocracy. Nepal has passed from democracy to absolute monarchy and back to democracy.

In a region of rich diversity-a mosaic of cultural heritage challenged by the problems of poverty, illiteracy, health, gender imbalance and religious fundamentalism-South Asian women have borne the greatest burden of poverty, deprivation, illiteracy and morbidity. They have also been the major victims of violence. Yet, contradictorily enough, it is also South Asia that has mobilised thousands of women through grass-roots initiatives in rural areas, as in the example of the Grameen Bank project in Bangladesh.

The issues that engage South Asian women politically are familiar to women elsewhere. These include resistance to militarism, the desire to become equal partners in new democracies, and a frustration about women's lack of representation in economic development programmes. Women's participation in political and social movements is evident in South Asia, as they have played important roles in mass mobilisation, and supportive roles in enabling the male leadership to remain in the forefront of political struggles.

Male dominance in the formal political systems of South Asia is universal, but the degree of dominance may vary from country to country or regime to regime. Even when women do become a part of the formal political process as members of elite political groups, they are usually assigned to soft portfolios 'appropriate' for women's concerns. The many barriers to political participation that South Asian women face exist at different levels, both formal and informal, and they arise from socio-cultural values and practices that are firmly entrenched in systems and structures of society. By and large, in the entire Indian subcontinent, women who interact outside prescribed relations are viewed with suspicion. The family still regards its female members as weak and in need of protection throughout their lives. It is a popular perception that politics is a 'dirty game' not meant for women.

The institution of purdah is widespread across Pakistan and Bangladesh, and in the northern regions of India. Purdah sharply demarcates and divides public and private spheres, in such a way that the former are designated as male domains, and the latter, female. Purdah and rigidly defined sex roles have also contributed to the low levels of female literacy, work participation and education. Combined with patriarchal structures, purdah has undermined women's access to traditional forums of adjudication and decision-making, like panchayats, jirgas, etc., on the one hand, and has become an obstacle for women's entry into formal electoral politics, on the other. Affirmative measures have ameliorated the situation to some extent.

Illiteracy further limits women's participation. The female literacy rate in South Asia, with the exception of Sri Lanka, is much lower than the male. But even beyond basic literacy, information about political processes-for example, which levels of government to access for policies that respond to women's interests, or even how and where to vote-is often difficult for women to obtain. Trade unions, political parties and other organisations-the most common sources of such information-are virtually inaccessible to most women.

Violence against women further restricts their political activity. Where women raise their voices, challenge the authority of men, or devote time and resources to political activism, they often risk provoking the violent anger of male relatives, neighbours and community leaders. Ethnic and religious violence further exacerbates the situation. There are broad regional variations, as well as rural and urban differences, with regard to women's opportunities and access to resources. But, throughout the region, women operate within fairly stringent manifestations of patriarchal structures and attitudes that devalue women's remunerated work, and promote her role as wife and mother. These attitudes permeate policy-making bodies, where women's representation is too small to make a significant impact. Development policies and, more importantly, budgetary allocations for women's programmes are insufficient. Priority is given to economic development rather than social sectors.

Political Struggle

India was under British colonial rule for approximately 200 years, and became an independent State in 1947. India then encompassed today's Pakistan and Bangladesh. Indian women's involvement in politics started in the late 18th and early 19th centuries. Although British imperialism profoundly influenced the political engagement of both elite and non-elite women during this period, its impact on the character and purpose of their engagement was very different. Non-elite women fought against the British colonialists. Moved by the hunger of their children, the British confiscation of their land, and oppressive taxes, women participated alongside men in 'famine revolts' in the late 18th and 19th centuries, and other revolts in the 19th century.

In 1947, with the end of British colonial rule and partition from India, Bengal became East Pakistan. The marriage with West Pakistan proved incompatible over issues ranging from language to economic exploitation of the east wing, and domination by the bureaucracy and military of West Pakistan. In 1971, Bangladesh was born to fulfil the dreams and aspirations of the people. Historically, two important movements characterised South Asia. One was the political movement of challenge and resistance to British colonialism, and the other, the social movement to reform traditional structures.

The national movement against British colonial rule in undivided India, spearheaded by Mahatma Gandhi, was instrumental in bringing women in large numbers into the public space. Gandhi played a crucial role in creating a favourable atmosphere for women's participation in the freedom struggle by insisting that the struggle for women's equality was an integral part of the movement of swaraj. His choice of non-violent satyagraha as the mode of struggle also allowed women to play a far more active and creative role than was possible in more masculine-oriented movements.

While he wanted a vanguard role for women in the freedom movement, Gandhi did not encourage women to compete for power. Rather, he wanted them to enter public life as selfless, devoted social workers to undertake the crucial task of social reconstruction. He wanted women to cleanse politics, to feminise it by bringing in the spirit of selfless sacrifice, rather than compete with men in grabbing power, and thus prove their moral superiority even in the realm of politics. In Gandhi's view, "Women are the embodiment of sacrifice, and her advent to public life should, therefore, result in purifying it, in restraining unbridled ambition and accumulation of property." Gandhi, therefore, created a political space for women within the patriarchal system, projecting the concept of women's role being complementary to men's, and embodying virtues of sacrifice and suffering.

Gandhi, however, was very conscious of the power that women could have in a struggle based on the concept of non-cooperation. He stressed the importance of their participation in political and social matters, and exhorted them to join the nationalist struggle. Gandhi, therefore, played a vital role in attempting to feminise the nationalist movement in India. In the process, the values and views that he espoused influenced and shaped the women's movement in the early phase of independence of the other nations of the region.

The leading South Asian social and religious reformers in the 19th century were males, whose principal objective was to cleanse and reinforce family life. For those early pioneers, women were, at first, objects of their emancipatory efforts. But, in the course of the 19th and 20th centuries, they became more and more subjects in the political and social spheres, as is clear from the examples of women's political struggles around a variety of issues in the countries of the region. Yet, the basic understanding of the national movement's leaders on women's issues continued to be filtered through the existing patriarchal system.

Women of India participated in demonstrations such as the all-night dharnas of 1930 against foreign cloth, and in selling `the salt of freedom' during the salt satyagraha. These campaigns succeeded in breaking the myth of segregation. They also articulated liberal sentiments like suffrage rights. To advocate women's equality and their right to participate in nationalist politics, the All India Women's Conference (AIWC) was formed in 1927 through an amalgamation of various regional women's groups. It also spearheaded constitutional reforms and other provisions for women. Consisting of reformist, revivalist and radical streams, the AIWC played a critical role during the freedom struggle, and helped women systematically articulate their political rights in public forums.

The 1946 election in Pakistan, two Muslim women, Begum Jahanara Shahnawaz and Begum Shaista Ikramullah, were elected to the Central Constituent Assembly. That same year, Muslim women organised and held demonstrations to prevent the government's refusal to allow the Muslim League to form a ministry. Violence was used against the women demonstrators, and they were arrested as well. Initially, most of these activities were confined to Lahore and Karachi. However, the civil disobedience movement of January 1947 mobilised even the Pathan women, considered the most conservative in the subcontinent. They marched in support of the movement, publicly unveiled for the first time. The most interesting form of political participation was the secret organisation called the War Council, formed by the Pathans, in which women helped run an underground radio station until independence.

By 1947, Muslim women were organising funds for the Pakistan movement, fighting oppression on the streets, and addressing issues such as education. The greatest numbers of women were not mobilised around issues relating to women's rights or their political and legal status. Instead, the rallying cause was the Muslim homeland. The women believed that the newly created government would automatically expand women's rights and open avenues for their participation at all levels.

In Bangladesh, the provincial education minister, Abdul Hamid, decided to close down the girls' schools, as there were not enough teachers and students. Jobeda Khatun Chowdhury, the first Muslim woman politician of East Pakistan, resisted the closure of Sylhet Women's College. She sought an interview with the minister on this matter. He stipulated a one-year period to enrol the requisite number of students; otherwise, the college would be closed down. Jobeda and a few other dedicated women then began a door-to-door campaign in search of students. They succeeded, and the college remained open.

In the 1940s, the people of Nepal were greatly influenced by India's freedom struggle against British colonial rule. They rose against the Rana regime, which had suppressed the growing people's movement for democracy. Women started coming together, and from 1947 until 1952, several women's organisations were born to raise the political and social consciousness among women in Nepal. In 1960, the King of Nepal subverted the democratic panchayat system to an autocratic one. This put a sudden end to all associations and their activities. Women, however, remained politically active.

In protest against the undemocratic royal proclamation of 1960, a group of women openly waved black flags in a public procession, and were imprisoned. Later, in the people's movement of 1989, women actively participated to get rid of the autocratic panchayat system and to usher in a multiparty, democratic system. Women of various regions and ideologies contributed greatly to the success of this movement.

In Sri Lanka, the erstwhile Ceylon, several movements characterised the fight against British rule. The Suriyamal campaign, which was started as a counter to the sale of poppies to assist British soldiers, was the training ground for the rise of the leftwing socialist movement in Sri Lanka, which spearheaded activities against British imperialism. For the first time, women entered radical politics. They became vocal and visible, and a variety of women's organisations emerged, like the Mothers' Union, the Ceylon Women's Union, the Women's Franchise Union, the Women's Political Union and the Lanka Mahila Samiti. The formation of the Eksath Kantha Peramuna was another great event in the political history of the country. It was the first autonomous socialist women's group in Sri Lanka. This party asserted its socialist policies in its declaration seeking changes in the fundamental structure of society. The women of these organisations continued to take part in active politics as members of parliament and cabinet ministers.

The fight for women's suffrage was a long-drawn one. The debate about women's voting rights go back to the early part of the last century, and the course of its articulation acquired a very urban and elitist character in undivided India. In 1917, when Lord Montague discussed Indian demands for political representation, women's wings of political parties raised the issue of women's suffrage. With the support of two national political parties, the Government of India Act was passed in 1919, which granted voting rights to the provincial assemblies, albeit based on wifehood, property and education. In 1935, the Act was extended to allow women to participate in elections to the Central Assembly. These rights were not donated to women by male leaders, but arose spontaneously as demands from the women themselves. Women's advocacy came mainly from the upper echelons of society, from those who had a close rapport with the leaders of the Indian national movement.

The urban and class bias of the Act that granted women suffrage was evident even a decade later. Women in modern Bangladesh first gained the right to vote in the Calcutta municipal elections. In the 1946 election, under the Government of India Act, special enfranchisement provisions were made. Around 6,600,000 women voted under this arrangement. To vote, a woman had to have one of these attributes: be a tax payer; an owner of property worth Rs 5,000; be at least 21 years old; be literate enough to be able to write her own application for registration; or be the wife of a voter. This arrangement did not provide for universal adult franchise, and restricted voting privileges to urban women. Therefore, very few women qualified as voters. Rural women acquired the right to vote in local government elections as late as 1956. Though they had the right to vote, they were not encouraged to run for office.

The class character of women also had a bearing on women's suffrage in Sri Lanka. The Ceylon National Congress formed the Women's Franchise Union to demand universal adult suffrage. The women who were instrumental in forming the Franchise Union were all from aristocratic families and, interestingly, were actively supported and encouraged by their husbands and sons. As a result of their efforts, women of Sri Lanka have had equal political rights alongside men, and universal franchise was introduced in 1931, when the country was still a colony of Britain. Women have, since that period, exercised their votes, and engaged in other forms of political activity.

In Nepal, the Nepal Women's Association mobilised women to fight for women's suffrage during the first election in 1948. However, despite South Asian women's long history of struggle to win suffrage from the State, their battles have moved to the family and the community, where decisions are made by the men. "When, in the 1970 national election, I wanted to cast my vote in favour of the candidate I thought best, my husband beat me, tied me and locked me up with the cows in the cattle shed for 24 hours, without food," recalls Bulu, a woman from Jessore in rural Bangladesh, a survivor and fighter, who is now a videographer of Banchte Sheka, an NGO in Bangladesh.

Bulu is one among the millions of women who have to struggle within the family and the community. In Bangladesh, as recently as 1991, 5,000 women voters were barred from exercising their franchise by a fatwa (religious edict) from religious leaders in Feni constituency. In 1996, the fatwa was passed in other constituencies too. Election-related violence is another factor that prevent more women from exercising their franchise. However, stories of subversion by women, thanks to the secret ballot, emphasises the struggles women wage to exercise the right to vote for a candidate of their choice.

South Asia presents a unique paradox. Almost every country in the region, with the exception of Nepal, has had a woman leader at its helm at some point in time, a phenomenon unparalleled in other regions of the world. Sri Lanka and Bangladesh have had the unique distinction of two women leaders in the course of their political history. This is in stark contrast to the dwindling numbers of women who are elected to national parliaments and legislatures during each election. The high visibility of women leaders is fully matched by the invisibility of women representatives in the national assemblies. This apparent paradox can be explained in terms of a unique phenomenon termed as `over-the-dead-body syndrome' by Diane Kincaid. She observed that, between 1920 and 1970, American women legislators assumed political roles after the deaths of their husbands. The same is true with women leaders of South Asia.

A woman leader derives her legitimacy for leadership from being a close relative of a dead leader, as a wife or a daughter. This phenomenon of catapulting women as leaders from `dynastic' families, and offering limited options to the others for contesting elections, is a part of the common patriarchal legacy of South Asia.

In the case of India, a land of one billion people and the world's largest democracy, representation of women in parliament is very low. With 545 members from across the country, the Lok Sabha, or the lower house of parliament, is a major decision-maker that charts the socio-economic and political lives of the people of India. Although the constitution of India guarantees equal political rights to women under Articles 15 (1) and 15 (3), the proportion of women members in the Lok Sabha, since 1950, has ranged from a low of 3.4 per cent in 1979-80 to 8.1 per cent in 1985-90. Subsequently, to date, the percentage of successful women candidates has not altered much, as Table 1 indicates.

Women's representation in the Rajya Sabha, or the upper house of parliament has, however, increased from 7.7 per cent in 1952 to 15.5 per cent in 1991. The marginalisation of Indian women in politics over the decades is evident from the example of one political party. During the 1930s and 1940s, the number of women leaders at different levels in the Congress party alone outnumbered those found in all parties put together today. Similar instances can be cited for other Indian political parties as well. While all parties claim to be vehicles of social equity, they are unable to encourage women to formally institutionalise their participation.

Table 1. Women's Representation in Lok Sabha

Lok Sabha	Total Seats	No. of women who contested	No. of women elected	Percentage to the total
First	499	—	22	4.4
Second	500	45	27	5.4
Third	503	70	34	6.7
Fourth	523	67	31	5.9
Fifth	521	86	22	4.2
Sixth	544	70	19	3.4
Seventh	544	142	28	5.1
Eight	544	164	44	8.1
Ninth	517	198	27	5.2
Tenth	544	325	39	7.18
Eleventh	544	599	39	7.18
Twelfth	544	271	48	8.8

In the case of Pakistan, in 1985, there were 22 women in the National Assembly of 200 members. Women's representation in legislative bodies peaked in 1988-90, when four women successfully contested in general seats, in addition to the 20 reserved seats, raising their total number to 24. Pakistan also elected its first woman prime minister during that period, and the elections saw a peak in the number of women contesting provincial seats (19), though only one was successful.

However, in 1988, the provision for reserved seats for women lapsed, with disastrous consequences for women in legislative bodies. In the absence of this enabling provision, in 1990, women's representation dropped to two and three women respectively in the National and Provincial Assemblies, with one additional woman being elected on a seat reserved for minorities. The situation in 1995 was hardly better, with

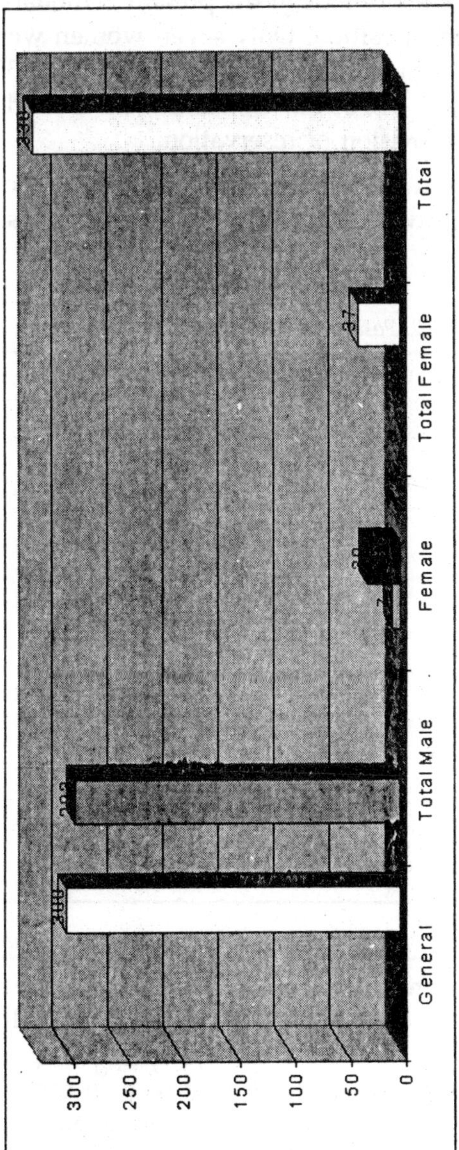

Figure 1. Parliament Members in the National Assembly of Bangladesh

four women sitting in the National Assembly and an equal number in the Provincial Assemblies. In the case of Bangladesh, a cursory look at the present National Assembly reflects women's position. Only seven women were elected directly, and, in a parliament of 330 members, 30 women occupied seats through nominations based on the constitutional provision of reservation.

The position of women in Bangladesh's political parties, of both the rightwing and leftwing ideology, has not been encouraging.

Table 2. Position of Women in Political Parties

Name of party	Party Organ	Total Incumbents	Female Incumbents
Awami League	Presidium & Secretariat	23	4
Awami League	Working Committee	27	Nil
Muslim League (Sabur)	Central Executive	11	3
BNP	National Standing Committee	11	1
BNP	National Executive	114	14
CPB	Central Committee	34	Nil
Democratic League	Central Committee	61	5
JCD	Central Committee	59	1
UPP	Executive Committee	24	Nil

The election manifestos of Bangladesh's major political parties do not incorporate any comprehensive programmes to ensure and encourage women's participation in politics. In both the 1991 and 1996 elections, the major political parties gave election tickets to only three or four women candidates. The manifestos of the political parties did not explicitly deal with women and their issues or concerns, but merely carried small statements on women and development. Only the Jamaat-e-

Islami clearly stated that women could not contest in elections. Though they hold positions in the party, these are nominated ones. The other political parties remained ambivalent on women in politics.

In the case of Nepal, women's access to positions of power in executive bodies and the courts has been limited. In the 25-member panchayat cabinet that was dissolved on 8 April 1990, there was only one female minister, who held the health portfolio. Very few women attained positions of office in panchayat institutions. Of the 140 members in the outgoing national panchayat, eight (5.7 per cent) were women.

In the May 1991 election to the House of Representatives, the final list of the 1,345 candidates included only 81 women (6.6 per cent). In the case of the two leading parties, the Nepali Congress Party had 11 women among its 204 candidates, while the United Marxist-Leninist (UML) party included only nine women among its 177 candidates. At the district and village level, the percentage of women candidates was a dismal 0.3 per cent and 0.9 per cent respectively. The results declared showed that of the 205 candidates elected, seven were women-five from the Nepali Congress Party and two from the UMI. Since the constitution requires that women make up five per cent of the upper house, three women were also nominated to fill the quota.

In Sri-Lanka, the high literacy and education status of women has made little difference to their representation in institutions of governance. There is a glaring gender disparity at all levels, within the national parliament, in local municipal councils, urban councils and pradeshiya sabhas. At present, the representation of women in the national parliament is 4.9 per cent, in provincial councils (which have just completed their five-year term), 3.1 per cent, and in local authorities, at the last elections held in 1997, only 1.1 per cent in the pradeshiya sabha. The 1997 local government elections showed a drop in female participation since 1991. In fact, there is a consistent decline in women's representation. In municipal bodies it came down to 2.3 per cent in 1997, from 2.9 per cent in 1991; in urban councils, from 2.4 per cent in 1991 to 1.0 per cent in 1997; and in the pradeshiya sabha, from 1.6 per cent in 1971 to 1.1 per cent in 1997.

During the recent provincial council elections in Sri Lanka, women's organisations appealed to political parties to field a minimum number of women candidates and to include women's issues in their manifestos. But the escalation of violence, witnessed at recent elections, kept women away from politics. Due to these structural impediments, women's presence in Sri Lanka's parliamentary politics has been low. Though political parties do have women's wings, few nominate women to contest elections. Except for Sirimavo Bandaranaika and Chandrika Kumaranatunga, who headed political parties after their husbands were assassinated and who are at present in power as prime minister and president respectively, no woman has headed a Sri Lankan political party.

An examination of the statistical records of the Department of Elections reveals the small percentage of women candidates who contested both at the national level and in local government elections. In 1970 and in 1977, the percentage of women was 3.4 and 1.9, respectively. These figures have not improved. Though the percentage in the general elections increased to 3.2 in 1989, it dropped to 2.7 in 1994. The only visible improvement, albeit amidst some fluctuations, is the number of women ministers in the cabinet. In 1977 it was 7.1 per cent, and in 1989, just 3.7 per cent, while the present cabinet has 13.7 per cent women ministers.

Several reasons account for the low representation of women in South Asia's national political bodies. Among them is a low priority accorded by political parties to women's candidature. This situation is consistent throughout South Asia. While women form a sizeable proportion of members of political parties across the spectrum of right, centrist and left, they are mostly absent from party leadership and `ghettoised' into women's wings of the parties.

Legislative Reforms and Affirmative Measures

All the countries in South Asia have initiated legislative reforms and undertaken affirmative measures for women's inclusion in politics at various levels, from the national to the grass roots. They differ vastly from one country to the other and present a variety of experiences for women. Since independence, various government initiatives have tried to promote women's political participation, or at least ensure that women are not entirely excluded from political structures. These included the introduction of a quota of reserved seats for women in public office.

At the national level, Pakistan's National Assembly and Bangladesh's Parliament have experimented with a system of reservation for women through indirect elections. The constitutional provision in Pakistan elapsed in 1988, while it is continuing in Bangladesh. In India, the 81st Amendment Bill, which proposed the reservation of one-third seats for women in the parliament and State assemblies, has been through a tempestuous history and is yet to be passed. Over the last few years, the Bill has been subject to acrimonious debate in the parliament and subverted by physical and other means from being passed. A section of parliamentarians who oppose this Bill, base their objections on the provision of blanket reservation for women without ensuring representation of women from socially backward groups.

The new constitution of Nepal, promulgated in 1990, provided women with equal political rights. It states that women can vote, compete in local and national elections, involve in political parties, and support and adopt any political ideology. In 1990, constitutional provisions were introduced that made it mandatory to nominate at least five per cent of women candidates for the House of Representatives, and to provide for seven seats for women in the National Assembly. The only provision added to appease women is the article on election rules (Article 114). The constitution now requires that women amount to at least five per cent of the candidates fielded by each political party in the elections for the House of Representatives.

In Sri Lanka, the ministry of women's affairs has taken an initiative to increase the level of women's participation in local and national bodies. To this end, the ministry's proposal to ensure 25 seats for women through elections has been welcomed in the parliament. The intention of the present government, as announced in its proposals for constitutional reform, is the introduction of a quota of 25 per cent for women in local government elections. Such a quota, at all levels, would make it imperative for parties to include women in their nomination lists. At the grass-roots level, constitutional provisions have ensured reservation for women in India, Bangladesh and Nepal. In India, there is a 33 per cent reservation for women through direct elections to panchayats or local-level self-governance institutions that function in almost every State.

National Level Reservations for Women

In Pakistan, reservation for women's representation in the National Assembly goes back to 1956, and 3 per cent seats were allocated for women through elections. Women voters enjoyed a double franchise to exercise their choice for the general as well as the reserved-seat women candidates. However, the constitutional amendments for this provision have been altered according to the whims of the leaders at different points of time. For example, General Ayub Khan changed the procedure for electing women from a direct to an indirect one in 1962. He mandated deputies of national and provincial assemblies (mostly men) to elect the women representatives. This principle of indirect elections continued, but the reserved seats were increased to 5 per cent in 1973, in both the National and provincial assemblies for a period of ten years.

In 1984, it was doubled to 10 per cent only for the National Assembly, paving the way for 20 women to be indirectly elected. However, this provision lapsed in 1988. In 1989, a bill was moved in the Cabinet, seeking consensus for extending the provisions in the Constitution for reserved seats for women. A decade and several governments later, to date, the bill has not been passed.

The constitution of Bangladesh provides for formal political equality of men and women. Women are entitled to the same fundamental rights as men, including those of association, assembly, speech and expression, which form the basis of political activity in a civil society. Article 65(3) provides for reserved seats for women in the parliament or Jatiya Sangsad. Article 9 promotes the special representation of women in local government. In the first two elections of Bangladesh, in 1973 and 1979, the reservation provision ended up in women being nominated to the parliament. Direct elections to the general seats have become a male privilege.

Women were provided with reservation to ensure a minimum representation in parliament and to give them a wider participation in national politics. However, the provision for reserved seats for women has ended up as a pawn in the hands of politicians, as the following case of President Hussain Mohammad Ershad indicates. President Ershad dissolved Bangladesh's parliament in 1986, to counter opposition moves to destabilise the government. In the election to the third parliament, President Ershad's party, the Jatiya Party, won 153 of the 300 parliamentary seats.

President Ershad desperately needed to bring a constitutional amendment to ratify his illegal usurpation of power from a legally constituted government, and the wrongs and arbitrariness of four years of martial law. To do this, he would have needed 200 votes in a normal 300-member parliament. But the results showed a hung parliament, with the main opposition party, the Awami League, threatening to take over by mustering support from other political blocs and the independents. Given the party positions then, it would have been difficult to win the required majority. However, in a 330-member parliament, President Ershad took all the 30 women seats, taking his party's total to 183.

With additional support from the independents, this rose to 215, just five short of the 220 votes needed for an amendment. As it happened, the Seventh Amendment, which ratified martial law and all actions under it, was introduced in the second session of the third parliament, on 10 November 1986. The session lasted just five hours, and the amendment was passed by 223 votes to nil, amidst an opposition boycott. President Ershad was so paranoid about winning the 30 women seats that he did not trust even his own party members in voting for the party women candidates. He promulgated a special ordinance, which said that if the returning officer receives a nomination paper proposed and seconded by more than half of the eligible voters (MPs), the candidate would be declared automatically elected. In other words, 30 candidates nominated and seconded by 151 MPs would be considered elected, without an actual election being held.

President Ershad's Tenth Amendment of the constitution was his gift to the future parliament, the beneficiary being the Bangladesh National Party (BNP) in 1991 and the Awami League (AL) in 1996. This amendment reintroduced 30 reserved seats for women in parliament. The present provision is that the members of parliament elect candidates for the 30 reserved seats. In practice, this means that the winner takes all. That is, the party that can muster 151 votes can take the 30 additional seats. The majority party nominates 30 women candidates, and since the election to these seats is seen as a foregone conclusion, other parties do not bother to nominate anybody.

The nomination process and the electoral principle of reserved seats for women render women's participation in the legislature dependent on the patronage of the male elite in the party in power. This only accentuates women's dependence and subordination in the political sphere. Reservation also undermines women's representative status. In 1990, the Tenth

Amendment to the constitution re-inserted Clause (3) to Article 65, providing for 30 reserved seats for a further period of 10 years from the first sitting of the next parliament. Several ideas were floated during this time. Among them were the abolition of indirect election of women representatives and filling the reserved seats by direct election from territorial constituencies, and establishing quotas for women nominated by the party to run for general seats.

However, indirect election for the reserved seats found support among a section of women politicians as well, because it eliminated the need for, as well as the risk of, electoral investments, both political and material. The parliament elected in February 1991 contained 30 reserved seats. Several women MPs in reserved seats attained greater political stature and visibility, with commensurate public and political roles, primarily through their association with the BNP and its leadership in the 1980s, personified by the then prime minister, Begum Khaleda Zia.

Today, the women's seats have become a deciding factor for almost all the political parties. The trend in recent elections, where no party wins absolute majority, means that there are only small margins of victory. In such a situation, the reserved seats can decide who forms the government. That is why, despite a decade's lobbying and advocacy by women's groups, Bangladesh's political parties have not amended the system. The women elected by nomination to the parliament do not really represent anyone, except the party that has selected them. Though they have a national geographical constituency, they have few links with it. They cannot be said to represent women in general, as Bangladesh's women themselves have no role in their election. As these women members of parliament have not gone through a competitive election process, they are taken less seriously by their directly elected colleagues, who regard them more as a `vote bank'.

The present trend in Bangladesh politics is for a two-party system. In 1991, the BNP formed a government, based on the support of 31 per cent of the voters. In 1996, the AL repeated the performance, with a 32 per cent share of the votes on its own ticket. It was helped by the `winner takes all' method of electing the 30 additional seats in parliament, a distortion of the concept of democracy. The introduction of direct election for the reserved seats is expected to address the problem to some extent.

More effective would be an amendment of the constitution to introduce a quota for nomination of women candidates by political parties. A mandatory 10 per cent provision would make a big difference in women's political participation. It would also contribute to the process of women building constituencies. Under the present arrangement, there is no accountability, and not many women are engaged in developing their constituencies to enable them to contest from the general seats in the next round. In fact, the method of indirect election has also gained popularity among the women MPs. The women's movement has been questioning the role of the women MPs. At every possible opportunity, they are reminded of their status in parliament and their accountability to women. This has led to an incremental, qualitative change. But the women still do not feel secure enough to question and pressure for major electoral reforms.

Local Level Reservation

India

In April 1993, the Indian government introduced the Panchayat Raj Act (the term panchayat means local, and raj means governance) to amend the constitution to introduce 33 per cent reservation for women in local-level self-government. In addition, it proposed one-third reservation for women as chairpersons and presidents among the elected women members at the different levels. The amendments to the Indian constitution that facilitated this act were the 73rd and 74th Amendments of 1992. The panchayat raj is basically a three-tier structure for local-level self-governance in the States of India, namely, at the district level, at the intermediary block level and at the village level. Together, they pave the way for local-level self-governance in India.

The Panchayat Raj Act legitimizes the role of a total of 2.25 million village councils, 5,100 intermediary councils and 4,750 district councils in the country. This confers decision-making power on around 22.5 million people at the village level. Reservation for women has ensured that one million women have emerged as leaders in the villages of India. The Act also ensures that one-third of the positions for chairpersons are reserved for women. In the first round of elections, five million women stood for elections to the one million seats.

The larger objective of strengthening the panchayati raj in India was to infuse the development process with social justice. Poverty eradication and helping people to access a broad range of rights was envisaged as a corollary to this process. In a society like India, where the process of implementing development projects for the people is circumscribed by power, hierarchies and patronage, the panchayati raj plays a critical role. In an ideal situation, it enables people to decide the course of development, according to their felt needs, and allocate resources to sectors prioritised by them.

The implementation of government-sponsored schemes is ideally decided within a framework of social justice for the poorest and the marginalised. However, the process and experience of substituting a corrupt system of governance with a socially just one has been fraught with problems. And one million women leaders, mostly in rural areas have been catapulted into this system with little experience, to tackle the difficult task of overhauling the system and process of governance.

Various experiences with panchayati raj have been reported from the different regions and States in India. With some exceptions, the common picture that emerges is one of the reluctance of the State governments to give up power and devolve financial resources, and of a bureaucracy reluctant to hand over their decades-old patronage. There is a great deal of scepticism about women leaders, who are viewed as proxies for men. These are very real problems. However, a select review of women's experiences is a fascinating story of how such affirmative measures do make a difference to the process of governance and to the women themselves, despite heavy odds.

Whether it is the backward State of Uttar Pradesh, where illiteracy and other conventional indicators of women's status are poor, or the State of Kerala, which enjoys the highest literacy rates in India and is considered to be relatively better off, women's agency in exercising their leadership roles against many odds in the panchayat is evident. The most common story across India that emerges is one of corruption-free governance strived for by the women leaders. This is not say that women leaders are not corrupt. But, by and large, the stories that emerge tell of women standing up to contractors, enforcing transparency in the system, and facing violence in return, in some instances.

The other common story is about changing priorities in development. Women's practical gender concerns, like water, sanitation, children's education, healthcare, domestic violence and alcohol abuse, are gaining currency within the development agenda of rural areas. A process of empowerment among the leaders is more than evident, particularly when there is access to support structures within the village, such as proximate women's organisations, women's awareness programmes or training and orientation programmes by non-governmental and governmental apparatuses.

Literacy makes a big difference to women's ability and sense of confidence. However, throughout India, whether it is women from the literate State of Kerala or illiterate women from a village in Karnataka, the initial years in office have been characterised by many struggles waged against a patriarchal society, and domination by men in the meetings. These teething problems were overcome in the first two years and "women have gained a sense of empowerment by asserting control over resources, officials and, most of all, by challenging men". Most women leaders report a sense of self-confidence in dealing with officials or giving public speeches, an increase of knowledge in administrative matters, writing reports and ability to conduct meetings.

Women's representation in local-level self-governance institutions has brought out the advantages of proximity. Leaders are available within easy reach to address the problems faced within their geographical constituencies. This has allowed for mobilisation of struggles around a variety of issues affecting the people. For instance, in Kerala, when a moneylender refused to return a woman labourer's jewellery even after she had paid her dues, the leaders of the panchayat went and met him. Though he promised to return the jewellery, he did not. A group of women gathered and sat on strike in front of his shop, threatening dire consequences. The moneylender had to relent. This is just one instance among many, of accountability being demanded from the system.

Bangladesh

In Bangladesh, women's representation to the local bodies has been through several amendments to the constitution. In 1976 and 1977, two presidential ordinances ensured women's representation in local bodies. Later, President Ershad's government passed two more ordinances, in 1982 and 1983, which changed the number of women representatives as well as the procedures for their nomination. Women members were to be nominated to represent each of three wards of a union. The local government Zilla Parishad (Amendment) Bill, 1993 provides for abolishing the system of nominating the chairman and members. Each zilla parishad would now consist of an elected chairman and elected male and female members. It also provided that from each thana of a district, two male and one female members would be elected by the chairman and members of the union parishad under the concerned thana.

Despite several attempts by successive regimes to reform local government institutions, elected local government officials have never enjoyed constitutionally guaranteed political rights since the birth of Bangladesh. Central bureaucratic control over administrative processes, lack of power and capacity to mobilise local resources, lack of women's participation in local government institutions, and institutional inability have all characterised local governance over the past decades. This has created a situation where local governments are neither promoted nor become effective in bringing women into the political arena.

The newly established Local Government Reform Commission, in its report published in 1997, suggested a four-tier democratic local government structure, namely gram parishad (at the village level), union parishad (at the union level), upazilla parishad (at the thana level) and zilla parishad (at the district level). While the report and the new legislation did emphasise the issue of representation, little mention was made of the specific powers and jurisdiction of elected members. The core regulatory functions of administration and the magistracy and judiciary have remained outside the scope of recent reforms. These functions, considered `retained' under the absolute jurisdiction of the bureaucracy, have constituted the main basis of non-democratic governments since the colonial period.

In 1997, during the first year of the Awami League regime, a bill was moved in parliament that sought to reserve three seats for women in each union parishad. The women were to be chosen through direct election, for the first time. The participation of women voters in those elections to local bodies was the highest ever recorded. That was possible due to the creation of an institutional space for women through a constitutional amendment, the Union Parishad Ordinance, which required all women members to be directly elected. Previously, the three reserved seats for women in each union parishad were filled by nomination. The new ordinance provided for the direct election of women to all the three reserved seats.

The 1997 union parishad election significantly increased the participation of women as voters, as contenders for general seats with men and as candidates for reserved seats. Although there was some confusion about whether or not women should contest from the general seats, they did contest. The 1997 election saw more than 46,000 female candidates competing for 12,828 reserved seats. Nearly 4,000 female candidates competed for the general seats. In Gaibandha district, northwest of Bangladesh, 25 female candidates won the elections, defeating their male counterparts. Furthermore, as many as 20 female candidates were elected to the posts of chairpersons.

The negligible number of female chairpersons indicates the marginal political status of women in the local power structure. Nonetheless, the massive participation of women as candidates for directly elected positions will be considered a landmark in the institutionalisation process of women's participation in Bangladesh's politics.

The introduction of direct election to the reserved seats for the local elected bodies is undoubtedly a breakthrough for women in Bangladesh. In no other way could these women have moved into these institutions and participated in them. However, their experience so far has been riddled with diverse problems. In one extreme case, five women union parishad members were raped, one because she refused to give in to her male colleagues. The woman member was not, however, intimidated, and was bold enough to file a complaint with the police. The fact that the police have been negligent is another matter, but her courage will be an example for the other women elected to the parishad.

The entire campaign process was an uphill task for the women candidates. There were media reports of husbands hiding the only sari a woman candidate had, to prevent her from leaving home to campaign. There were also reports of physical abuse. The campaign period was trying, and, on being elected, the women found the situation more complex. They were not allowed to operate as elected members, and, within months, they were complaining against their male counterparts. The pressure they created, along with help from NGOs, led to a meeting with the minister for local government and rural development, and then with the prime minister, at a national convention. The elected women submitted a memorandum of their complaints. That was the first case of assertiveness from women at the local level in Bangladesh.

There is also a gender imbalance in the ratio of men and women. There are more men on the general seats than women. The union parishad functions within a centralised set-up. It is only the chairman and the secretary who have any influence or power in these structures. As a result, participation by the majority of male and female members is a mere formality. The men have also learned to manipulate the system. When convenient, they push their wives or female relatives into electoral politics to perpetuate their own control. The women are elected to the parishad from a constituency of three wards, thus by an electorate three times the size of the voters who elect the male members. Thus, the expectations of, and demands on, the women are greater. This puts them under serious difficulties.

The lack of clear guidelines on the roles and responsibilities of the women members compounds the problem. There is worry that the gap between the expectations of the electorate and the performances of the representatives may end in alienating the women and negatively affecting their future in politics. As it is, the women have no, or very little, experience in running local elected bodies. The elected women now bear an additional burden, as there is no support system to relieve them of domestic responsibilities. Financial dependency is also a serious drawback.

In Bangladesh, religion continues its grip over politics. For the first time, in the 1980s, the government introduced compulsory religious education at the school level. Finally, the Eighth Amendment removed secularism from the constitution, replacing it with Islam as the State religion. Though the local government laws in Bangladesh are progressive, they exist in an entrenched system of patriarchy. It is perhaps too early to expect major changes just because women have been placed in these new political positions

Nepal

At the local level, the new ordinance of 1997, which ensured a 20 per cent reservation of seats for women, has been a breakthrough, and has contributed to the increased participation of women in local elected bodies. One seat is reserved for women in each ward of the Village Development Committee. The new ordinance forced all political parties to support at least one female candidate. This fact encouraged women to get more involved in political activities in Nepal. About 40,000 female candidates were elected in the local elections of 1997. This provision has increased the numerical involvement of women in the local government units. However, their involvement in positions of decision-making and influence is insignificant. Overall, a strong male domination prevails..

Women Leaders

Sirimavo Bandaranaike is the first women prime minister of the world. That was an ominous beginning. It laid down the emotional tracks, which carried all the subsequent women leaders of the region to the most prominent political position in their respective countries. Sirimavo Bandaranaike in Sri

Lanka, Indira Gandhi in India, Benazir Bhutto in Pakistan, Khalida Zia and Hasina Wajed in Bangladesh, and more recently, Chandrika Kumaratunga (Sirimavo Bandaranaike's daughter) in Sri Lanka - all are daughters or widows of Prime Ministers who, with the exception of Jawaharlal Nehru, faced brutal and violent ends.

Benazir Bhutto's father Zulfikar Ali Bhutto was hanged by General Zia; Sirimavo Bandaranaike stepped into her role as the country's Prime Minister after her husband's assassination - so did Khalida Zia in Bangladesh. The present Prime Minister of Bangladesh - Hasina Wajed - is the daughter of Bangladesh's first Prime Minister Mujibur Rahman who was killed one morning, together with 15 members of his family, by four young army officers. These women rode the crest of a massive sympathy wave that landed them in an office they were neither qualified nor trained to hold. All were inexperienced as politicians and some were homemakers and mothers.

In a strongly patriarchal south Asian society, this pantheon of women leaders, Stanley Wolpert feels, may be an "accident of gender". Indira Gandhi was an only child, Benazir Bhutto and Chandrika Kumaratunga are the eldest among siblings - the younger of Benazir's two brothers was found dead in his apartment in France, while Murtaza, seen by many as a political heir to Zulfikar Bhutto, was assassinated in Karachi a few years ago; Hasina Wajed is the sole survivor of a family that was massacred; Chandrika Kumaratunga's younger brother Anura Bandaranaike, unable to deflect his older sister from her political ambitions, joined the Opposition. Sirimavo Bandaranaike and Khalida Zia - were housewives at the time of their personal tragedies, and did not have children old enough to be seated in their father's office.

When Indira Gandhi (1917-1984) first became the Prime Minister of India in 1966, she was 49 years old, had a fine political pedigree, and also a track record of 28 years of close association with the Congress (she had been a member of the

Working Committee and also the President of the party); she had served on various Boards and had also headed a Ministry. In retrospect, even these credentials are not enough for the Prime Minister's Office - it is wisdom and vision that matter. Many groups and Governments were alienated by her myopic policies, not least by her younger son Sanjay, who was feared for his muscle-flexing bully-politics.

Sirimavo Bandaranaike passed away in October 2000, in Colombo. She had just finished serving her third term as Prime Minister - this time under her daughter President Chandrika Kumaratunga. Sirimavo Bandaranaike came from an influential family of Sri Lanka, studied at St. Bridget's Convent in Colombo, married Solomon Bandaranaike, raised a family, and her life was devoted to her role as a mother and a wife. Her husband became the Prime Minister of Ceylon (now Sri Lanka) in 1956 and three years later, in 1959, was killed by a Buddhist monk. Sirimavo stepped into her husband's shoes, aged 44. Her first two terms as Prime Minister were marked by unpopular policies that alienated the country's minority groups, led to ethnic strife and dissension, and also economic stagnation. In 1980 the Parliament barred her from political office but was pardoned six years later.

Benazir Bhutto was 24 years old when General Zia staged a coup, imprisoned her father Zulfikar Bhutto, and executed him in 1979. Benazir and her mother Nusrat Bhutto were put under house arrest, later imprisoned for a while. Benazir spent 5 years in detention. Educated at Radcliffe and Oxford, Benazir won the 1988 elections. She had the nation's goodwill but her focus remained misdirected. She was dismissed 20 months later on charges of incompetence and corruption. Benazir came back to power in 1993 and there was little or no change in her agenda. She was once again dismissed on accusations of corruption. Her husband Asif Zardari is in prison on charges of corruption, she is estranged from her mother, her brother Murtaza was assassinated in Karachi in 1996 - a heavy price to pay for lust of power.

Bangladesh's first woman Prime Minister, Khalida Zia, had led a quiet existence, married to General-turned-President Zia Ur Rahman, and was totally involved in raising their two sons. In 1981 rebel military officers gunned down her husband. She got inducted into politics and a decade later won the election to the Prime Minister's Office. Five years later she lost to Hasina Wajed, daughter of Bangladesh's first Prime Minister Mujibur Rahman, who was assassinated in 1976.

Hasina Wajed was in Germany with her nuclear physicist husband when a group of four young army officers stormed into her father Mujibur Rahman's house in Dhaka and killed all members of the household, including Mujibur Rahman's young grandchildren. The lone survivor of Mujibur Rahman's family, Hasina Wajed was the natural choice for her father's party leadership. She lost the election to Khalida Zia in 1991 but defeated her in the following elections in 1996 to become the country's Prime Minister.

Chandrika Kumaratunga, the current President of Sri Lanka, is the daughter of two Prime Ministers - Solomon and Sirimavo Bandaranaike. Born into a privileged family, Chandrika was educated in Sri Lanka and later studied Political Science at the University of Paris. Her husband, an actor and an aspiring politician, was killed in 1988, and it was after his death that Chandrika Kumaratunga rejoined her mother's party that won the parliamentary elections of August 1994. Only six years after her formal foray into politics, Chandrika, aged 49, first became Prime Minister in 1994, and then, in November of that year, she won the presidential election. She appointed her mother, Sirimavo Bandaranaike, to serve as Prime Minister in her new government. The ongoing ethnic crisis that arose during her mother's tenure, has cost the country heavily in terms of its people, productivity and resources.

Sonia Gandhi, wife of the assassinated leader and former Prime Minister of India, Rajiv Gandhi, was elected to the Office of the President of the Congress party. Sonia shied away from politics for a long time, devoting herself to her children - Rahul and Priyanka - but eventually succumbed to the pressures of the Party stalwarts who needed a 'man' to keep the fortunes of the party together. Her mother-in law Indira Gandhi was often referred to as the only man in her Cabinet. She, however, declined the offer and the opportunity of becoming the Prime Minister of India after the elections earlier this year.

Margaret Thatcher, became the Prime Minister of Great Britain after 27 years of work experience. She had worked as a research chemist and a tax lawyer before she joined the Conservative Party. When she got elected to the Parliament, she was still a long way from 10 Downing Street - it would take her another twenty years to get there. Similarly Golda Meir, Israel's Prime Minister (1969-74), spent forty odd years working hard for various organisations and working her way to the top through sheer devotion and dedication. They were neither wives nor dynastic daughters.

Democratic institutions evolve with vision, hard work and foresight of wise leaders - and leadership is not created overnight. People brought in for emotional reasons interrupt and halt the democratic process, and at times have easily undermined democratic institutions. The quest, and consequent, lust for power is not gender specific. Corruption and insatiable ambition are the hallmark of many a leader in the south Asian region - man or woman. South Asian women need to change this record of political inheritance. There are among them, many who are talented and politically gifted to enter the political arena on their own merit. Asma Jahangir of Pakistan maybe one of them.

Role of Goddessess

The role of the Goddess in Indian political life has been fairly well documented, women's participation in the anti-colonial movement; and the political career of Indira Gandhi. The renewed interest of indology for the Goddess, in order to sketch her successive incarnations and functions, before and after independence. The first political participation of Indian women as a group coincides with the symbolic representation of the Indian nation as a beloved, suffering, deified mother Bharatmata, i.e. "Mother India", a character created by the nationalist Bengali writer Bankim Chandra Chatterjee in a novel published in 1882, Anandmath.

Bharatmata starts her political career, one might say, when the partition of Bengal ordered by the British in 1904 - ostensibly for administrative purposes - gives way to the first mass agitation of Indian nationalism the Swadeshi ("one's own country") movement (1904-1907), advocating the promotion of indigenous productions and national schools freed from the control of the colonizer. Women then participate for the first time in political agitations, demonstrate in the streets, organize big boycotts for imported textiles etc. Bharatmata then comes to embody India, both as a territory and as a people, struggling for her freedom; while Vande Mataram, a hymn to the motherland also found in Anandmath, becomes the anthem of the nationalist movement.

Thus real women find a place for themselves within the anticolonial struggle at the very moment when the Goddess becomes the omnipresent representation of the nationalist cause. Bharatmata has much in common with Durga, as her iconography shows. Like Durga, she rides a lion (or a tiger), and she has the same matronly, smiling face. Durga in fact is the most popular of all incarnations of the militant mother-goddess. In India she is mostly worshipped as Mahisasuramardini ('killer of Mahisasura") during the autumn festival of Dussehra - also called Durga Puja in Bengal, where it is the most important of all Hindu annual festivals. Durga is then represented as a ten-armed woman warrior, brandishing her weapons, riding her lion, and vanquishing the demon-buffalo Mahisasura.

This image refers to a well-known mythical event related in the Devi Mahatmya ("Praise of the Goddess"), a text dating back to the VIIth century AD, which is being read or recitated as an essential component of Durga Puja. The Devi Mahatmya relates how the gods, helpless in front of a formidable demon, Mahisasura, who could be vanquished only by a woman, created Durga, who then indeed slayed him. Bharatmata is a favorite theme of Indian nationalism; a theme illustrated on banners and flags, as well as by artists such as Abanindranath Tagore and Amrita Sher-Gill. From 1930 onwards she is represented as a woman whose body defines the frontiers of the subcontinent, and she definitely becomes, in the words of S.Ramaswamy, "the fetish object of Indian nationalism". As such, she moves, appeals to, in short mobilizes, in the fullest sense of the term, both women and men.

But two leaders, in the Indian Freedom movement, designed mobilization strategies specifically aimed at women. The Mahatma Gandhi on the one hand, and Subhas Chandra Bose - a prominent Bengali leader of the Indian National Congress -on the other hand, were deeply concerned with women's participation in the nationalist struggle. Both were convinced that a new India could be born only with women's full contribution, and both invented new political roles for them, invoking the Goddess as an example for Indian women. In 1930, for instance, he toured Bengal, declaring that, "...women had not only duties to their family, but they had also a greater duty to their country. When the gods found their silver almost vanquished in their fight with the demons, they invoked the help of 'sakti' in the form of mother. The country was in a sad plight, therefore the country looked up to the mothers to come forward and inspire the whole nation."

This epitome of wifely virtue, the chaste, dutiful spouse of the god Ram in the Ramayana (the most popular epic in north India), was invoked by the Mahatma as an example for women. Gandhi was convinced that the participation of women was necessary for India to gain its independence. His political method, relying on nonviolence and the highly symbolic value of activities such as spinning, was meant to involve women fully into the nationalist struggle. Gandhi often drew explicit parallels, in his addresses to women, between Sita's legendary fight against the demon Ravana, and Indian women's fight against the British.

The Goddess thus appears to fulfill one crucial function for any mass movement that of mobilization. Bharatmata is a representation of the nation that deeply touches men and women, because of her striking resemblance with the most popular image of Durga, and because of her emotive appeal as a suffering mother. Sita, on the other hand, is a popular deity called upon by Gandhi mostly for women's use. Sita, the beloved heroine of the Ramayana, is here deliberately construed as a role model for women to engage in the nationalist movement. The mobilization effected by the reference to the Goddess draws upon two distinct, if combined, processes.

Firstly, the ongoing struggle is recast in terms which are familiar to the masses. Durga (through Bharatmata) and Sita lend their popularity to the nationalist cause, conferring upon her an emotional appeal. Secondly, the invocation of the Goddess translates a political endeavour into a religious mission. The ongoing struggle is then endowed with a sacred dimension, simplifying the fight as one of good against evil. The invocation of Sita, which casts, by analogy, the British colonizer into the role of the demon, shows this very clearly. As a result of these two processes, and this is particularly important as far as women are concerned, the invocation of the Goddess legitimizes people's participation in the movement.

The translation of political activism into religious terms transforms its very nature engagement with politics, hitherto synonymous with the public sphere, and thus the preserve of men, can then be construed as performance of one's religious duty, which is opened to women as well. The translation operated through the invocation of the Goddess thus prevents potential role conflicts for women. They can then walk in the streets, mix with strangers, even with men who are not family members, without losing their respectability. They can engage in a traditionally masculine activity without threat to their femininity.

In independent India, the Goddess seems to be associated exclusively to individual women, that is, to women leaders. Foremost among them, of course, is Indira Gandhi, an exceptionally powerful and enduring woman politician. The daughter of Jawaharlal Nehru became the Prime Minister of a country of 500 million people at the age of forty-eight, in 1966; she remained at the head of the Indian government until 1977, and then again from 1980 till her death, in 1984. She was associated to the Goddess in two crucial moments of her political career: after India's military intervention against Pakistan in 1971; and after the declaration of the internal state of Emergency in 1975.

After the Indian army's successful intervention in East Pakistan, which later became Bangladesh, Indira Gandhi was widely represented, on calendars and chromos, as Durga. This was the highest point of her popularity, the moment in her career when her dynastic charisma became a personal one. She then appeared as the champion of democracy, both soldierly and motherly, just like Durga Mahisasuramardini. Five years down the line, her popularity had greatly diminished. Her government was facing a number of economic and political problems, and she was personally accused of favouring corruption through excessive concentration of power. After being accused of electoral fraud, in June 1975, she refused to surrender to what she considered as the forces of disintegration she declared a state of Emergency, jailed her opponents, cancelled elections, put a ban on demonstrations, and, for the first time in the history of the Indian democracy, censored the media..

This interpretation of the painting by Mrs. Gandhi's biographer, the poet Dom Moraes, highlights the degree of criticism that could be conveyed by the reference to the Goddess. The righteous Durga, triumphant on slaying the demon, has indeed another face, that of the more ambiguous Kali, the "Black one", a figure of fury and destruction - although Kali, too, ultimately fights evil. In the Devi Mahatmya, Kali is born from Durga's frown; she seems to embody Durga's furor, surging when Durga loses control or when she faces an awesome enemy. Kali generally threatens stability and order; yet for her worshippers, Kali is also the divine mother, full of compassion. Despite her fearful appearance, Kali, the most important of Hinduism's "fierce" goddesses, is widely worshipped in most of north India, particularly in Bengal, where she is the object of the shakta cult.

Astride on her lion, the Goddess Durga is riding again in our midst. But all are not agreed about who the demons are that she should destroy. Also, most of us wish that the Devi will send her awesome form and appear again as the loving Ambika or the Mother Goddess. Lastly, even Indira Gandhi seemed to identify herself with Durga. More recently, another important Indian female politician has been regularly associated with the Goddess Jayalalitha Jayaram, who was the Chief Minister of the southern state of Tamil Nadu between 1991 and 1996.

Jayalalitha was first known as a popular actress. In Tamil Nadu, cinema has long been a "cultural springboard of politics". MGR built a successful political career on his popularity as an actor, and was the Chief Minister of the State from 1977 to his death in 1987. Jayalalitha, however, had to build her political career not upon her fame as an actress, but against it. Jayalalitha started representing herself as a Goddess during the electoral campaign of 1991 alleging that she had been assaulted within the State's Assembly by members of the rival party, she referred to this incident presenting herself as Draupadi, the famous heroine of the Mahabharata.

The metaphor used by the woman politician casts her in the role of the pure - and ultimately triumphant - heroine, and her political opponents in that of the villains. After the victory of her party, Jayalalitha became Chief Minister and unleashed a personality cult which manifested itself through her representation as a variety of goddesses - including non-Hindu ones. During Christmas of 1994, for instance, she appeared as the Virgin Mary on huge, wooden cutouts all over Madras. In 1998, to celebrate her party's 25anniversary, she was portrayed as Kali, wearing a garland of skulls, depicting M.Karunanidhi, the leader of the rival party,. All these representations, unlike in the case of Indira Gandhi, are directly produced by Jayalalitha and by her party. The material supports of these images are those of electoral paraphernalia - posters, banners, paintings on the walls, cutouts.

These visual metaphors clearly are part of a deliberate political communication. Yet other women, in the last decade, have gained access to some of the highest positions on the Indian political scene. Mayawati - a Scheduled Caste, i.e. untouchable woman - was, for a brief period, the Chief Minister of Uttar Pradesh; so was Sushma Swaraj in the Capital region of Delhi; Rabri Devi has been Bihar's Chief Minister since the past three years; and the leader of the Opposition at the Centre today is Sonia Gandhi. None of them have used the Goddess in their political communication. They are, however, regularly compared to goddesses by the Indian media.

When Sushma Swaraj, an eminent personality of the ruling Bharatiya Janata Party (BJP), was nominated as the Chief Minister of Delhi in 1998, a leading political magazine called her a "modern Sita", even though she is far from being a submissive wife. When the coalition government led by the BJP lost a confidence motion, in April 1999, a political commentator assigned this defeat to three women party leaders - Jayalalitha, Sonia Gandhi and Mayawati -comparing them respectively to Laxmi (the goddess of wealth), Saraswati (the goddess of knowledge) and Durga.

The media are an essential component of women's image and visibility on the political stage. On the one hand, the reference to women politicians as goddesses singles them out, on the basis of their gender, among politicians as a whole. The metaphor makes them more visible, and it prevents the banalization of women's leadership :if any woman leader has to be a goddess, it means that this is a role unfit for normal, human females. In Indian politics over the last century, then, the Hindu Goddess has performed a function of mobilization for groups - males as well as females - and a function of legitimization for individuals, more particularly for those female leaders who identified themselves with her.

The political history of the small Himalayan kingdom of Nepal in the twentieth century is very different, if often dependent, from that of its big neighbour. There was no colonization in Nepal, even though a British Resident, representing the Empire, was permanently posted in Kathmandu after Nepal's defeat in its war against Great Britain (1814-1816). The kingdom was actually kept in deliberate isolation from the rest of the world from 1856 onward by the Rana dynasty, who occupied the position of Prime Minister in a hereditary fashion. Democracy was restored only in 1951, when the democrat forces, allied with King Tribhuvan (whose family had been maintained in a purely symbolic function), overthrew the Rana rule. Ten years later, however, the son of Tribhuvan, King Mahendra, staged a coup in his turn, and established the so-called "panchayat system", which actually was an absolute monarchy.

The only mass movement in the country's history, the so called Jana Andolan ("People's Movement") brought back democracy in 1990. The history of people's political participation at the national level is thus a short one, comprised between 1951 and 1960, and then between 1990 and today. In between these two periods, in fact, political parties did continue their activities, but on a very modest scale, since they were officially banned. Yet two important facts ground this comparison with India. Firstly, Nepal is a Hindu kingdom, the only one of its kind, and Durga is the central Goddess of tantrism, a form of Hinduism prevalent in the Kathmandu

Valley. Secondly, most Nepalese political cadres have been formed in India both before the Freedom movement and during the Panchayat system; they have imported ideologies and party structures from India; one can wonder if they have also imported the political use of the goddess.

The 1990 "Movement for the Restoration of Democracy", led by an alliance between seven communist parties and the Nepali Congress, was the only mass movement in the history of the country. Indeed when the Rana regime was overthrown in 1951, this was the work of a small number of exiled democrats, benefiting from the support of the King and from the help of India. One of the major effects of the national isolation imposed by the Rana was the non-development of a middle-class who could have supported such a political endeavour. Evidence exists, however, of the active participation of some women at that time; but these were mostly the close relatives of democrat leaders, and they were usually confined to the "women's sections" of the clandestine political parties created between the 1930s and the 1950s.

The first mobilization of women as a group thus occurred in the spring of 1990. Women's large participation in the movement was actually one of its most remarkable features. Moreover, the leader of the communist coalition, called the United Left Front, was a woman Sahana Pradhan, the widow of Pushpa Lal Shrestha, who was the founder of the first Nepalese communist party. In 1990, women joined mixed demonstrations, organized demonstrations of their own, and were mobilized in a variety of inventive, significant ways. They would, for instance, march on the streets with the copper pots in which they traditionally carry the water; in another place, they would carry with them the metal plates in which they serve meals; in yet another demonstration, they would carry their babies.

Mobilizations of these kinds were most often initiated by the women's section of the main communist party. They obviously intended to convey a specific meaning that women, as housewives - i.e., in a conservative social context, as women - were demanding the restoration of democracy. Other symbolic actions specifically carried out by women included the performance of the Swasthani vrata which is a very popular Hindu ritual, performed uniquely by women, in order to ensure the stability of their homes. In the spring of 1990, this ritual was invested with a new meaning: all over the Valley, groups of women gathered to perform "vratas for democracy" in sacred places associated to power. These examples show the importance paid to the symbolic dimension of people's, and more specifically women's, mobilization.

The choice of "props" synonymous with womanhood, or of ritual acts which are traditionally performed by women, manifest the will to translate politics for women's use, and at the same time, to harness women's social role in favor of the political cause at stake. Unlike in the Indian Freedom movement, however, the Hindu Goddess was remarkably absent from the whole Movement for the Restoration of Democracy. Very few women have reached important political positions since 1951. Sahana Pradhan and Shailaja Acharya might be the only women leaders in Nepal today. Both of them have held important positions in their party and relatively important portfolios in the government, but neither seems likely to ever become Prime Minister. Neither of them, nor any other woman politician, since 1951, have used the Goddess' image in their political communication.

Another potential explanation might be that of the local incarnations of the Goddess, which do not allow easy identification for real women. The Goddess has two main faces in Nepal the Kumari and Durga. On the one hand the Kumari, a little girl chosen to embody the Goddess for a few years (until her puberty), is the living image of Durga. The Kumari is not a woman, she's a little girl, and a very unchildlike little girl; she is a most unlikely role-model for women. On the other hand, Durga as she is represented in statues and paintings, doesn't exhibit any of the conventional attributes of femininity; she is a fearful warrior, concerned only with war. As such, she is celebrated during Dasain, the Nepalese equivalent of the Durga Puja festival. The rituals enacted for Dasain actually provide the answer to the question of the political uses of the Goddess in Nepal Durga's alliance with the King.

Only men are concerned with Dasain, which explicitly excludes women. This contrasts with Bengal, where Durga Puja celebrates not only the slayer of the demon, but also the married daughter's return to her parents'home for a few days; the wide representation of Durga as a smiling matron, notwithstanding her armed arms, is evidence of this dual aspect. The Nepalese Durga, on the other hand, is a bloodthirsty warrior, who is sometimes symbolically represented only by a sword. But even more significant than her fearful appearance, is her explicit alliance with the King. The anthropologist V.Bouillier sums up thus the different meanings, and the different roles, of Durga in the Himalayan kingdom.

Dasain is a ten day festival, divided between the first nine nights, called the Navaratra, and the tenth, climactic day. The first nine days are devoted to the goddesses who compose the group of the Navadurga ("the nine Durga"); while the tenth day, which is that of Durga Mahisasuramardini, is "more specifically centered on war and on the king". But "All the goddesses who manifest themselves during Dasai are either warrior divinities, or divinities closely associated to the royal power. These female deities are all mobilized by the king for the survival of his kingdom and for the upholding of his power. "Moreover, each year, the Kumari puts a tika, i.e. a red, auspicious mark, on the forehead of the king, a gesture which signifies that she, the Goddess, protects his legitimacy over the kingdom. The comparison of the political uses of the Goddess in the political life of India and Nepal now allow me to qualify her value as a symbolic resource for women's political representation.

Firstly, the Goddess is indeniably a symbolic resource in the political life of these two countries. Even though it might prove difficult to measure her real impact on people's minds, her prominence in the symbolism of the Indian nationalist movement, her instrumentalisation by leaders such as Indira Gandhi and Jayalalitha, and her omnipresence in the rituals connected with the legitimacy of the King in Nepal, all testify to her political efficacy. The very diversity of the situations mentioned here points to the versatility of this resource, which is tapped by mass movements as well as by individual leaders, and by revolutionary forces as well as by a conservative ruling order. This versatility also shows that the Goddess does not constitute a resource for women's political activity. The essential femaleness of the Goddess does not prevent her close association to a male ruler, nor her efficiency in mobilizing men.

Moreover the comparison of India with Nepal highlights, on the one hand, the construction of the Goddess, in India, as the emblematic figure of the struggling nation; and on the other hand, the specificity of the Nepalese democratic movement, which had to fight, from 1960 onwards, the very symbol of national unity - the king. As such, the comparison underlines the importance of the identity narrative in India, as well as its utter absence in Nepal. These two facts point at the specific circumstances which can account for the major symbolic role played by the Hindu Goddess in the Indian Freedom movement. The great political destiny of Bharatmata owes much to the fact that the cradle of the Indian freedom movement was Bengal, a region characterized by its tradition of Shakta cult.

The dominant image of authority in the peasant cosmology of Bengal has always been feminine. It was that of a mother goddess who was the original or basic power, Adyashakti, and the ultimate principle of nature and activity, Prakriti. The personification of this principle was Chandi, the traditional goddess of the region. Though apparently associated only with the Shakti cult, a cult in turn associated with the elite castes in Bengal, the mother goddess constituted the basic irreducible elements in the Bengali cosmology. "Because the nationalist struggle became a mass movement in Bengal, with the Swadeshi movement, the Goddess was more likely to play a political role. But a more important factor, perhaps, was the anti-colonial dimension of the Freedom movement. In order to assert the existence of India as such, and its legitimate right to self-government, the movement needed symbols expressing the identity of the nation.

Firstly, the figures concerning the overall political representation of women in India suggest that the goddess does not generally play a significant role. Even if a number of women have reached some of the highest political positions in the last decade - and significantly only half of them fall into the category of "political heiresses" - the composition of the Indian Parliament as well as that of state assemblies over the past 50 years show that women's electoral representation in India is actually lower than the average for developing countries.

Legitimacy in Democracy

The India-Nepal comparison seems to illustrate part of the Weberian distinction between different types of legitimacy. The Goddess appears to be both the instrument and the expression of either a traditional type of legitimacy - as in the Nepalese monarchy; or of a charismatic type of legitimacy - as that of Indira Gandhi and Jayalalitha. In Nepal, where the 1990 democratic movement has ushered in a constitutional monarchy, the King is now largely relegated to a purely symbolic function, that of representative of the national unity. The rituals such as those performed during Dasain, asserting his legitimacy as the ruler of the kingdom, express a traditional, sanctified order, which has no relevance in today's political configuration other than that of providing a sense of continuity between the different episodes of Nepal's political history.

The clear association of the Goddess with a traditional type of legitimacy in Nepal points at the charismatic character of the legitimacy of both Indira Gandhi and Jayalalitha at those times when they use the Goddess in their political communication. In both cases the reference to the Goddess occurs when a personality cuit is being developed by the leader and/or her party. In the case of Indira Gandhi, this starts with her victory over Pakistan, and culminates under the Emergency with the slogans "Indira is India, India is Indira"; in the case of Jayalalitha, the personality cult is encouraged as soon as 1991, and has continued since then.

In both cases the leader, through her identification with the Goddess, is put on a superhuman, extraordinary plane; as such she escapes the usual difficulties of political life, ranging from character assassination to political criticism, and to the loss of political power. The political use of the Hindu Goddess can indeed appear as an indicator of the evolution of political legitimacy in the countries studied here. The authoritarian, extremely personified aspects of the leadership of Indira Gandhi and Jayalalitha can be interpreted as traces of a pre-democratic organization of power in India.

On the one hand we have seen that the reference to the Goddess in the Indian Freedom movement allowed women a real transgression of the ordinary limits to female behaviour; but on the other hand the prominence, at the symbolic level, of a Hindu deity during this founding episode of contemporary India, reasserted the pregnance of religion in social life - and religion is the main source of social norms concerning women. Moreover the Goddess referred to was always a (supreme) mother, even when she was a militant mother. Her instrumentalisation in the Freedom movement probably reinforced the social legitimization of women through motherhood only. The reference to the Goddess in connection with women leaders prevents the banalization of women's leadership by placing them on a superhuman plane. These leaders thus cannot serve as role-models for other women.

Enhancing Women's Movement

The women's movement in South Asia has developed strong networking across borders to strengthen advocacy for women's political participation. Exposure to the international context, as well as sharing of experiences within the region, have thrown up various formulations that have helped the women's movement to engage with the State in their respective countries. Along the way, these activities also succeeded in raising awareness amongst women across parties.

In Bangladesh, NGOs took on programmes for dialogues with political parties, voter education, leadership training, candidate training, etc. The specific activities of NGOs focused on raising awareness and sensitisation on politics, and political empowerment of the rural citizens, particularly women. Several NGOs have been advocating, among themselves, academics, activists and policymakers, an increase in women's representation in politics.

In India, both governmental and non-governmental organisations are conducting capacity-building programmes for elected women members. An illuminating example is one from Kerala State, where systematic gender training programmes for women in panchayats have been conducted by the government and technical training on gender-budgeting of projects imparted. Elsewhere, in the backward States of northern India, NGOs train elected women members to intervene in panchayat meetings, to read and write, and to abandon their purdah (seclusion), both symbolically and functionally.

In Nepal, after the first general election of 1991, and the first local elections of 1992, women activist organisations began raising the issue of the need to increase women's participation in politics. Various workshops and seminars were organised, alongside regional initiatives, including the establishment of a regional network on issues relating to women in politics.

In Sri Lanka, the Sri Lanka's Women's NGO Forum (SLWNGOF), set up in 1993, has been launching several media campaigns to raise awareness at the national level on women's concerns. Political participation of women was the focus of the first theme of the media campaign.

Recently, the SLWNGOF mounted an intensive media campaign that came out strongly and actively against the spread of political violence during elections to local/provincial councils. In view of the forthcoming provincial council elections, the forum has launched a campaign to appeal to:

— political parties to include more women candidates in their electoral lists and to address women's concerns in their campaign manifestos;

— women to exercise their votes; and

— all citizens to ensure a violence-free election.

The Forum hopes to publicise this campaign through the mass media. In addition, it will personally address the women's branches of all political parties. The Forum will also actively work in collaboration with other civil organisations to achieve a free and fair election. SLWNGOF deems it necessary, given the current climate of violence and fear during and after elections, for women to come together to demonstrate their concern about violence in the political process.

The Centre for Society and Religion has launched a series of workshops on women's rights, with the long-term objective of voter education to help women voters identify candidates who are gender-sensitive, responsive and who promote democratic practices. The workshop participants are drawn from all walks of life. They include members who are politically active as well as those who have themselves been candidates.

The Sinhala Tamil Rural Women's Network, in the central province of the country, has a membership of about 36,000, comprising mainly peasant women. The Network has women representing all the three major ethnic communities, namely, Sinhala, Tamil and Muslim. For the first time in the history of NGO activism in Sri Lanka, the Network has been able to field a group of active members as independent candidates in the local government elections, in 1997. The Network has systematically promoted women as candidates with a substantial mass base, who could be a decisive factor in determining the final outcome of the election. The Network has already submitted nominations for the forthcoming provincial council elections.

3

Minorities in South Asia

In each of the South Asian countries finds national minorities, almost all of them living in their historical homelands and possessing distinct cultural and linguistic identities. All of them, except Nepal and Bhutan, entered the modern period in history under British colonial dispensation which gave them the concepts of constitutionalism, representative government, autonomy and safeguards, and even Nepal and Bhutan did not remain unfamiliar with these ideas. In nearly all of these countries the British reinforced the distinct identities of the various groups, majorities as well as minorities. They identified the religious, tribal and caste identities of these groups in the census and in the manuals for administrators, allowed them the freedom of religion, personal laws and customs, and took steps to safeguard the interests of the weaker groups by reservation of quotas in elected bodies, educational institutions and services.

The various communities were told to coexist, avoid attacking each other and remain firm in loyalty to the British Crown. Most of them were given first lessons in democratic elections, though on a restricted franchise, leading up to assemblies at the national level, in impartial justice between the natives, and in dealing with their neighbours and the world beyond. They were not interested in either pushing for the integration of diverse groups into new communities in any sense except for their shared bondage or allowing the assimilation of smaller groups into the bigger ones. Two factors greatly contributed during the colonial period to the strengthening of national, cultural and other identities.

The introduction of democracy, however elementary or imperfect, gave rise to the politics of power at the various sub-national levels and sowed the seeds of majoritarianism. Each group looked upon accession to power through the election system as means of garnering the benefits of the new experiment in its limited interest and used religious, cultural and other affinities to acquire power and forced the weaker elements to demand protection, safeguards, minority status, and ultimately the right to self-determination. Most of these South Asian states moved towards independence during the Second World War and the years after its end when the rhetoric of self-determination and human rights was running strong in international discourse, and the Universal Declaration of Human Rights in most cases came while discussions on post-independence national constitutions had begun.

This discourse attracted all groups but while it had a special appeal for majority groups in the context of decolonisation it gave the minority groups a strong instrument to defend their identities - the argument of human rights. A change in the entitlement to form nation-estates, regardless of the size of a community, the area occupied by it and its economic viability as a state, and the application of this idea first in the proposed division of Palestine and then in the partition of India made sizeable minority communities aware of the possibility of escaping the rule of majorities by establishing their own power centres.

The high level of hostility between India and Pakistan since the Kargil conflict and General Musharraf 's coup of 1999, followed by the war on terrorism, has fed into Pakistan's rapid plunge downhill. The Islamic right, which gained steadily through the 1980s, rose sharply again in the late 1990s, this time with India as an avowed target. If the standoff between the two countries continues, as it has done over the past four years, Islamic radicalism will grow exponentially in Pakistan. Peace with India, on the other hand, could give Pakistan the chance to stabilize itself and turn its intelligence services and religious activists to reform. But peace with India is harder to achieve today than it was five years ago. India too has been radicalized by the years of mounting hostility.

The escalation of Islamic militancy in Kashmir,backed and increasingly manned by Pakistan, as well as its spillover into terrorist attacks in other parts of India, including the capital, Delhi, has given Hindu nationalism an enormous spur. Thanks to the end of state controls over the media and the rapid growth of Internet communication, millions of Indians are now familiar with the Islamists' hate speech against India and in particular against Hindus. As a result, Hindu xenophobia seems less wild to many Indians than it did earlier. The Pakistan government's politics of denial and increasingly offensive allegations that terrorist attacks in India are engineered by the Indian government and security forces have further fanned Hindu grievance. They have also contributed to a wider, or perhaps more open, wariness toward Islam, which has increased after 9/11 and permits quite unrelated issues to be linked, such as Pakistan-backed terrorism in India and the February 2002 pogrom against Muslims in the Indian state of Gujarat.

The Gujarat pogrom, in which more than a thousand Muslims were killed in a state-tolerated-perhaps even sanctioned-revenge for the brutal slaying of fifty-eight Hindus, came as a considerable shock both domestically and internationally. India's Hindu nationalists, the general belief was, had moderated with experience in government. The contentious issues that led to the 1993 Hindu-Muslim riots had been shelved by the Bharatiya Janata Party (BJP) at the center, and they would control their more radical Hindu partners. India, after all, was poised to be a regional and maybe global power. In the wake of the Gujarat riots, many concluded that this was an optimistic assessment. The BJP government at the center might have put aside contentious issues, such as the campaign for a Hindu temple on the site of a mosque that Hindu radicals destroyed in 1992 (the Babri Masjid),but it was unable to restrain its radical wings in the states.

The BJP-led Gujarat government revived the temple agitation when its allies tried to bury it; at the same time, Gujarat's extremist chief minister, Narendra Modi, made great play on Pakistan-backed terrorism in India.Gujarat's Hindus and Muslims were polarized, and one of Gujarat's previous hot spots, Godhra, erupted when Hindu temple activists came to blows with local Muslims at the railway station. Muslim radicals set fire to a carriageload of men, women and children, killing fifty-eight. Revenge riots broke out across Gujarat, many of them led by Hindu activists affiliated with the Gujarat government. The state government failed to stop the riots until more than a thousand Muslims were killed, some literally torn apart.

The Gujarat government's policy of "turning a blind eye" to the carnage, and the central government's decision to opt for pressure on the state government instead of dismissing it and placing the state under Governor's rule, allowed more than a thousand preventable deaths. Muslims continued to be harassed after the violence subsided. It looked as if India was beginning to undergo the same process of religious radicalization as so many of its neighbors-and with potentially worse consequences for its minorities, especially the 120 millionplus Indian Muslims. The Bush administration especially criticized foı not having reacted to the Gujarat pogrom more strongly than it did. The Europeans, who had reacted strongly, were under pressure to do more.

It is still largely concentrated in diasporahomeland ties, and the two countries will take time to overcome the estrangement of the Cold War years, the U.S. administration has worked hard with the Indian administration to chart steps toward a long-term alliance on several levels, including security and trade. The U.S. interest, therefore, is in a stable and prosperous India. Indian Muslims did not support al-Qaeda or the Taliban, nor did they believe the 9/11 attacks were justified in light of U.S. support for Israel against the Palestinians. Though there was enormous anxiety about the air campaign on Afghanistan, public protests were few.

Indian Muslims were beginning to emerge from a partly selfimposed isolation following the terrible violence that accompanied the partition of India in 1947, the three India-Pakistan wars that ensued, and the 1992-93 Hindu-Muslim riots that were sparked by the temple agitation. Over the past decade, Indian Muslims had begun to enter the mainstream in larger numbers than before. In several southern Indian states, a government policy to rapidly increase the proportion of Muslims in the civil services generated enthusiasm and spurred Muslim enrolment in educational institutions. India produced South Asia's first Fortune 500 Muslim billionaire. It looked as if Indian Muslims were beginning to seek benefits from India's new economic opportunities. The Gujarat riots dealt a body blow to this process. Ironically, Gujarat's new assembly and service sector opportunities drew a wave of Muslim immigration from poorer regions, in particular to the state capital, Ahmedabad. Many of these economic migrants died in the riots; others were forced to return to the poverty-stricken villages they had left in search of a new life.

As subsequent events show, however, Gujarat is an aberration rather than the norm. Hindu-Muslim violence tends to be heavily localized in India-the bulk of it takes place in five out of India's twenty-one states and in a handful of cities-and it only rarely spreads to other parts of the country. The Gujarat riots did not trigger violence across India; in fact, 80 percent of the deaths occurred in Ahmedabad alone. After the riots, India's elephantine government slowly lumbered back to rule. The BJP government at the center acknowledged the "blot" the riots had stained India with, partly under pressure from their allies in the ruling coalition. Important watchdog institutions stepped in to pressure the Gujarat government. The National Human Rights Commission indicted the state government for its failure to stop the riots, and the Indian Election Commission forced the state to restore order by setting benchmarks for an assembly election.

There was, too, enormous domestic outcry against the center's reluctance to intervene directly in the state to stop the violence. Human rights and women's groups combined humanitarian aid with investigative reports. The media called for immediate government intervention to stop the riots. Religious groups-in particular, the Hindu priests who called the Hindu nationalists to account-disavowed the Gujarat xenophobes and led peace initiatives with Muslim leaders. Business groups such as the Confederation of Indian Industries expressed their concerns collectively as well as through individual members. And finally, India's new President Abdul Kalam Azad, himself a Muslim, brought a healing touch when he chose Gujarat for his first presidential visit within a week of his inauguration. Perhaps for these reasons, Gujarat survived a second test peacefully when terrorists killed some thirty-five Hindu, Muslim and Sikh worshippers at the Akshardham temple in September 2002.

This time the Gujarat government deployed security forces around all vulnerable areas. More important, there were no mobs baying for blood. Instead, Gandhians reported crowds of two thousand at their peace meetings. It would be over-optimistic to conclude from this sequence of events that Gujarat has turned to lasting peace. The state has suffered from periodic outbreaks of Hindu-Muslim violence since the late 1970s-a period that is also marked by the rise of Hindu nationalism in Gujarat. Gujarat's Muslim-bashing chief minister shows little signs of post-conflict moderation. Much depends on how the December 2002 Gujarat assembly election turns out. The Indian government and elites, even under the leadership of Hindu nationalists, realize the danger of perpetuating Hindu-Muslim violence and will be more vigilant if another Gujarat is in the offing. Whether they are ready to take the larger lessons of Gujarat on board, however, is another matter.

The literature on ethnic conflict shows that multiethnic societies are most stable when they have achieved some degree of integration between their different communities-and the most potentially unstable when earlier integrative networks are in decline. Hindu nationalism rose in Gujarat as its once-flourishing textile industry gave way to the power loom sector, and the Textile Labor Association, one of India's most powerful trade unions, shriveled.Recent research shows that even small steps toward integration can keep the peace. India's south, where a large proportion of Indian Muslims live, is largely free of violence. This is chiefly due to a combination of government and civil society initiatives, such as minority education funding and open reading rooms, avenues that have crumbled in the five states where Hindu-Muslim violence recurs. Gujarat has become one of the most highly segregated states in India. In other words, we now know what India can do to prevent riots such as the ones in Gujarat from recurring, and the task is not Herculean.

Indeed, the majority of Hindu-Muslim deaths occur in a handful of cities. It is only a few areas that require concerted effort. We also know that the two most important avenues of integration are education and employment. Both are highly segregated in India and there is as yet limited readiness for change among educators and employers. The issue has, however, begun to be discussed by businessmen, partly thanks to India's modest information technology billionaire, N. Ramamurthy, who ruefully disclosed that there were no more than six Muslims among his thousands of employees. The Reliance Group, too, has just announced a new program to link all Gujarat's villages through the Internet. They have yet, however, to announce a policy to increase minority jobs. Where education is concerned, the chief culprit is government. Most primary and secondary schools are government funded, as are most universities in India.

A proactive policy by schools and university boards to increase the enrolment of minority candidates could make a great deal of difference. India has in any case shown new commitment to education programs such as universal literacy. Civil society too can play a useful role here, through pushing for desegregation initiatives at the local level. But whether these policies will be undertaken is an open question. The fact that Hindu-Muslim violence is concentrated in a handful of areas in the north and west of India is both good and bad news. It is good news because it indicates that India is unlikely to go the way of the former Yugoslavia. It is bad news because many of these states are especially vulnerable to India-Pakistan hostility, either because, like Gujarat, they border Pakistan, or because they are politically powerful at the center.

In the immediate term it is difficult to imagine India-Pakistan hostilities decreasing. The Pakistan-based jihad groups opposed the Kashmir election of September-October 2002, which was marred by a series of terrorist attacks. More than eight hundred people died during the three weeks of the election. The Pakistan election that followed hard on the heels of the Kashmir election yielded significant gains to the Islamists, who now have a critical mass in parliament. Their demands include the release of several militant leaders who were arrested between January and March 2002. In late October the Pakistan government released the chief of the banned Lashkar-e-Toiba group, Hafiz Saeed, and placed him under house arrest.Soon after, two alleged Lashkar-e-Toiba militants were killed while trying to attack a crowded shopping mall in Delhi.

These indications that Pakistan is continuing to lift the curbs that were imposed on militant groups following the attack on India's parliament in January 2002 have already rung alarm bells in India. Most Indian policymakers believe there will be more rather than fewer attacks in Kashmir and in the rest of India in the months to come-and the bulk of them will be by Pakistan-based jihad groups. Yet few Indian policymakers are counting the domestic costs of this escalation.

There has been a general rise in Hindu-Muslim insecurity during the years of India-Pakistan hostility, then this trend is likely to continue with more terrorist attacks forecast. The Indian government has shown readiness to take considerable risks in pursuit of peace with Pakistan. But it has not shown the same readiness to make Muslim integration a priority-as it should have-given the sharp escalation of India-Pakistan hostility. As long as this hostility continues Pakistan is bound to, and will, support Muslim disaffection in India. It is in India's vital interest, therefore, to prevent sources of disaffection.

The Indian government is supporting proactive steps in Kashmir, where the newly elected state government has released separatist leaders from prison, counter insurgency is being rolled back, and economic reconstruction and devolution top the agenda. A peace process has begun in the state and could be strengthened if Pakistan were to support it. There is too, as stated earlier, new awareness of the need to prevent Hindu-Muslim tensions India-wide in both government and civil society -though it would appear to flicker where government is concerned. As an ally with a large Indian American diaspora and a large Pakistani American diaspora, the United States could play a useful role in supporting Indian preventive action and encouraging Pakistan to do so as well. Indian government and civil society have been more receptive to international aid and ideas in the last decade, especially so to the diaspora.

International institutions, especially global trade organizations, could work with Indian partners to write minority employment and integrated education into programs for economic growth. Much depends, however, on whether Pakistan can be persuaded to aid rather than hinder India in these efforts. Anti-Indian sentiment has multiplied exponentially in Pakistan since the 9/11 attacks and the international spotlight on Pakistan's role in Kashmir-related terrorism in India that ensued-which Pakistanis blame on

India's stationing of a half a million troops on the border. Though the two countries took the major step of troops' withdrawals after the Kashmir and Pakistan elections, it was accompanied by a rise in shrill rhetoric that frittered away its confidence-building potential. Pakistan has added Gujarat to its litany of Indian crimes, a move guaranteed to raise Indian hackles further given the sorry state of Hindus and Christians in Pakistan.

There are appear to be fresh Pakistani initiatives to court anti-Indian lobbies in Bangladesh, whose Hindu population has more than halved since 1947. India can take unilateral steps to prevent serious domestic fallout from hostility with these two Muslim neighbors. But the political will and resources are likely to be uneven as long as the threat of Islamic terrorism is high, given that India's institutions of governance are already unable to keep pace with population growth and the rapid social and economic change that is taking place. Sad as it is, especially for Indians who believe their numbers, territorial size and democracy insulate them from their smaller and weaker neighbors, the subcontinent's minorities and majorities impinge on each other across borders. The Pakistani government could take a leaf from his book.

Though it does not trigger it, arming and sending Islamic militants into India compounds the vulnerability of Indian Muslims. This is one more reason for the United States, increasingly embroiled in Pakistan and more closely involved with the two countries than before, to support preventive action in each country as well as at a regional level. At the moment, and for the near future, containing Pakistani militancy and strengthening Indian democracy are key, especially as the two impinge on each other.

India

As the largest, most populous and most-resourceful of the South Asian states and the home of many cultural and some religious communities, India was expected to provide a role model for other South Asian neighbours, and possibly to the world at large, in evolving a workable pluralist democracy. It did make a good attempt and the effort continues despite the assumption of power by religious revivalists. The founding fathers of free India recognised the existence of many nationalities, with distinct ethnic and / or linguistic identities, within the country's fold. But they also entertained the view that the freedom struggle had moulded the various groups into a single nation, at least in the political sense, and the pre-independence plans to respect linguistic identities could wait. They were surprised by the intensity of the language agitation, and the administrative units created by the British had to be redemarcated.

India also opted to structure the State as a union of autonomous states (previously provinces) with some territories given special safeguards. However, faith in centralised planning and in the leading role of the party that had led the struggle for independence and reluctance in accepting the opposition parties' governments in states (such as West Bengal and Kerala) kept the autonomy question alive. Eventually the bigger states won the right to autonomy while smaller communities, particularly in the north-east, are still struggling for autonomous status. Some of them have also entertained the idea of gaining independence.

The Indian constitution recognises minorities and on the one hand it enjoins a policy of nondiscrimination in respect of basic rights, on the other hand it seeks to protect the socially and economically backward communities, such as scheduled castes and scheduled tribes. Quite a few states (Jammu and Kashmir, Nagaland, Sikkim, Assam, Manipur, Arunchel Pradesh) were assured of special status, and the process of creating new states (Jharkand, Uttaranchal) continues. A series of amendments to the constitution have testified to the resilience of the system. The scheduled castes and tribes have been allowed reservation of seats in elected bodies and tribal laws / customs and land rights are protected. Nondiscrimination is pledged in Articles 14, 15, 16, 19 and 29 of the constitution.

Freedom of conscience is guaranteed (Article 25) along with freedom for all communities to manage their religious affairs (Article 26) and the right to establish and run their educational institutions. Despite the range of forms of autonomy, demands for right to self-determination ranging from more autonomy to secession have arisen frequently, and if some have mellowed, others have persisted and have grown insistent notwithstanding massive state-suppression and loss of lives. It began with the Muslim demand for self-determination in the pre-independence time and continues in various forms and at various levels still today.

The constituent states have said that their legislative, administrative and financial autonomy is inadequate or has diminished. Kashmir says its autonomy is fictive. Insurgents in the northeast have said that grant of statehood is a ploy to subsume them in Indian polity. Religious minorities say that they are under unprecedented attack of the fascist communal forces belonging to the majority community backed by the State. The scheduled castes and tribes say that their deprivation, poverty and disempowerment have only grown. The legal-administrative measures for protection of autonomy such as the Minorities Commission, Human Rights Commission, Women's Commission, are severely limited in their powers.

These national commissions have their state counterparts even more limited in powers and functions. So are weak and inadequate the commissions in the states for protection of minority languages and cultures, and interests of scheduled castes and tribes. The problems of minorities have increased by the lack of their definition. The largest minority in India is the Dalits, about a quarter of the population. While the State has offered them concessions in political and service sectors they remain subject to the majority community's violence.

India has been even less successful in resolving issues related to religious minority.

The Muslims constitute the largest religious minority in India - around 12 % the population. They are scattered all over the country, constitute a majority in Jammu and Kashmir and have sizable pockets in West Bengal, Uttar Pradesh, Kerala, Andhra Pradesh, Karnataka and Rajasthan. The status of the Muslim minority has been affected by the pre-independence communal divide, the partition that allowed about half of the Indian Muslims to create Pakistan in their majority areas, the wars with Pakistan, and the fears aroused by the demand of Jammu and Kashmir Muslim majority for self-detemination. Despite the efforts of pre-BJP governments to meet the demands of the Muslim community, especially in relation to representation in educational institutions and state employment, and the election of two Muslims as the heads of the state (and now BJP has added a third), it suffered discrimination at the hands of both the administration and non-state elements. It was difficult to erase the public image of the Indian Muslims being more loyal to Pakistan than to their own country.

The deprivation of the Muslim community has been well-documented. According to the 1981 census, the share of Muslims in central government jobs was 4. 41% (their largest share 5. 12% was in class IV employees, and it declined in higher classes - 4. 41% in class III, 3% in class II and 1. 61% in class I). During the nineteen seventies, only 2. 86% of the officers joining the elite civil service (Indian Administrative Service) were Muslim, and they formed 2% of the fresh entrants to the Police Service, 3. 06% of the Revenue Service, and 2. 8% in the bank jobs. During this decade the Muslims accounted for 2% and 2. 5% respectively of the new graduates in engineering and medicine and constituted only 4. 08 per cent of the workforce. Their representation in the central and state legislatures has never corresponded to their demographic status.

Communal rioting had become an ugly feature of life during the nineteen thirties and forties and this menace has continued to cause misery to the Muslim minority. The rise of Hindu communal forces, especially in the last two decades of the 20th century, resulted in anti-Muslim rioting becoming fiercer. The more significant riots in which the Muslims suffered heavy loss of life and property have been at Biharsharif, Meerat, Baroda, Nellie (Asam), Bhiwardi, Ahmedabad and Bhagalpur - all during the 1980's. The threats to the Muslims' rights to security of life increased with the demolition of the Babri Mosque on December 6, 1992, and the Gujarat massacres of 2002 resulted in unprecedented Muslim casualties and loss of homes and work. The Muslim Community's fears of persecution have been strengthened by their view that judicial forums have been unable to punish the perpetrators of violence and hate-preachers. The creed of Hindutva followed by the extreme RSS Wing of BJP has heightened these fears.

The Christians constitute around 3% of the population (2. 63% in the 1981 census) and are scattered all over, with sizeable pockets in the southern states (Kerala, Karnataka, Maharashtra and Gujarat). Till recently they got a share in central government services corresponding to their demographic status and sometimes even higher. However, with the growing strength of Hindutva followers during the nineties, attacks on Christians, especially missionaries, have become quite frequent. Christian leaders now mention two forms of discrimination - the discrimination faced by the Christian community in general and the discrimination within the Christian community, the latter resulting in the emergence of the issue of dalits among them.

The freedom to profess and propagate one's religion is subject to restrictions that can be and are used to curtail the basic freedom. Missionaries are frequently attacked and the freedom to change religion has been affected by court judgments and state legislation. Where Freedom of Religion

Bills have been adopted by states the law is ambiguous and allows the administration to follow its biases in matters concerning recognition of religious groups, public information about minority groups, and giving permission to build or enlarge churches.

The Sikhs constitute around 2% of the population (1. 95% in 1981) and although they are found scattered across the country, they are concentrated in Punjab where they are in a majority. Their share in central services is roughly according to their population. The Sikhs have been aggressively conscious of their religious and linguistic identity for centuries and have two organisations - the Akali Dal to book after political issues and the Shiromani Parbandhak Committee to manage their religious places (gurdwaras) - and both are recognised by the State. During the seventies the Sikhs mobilised themselves to agitate for greater political autonomy. They also complained of less than due share in the country's industrial economy, considering that Punjab is the richest state in India. The Indian government's attack on the Golden Temple, the assassination of Prime Minister Indira Gandhi by her Sikh guards and the large-scale killing of Sikhs in New Delhi that followed fuelled an insurgency that continued for many years. The insurgency was put down with extraordinary use of force and the wounds caused by heavy loss of lives have not yet healed, though the pre-1970 political and social equilibrium has been restored.

There are several small religious groups - Buddhists, Jains, others - each less than 1% of the population. They suffer the discrimination faced by minorities in general. The rise of the saffron brigade (Hindu extremists) under the slogan of Hindutva has radically affected the rights of minorities. The destruction of Babri Mosque opened the way to destruction of more Muslim mosques and Christian churches. The constitutional safeguards are steadily being eroded and the protective policies are becoming increasingly ineffective. The Gujarat massacre, in which the state government was directly involved, and the return of BJP to power in the state elections, are considered models that may be followed in other states. There is much greater state patronage of temple rituals and on enhanced demonstration of majority's religious identity in public. Attempts to rewrite the constitution and educational texts frighten not only the minorities but also the secular elements.

In Tom Hadden's language, India followed for decades a policy of integrating the minorities into the mainstream with safeguards for backward communities and religious minorities. This policy of protection was, firstly, inadequately effective and, secondly, left the cultural aspirations and urges for political self-determination unsatisfied. Under BJP, India is seeking to replace the integrative approach with an assimilative one. Indian nationalism is being defined in terms of Hindu nationalism and all minorities told that their lives and rights depend on their adherence to Hindutva.

Fortunately, the anti-fundamentalist forces in India have not given up their resistance. While some observes commented favourably on the fact that the Gujarat violence did not immediately spill over into other states, others were alarmed at the collapse of secularists in Gujarat. An unfortunate aspect of the situation in South Asia is that minority problems quickly cross national frontiers. The consolidation of fundamentalism in India, even if does not get stronger, will have extremely adverse effect in all other South Asian States.

Pakistan

Pakistan comprises the traditional homelands of several ethnic communities - Punjabis, Sindhis, Pakhtuns (also called Pathan) and the Baloch. They are concentrated in units of the federation, called provinces, that are named after them - Punjab, Sindh and Balochistan - except for the Pakhtuns whose land still carries the name coined by the British - the North Western Frontier Province (NWFP). However, there is considerable ethnic or linguistic / diversity within each province. The Punjab has a sizeable Seraiki-speaking population. Sindh has a large proportion of the Baloch, and an even larger number of post-partition Urdu-speaking settlers who call themselves 'mohajirs'. NWFP has Hazara-speaking people who are concentrated in its south-eastern part, and a Seraiki-speaking community in the south-western district of Dera Ismail Khan. Balochistan has a large number of Pakhtuns besides a Brahui-speaking community and Punjabi settlers.

The population of Pakistan (132. 352 million, 1998 census) is distributed over the federating units (called provinces) as follows. Punjab - 73. 62 million; Sindh - 30. 44 million; North-Western Frontier Province - 17. 74 million; Balochistan - 6. 56 million; Federal Capital territory of Islamabad -. 8 (point 8) million; and Federally Administered Tribal Areas - 3. 18 million. In Pakistan, too, the absence of an agreed definition of minorities creates problems. The constitution does not recognise any ethnic and linguistic groups, it takes notice only of the religious minorities.

The problem is complicated further by the fact that the major ethnic-linguistic communities dominating three provinces (Sindh, NWFP and Balochistan) do not accept the label of minorities and instead insist on being accepted as nations or nationalities. Even the migrant-settlers in Sindh wish to be recognised as a distinct nationality. However, all of these communities are entitled to be treated as national minorities as together they are less than the population of the Punjab and their struggles for their rights have revolved around the question of provincial autonomy.

The question of provincial autonomy is rooted in history. The British introduced representative government only in the provinces albeit within the centralised state structure. When the All-India Muslim League formulated its demand for separate homelands for the Indian Muslims it had to recognise the provincial units' aspirations for autonomy and the Pakistan resolution pledged that these units would be autonomous, independent and sovereign. Without this commitment, it was believed, the demand for Pakistan could not have received the mass support that it did in the decisive elections of 1945-46. After Pakistan had come into being in the form of two wings - East Pakistan and West Pakistan, and the two divided by over 1, 000 miles of Indian territory-these pledges were disregarded. No demarcation of provinces on ethnic / linguistic basis took place.

Instead, the demand for provincial autonomy was suppressed with force and the federal constitution worked in the manner of a unitary state. East Bengal, which accounted for a majority of the population, was obliged to accept parity in legislature with west Pakistan till 1970. Attempts to deny its majority status eventually forced that part to break away, after a bloody conflict, in 1971. In West Pakistan the provinces were abolished in 1955 to form a single unit and this experiment was undone only in 1970. Unlike India, which had its new constitution in 1950, Pakistan was governed by the British statute, Government of India Act of 1955, till March 1956.

The continuance in force of this colonial-viceregal system sharpened the provincial identities and put their autonomy at the top of the political agenda. The first post-independence constitution largely denied provincial rights, and the second constitution (1962, imposed by a military dictator) repudiated parliamentary democracy. It was only after the debacle of Eastern Wing's separation that the constitution of 1973 conceded a somewhat reasonable measure of provincial autonomy. Problems arose when this constitution was not respected in practice. The document has lost a great deal of its sanctity as a result of drastic changes introduced in it by military regimes.

The constitution defines the State as a federation comprising four units (provinces), each having its own elected legislature and an executive answerable to it. The provincial chief executive (Governor) is a nominee of the federal chief executive (President). The federal parliament is bicameral - National Assemby, the lower house directly elected by the people, and a Senate, the upper house in which all provinces have equal seats that are filled through indirect election, the members of the provincial assemblies being the electoral college. The National Assembly can be dissolved by the President in his discretion. The federal executive comprises a Prime Minister and his cabinet who are answerable to the parliament. The division of legislative powers between the federation and the units is done on the basis of lists of subjects - one comprising matters on which the central parliament has exclusive jurisdiction and the other comprising subjects on which both the federal parliament and a provincial assembly have power to legislate.

If both authorities adopt legislation on a subject in this list the federal legislation prevails over the provincial one. The federation collects most of the revenues and its expenditure is the first charge on them, while the rest is divided amongst the provinces on the basis of population through an award by a National Finance Commission. A council of common interests deals with matters related to interests / services shared by the provinces, such as rivers, railways, and electricity. Fundamental rights are guaranteed in a chapter of the constitution. The judiciary is presided over by the Supreme Court at the federal level with a high court in each province and a subordinate judiciary under it.

The constitution has remained suspended for long years; from July 1977 to December 1985 in one instance and from October 1999 to November 2002 in another instance, a total of eleven and a half years out of the 29 years since it was enforced. Only one elected government - 1971-77 -- completed its term and all others formed between 1985 and 1996 were removed by the President by dissolving the National Assembly (elected in 1985, 1988, 1990, 1993 and 1996). The Senate cannot be dissolved but has been dissolved twice. Suspension of the constitution and its inadequate enforcement even when it is supposed to be in force have kept the questions of autonomy unresolved.

The autonomy demands of the federating units and ethnic communities now can be summed up as follows. The Pathans (also called Pakhtuns or Pashtun) assert that they have been arbitrarily divided into three units - NWFP, Balochistan and Tribal Areas. The demand for their unification into a single unit through reorganisation of provinces on ethno-linguistic basis has often been raised but is yet to gain the support of a majority of elected provincial representatives. The Pathans in NWFP also demand the right to name their province Pakhtunkhwa (the land of Pakhtuns) just as other provinces (Punjab, Sindh and Balochistan) bear the names of their dominant ethno-linguistic communities. The Sindhis have been resisting being turned into a minority through continued influx of migrants from India and other parts of Pakistan. Balochistan, which is the largest of the provinces in terms of its territory and has the smallest population of them rejects the division of revenues on population basis.

All the three provinces have a grievance that they are under-represented in armed forces and civil services. They also complain of denial of control over their natural resources. They are unhappy with the emergency provisions of the constitution under which the centre can dismiss their governments and dissolve their assemblies through its Governors. They argue that the upper chamber that is supposed to protect the provincial rights lacks effective powers. The 'Mohajirs' demand share in power in Sindh in accordance with their population but support the demand for provincial autonomy.

These problems have been aggravated because Pakistan does not recognise ethnic-linguistic minorities, although it does accept the right of provinces to develop their languages without affecting the status of the national language, which incidentally is the language of a small minority. This posture was adopted during the freedom struggle when it was presumed that all communities had dissolved their ethnic-linguistic and cultural identities into their common religious identity. The argument has been summed up in a few paragraphs on a single page in the report of the 1998 census.

Pakistan has been the habitat of various immigrants prominently called Dravidians, Aryans, Persians, Greeks, Arabs, Turks, Afghans and Mughals, who entered this land on different occasions. Hence, Pakistan's population is marked by diversity of castes and races as a multi-ethnic society. In general, ethnicity of Pakistan society may be identified according to geographically and administratively defined limits as Punjabis, Sindhis, Pukhtuns and Baloch. Similarly these ethnic groups may be divided into more than one category as well as into various castses. However, the notable races can be classified into three socio-culture groups Indo-Aryan. Turco-Iranian and Mongola-Dravidians. The people of Pakistan are further divided into linguistic groups. The main languages spoken in well defined areas are Urdu, Punjabi, Pushto, Balochi, Sindhi, Seraiki, Dari and Gujrati. Among all these languages and dialects.

Urdu occupies a very significant place. It enjoys the status of our national language. It is widely spoken and understood all over the country and serves as "lingua franca" throughout Pakistan. Most of people in Pakistan are bilingual, speaking their regional language and Urdu with almost equal facility. The diversity of castses, races and linguistic groups is however not so great as to create fissiparous tendencies. The people are fully conscious of common nationality. This feeling of unity is mainly based on religious, historical, geographical and political factors. Islam is a great unifying factor and the population is overwhelmingly Muslim and being Muslims they share common history in the Indo-Pak subcontinent. The assumptions underlying such statements have never stood the test of time or pressures of politics and it can be asserted that the national minorities do not fully enjoy their rights and will not do so until the national, ethnic diversities are not only recognised but also respected through firm and operative constitutional instruments and functional institutions of democratic governance are stabilised.

Pakistan is a predominantly Muslim country. The number of all the non-Muslim minorities is 4. 919 million in a population of 143 million. These minorities are Christians, with their largest pockets in Punjab. Hindus, with their largest pockets in Sindh; a small number of Parsis, mainly in the city of Karachi; a small number of Sikhs in Balochistan and NWFP; a small number of Bahais in some urban centres; pockets of indigenous people in Northern Areas and of scheduled castes in Sindh. These are distinct religious groups recognised as such since the British period. In 1974 Pakistan created a new religious minority, Ahmadis. They claim to be Muslim but were declared outside the pale of Islam through a constitutional amendment. Attempts have been made off and on to get the Zikris, a sect in Balochistan, declared as non-Muslim but so far these moves have failed. There are also minority Muslim sects, such as Shias, Ismailis and Bohras, that are not treated as religious minorities.

Starting as a secular democracy, Pakistan has gradually moved close to a theocratic state. It is known as an Islamic republic though its political structure is based on the Westminister type of parliamentary democracy, Islam is its state religion, the Objective Resolution according to which sovereignty belongs to God alone and the parliament exercises authority within the limits prescribed by Him, is a substantive part of the constitution. No law which is repugnant to Islamic injunctions can be enacted and all existing laws are to be brought in conformity with these injunctions. A religious court titled the Federal Shariat Court has the power to strike down any law on the ground of repugnancy to Islam and also to suggest amendments in statutes. The constitution also provides for a Council of Islamic Ideology, comprising religious scholars, to advise the government on Islamisation of laws and state policies and practices. Five Hudood laws prescribe Islamic punishments for crimes. The head of state can only be a Muslim and in practical terms the Prime Minister too can only be a Muslim.

The constitution does not explicitly recognise national or ethnic minorities, while it refers to religious minorities at several places. In addition to the provisions of the Objectives Resolution, which guarantee them freedom of belief and safeguards for the legitimate interests of all minorities, the fundamental rights are guaranteed to all citizens. A non-Muslim has the right to freedom of belief, every religious denomination has the right to maintain its religious institutions and is exempted from payment of any special tax raised in the interest of a religion other than its own. No-one can be required to receive instruction in a religion, or join a religious ceremony related to a belief, other than his own.

Apart from the discriminatory provisions of the constitution noted above, the biggest cause of discrimination against religious minorities till 2002 was the system of separate electorates. Under this system Muslims elected legislators on an exclusively Muslim list of voters while non-Muslim denominations voted only for their co-regionalists on separate voters' lists. The religious minorities opposed this system as it kept them out of the political mainstream and led to discrimination in education and services and also in social and economic fields. In 2002 the system of a common voters' list was adopted except for the Ahmadis. The religious minorities have reserved seats in all legislatures, except for the Senate, but these seats are filled with candidates appearing on political parties' lists in proportion to the seats won by these parties in the various legislatures. These political parties are largely all-Muslim outfits.

The freedom of belief, guaranteed to all, is subject to laws and public order. The Ahmadis are forbidden by law to preach their belief, cannot call their prayer houses mosques nor pray in public in Muslim style. They can be punished for displaying epithets belonging to Islam and they are not allowed to hold congregations on the ground that these will hurt the feelings of Muslims and create law and order problems. The judiciary has consistently failed to recognise the Ahmadis' basic rights. The constitution does not recognise the right to change one's belief. While non-Muslims' conversion to Islam is welcomed a Muslim converting to any other faith runs the risk of losing his life. Several laws have built-in discrimination towards the religious minorities. These include the Islamic laws under which compensation for killing a non-Muslim is less than that for killing a Muslim, cases against non-Muslims can be heard by religious courts but they cannot be represented by non-Muslim counsel. Under the blasphemy law even a non-Muslim faces mandatory death-penalty for insulting the Prophet of Islam.

Pakistan is deficient in watchdog bodies to protect the rights of religious minorities. It has a division in the Ministry of Minority Affairs, Culture, Sports and Youth Affairs but its mandate is limited. A broader mandate has been allowed to a minorities' commission but it is an appendage of the Minority Affairs Division and has done little to protect the minority rights. The constitutional scheme treats Muslims as a privileged majority while religious minorities are promised only protection. In the presence of Islamic provisions the minorities will always be at a disadvantage. Laws that practically deny the freedom of belief (such as the blasphemy law and provisions of the Penal Code targetting only Ahmadis) need to be scrapped. The minorities do not enjoy equal right to public service. Non-Muslims are restricted to nominal quotas in educational institutions and are denied admission on merit.

Girls belonging to minority communities are abducted and forcibly converted to Islam and the state machinery often denies them justice. The properties belonging to minorities' shrines and trusts have been taken over under the pretext that the owners have migrated to India while only the managers may have gone away and the community owning these properties is still here. The minorities' lives and properties are threatened as a reaction to events abroad. When the Babri Mosque was demolished in India many temples and churches were demolished in Pakistan. Christians have come under regular and intense attacks after the September 2001 events. To conclude, all minorities are at a disadvantage in Pakistan and suffer discrimination in many ways. State institutions and policy frameworks need to be remodelled and mechanisms to guarantee minorities' equal rights and redress in the event of their violation made effective.

Bangladesh

Bangladesh has a significant minority population, estimated in the 1991 census at 12. 6 per cent of the total. It includes Hindus (10. 5 per cent), Buddhists (0. 6 per cent), Christians (0. 3 per cent), and other religious minorities (0. 3. per cent). The Buddhists are largely concentrated in the Chittagong area while the other communities are spread across the country. Besides, there are 27 ethnic minorities, accounting for 1. 13 per cent of the population, that are concentrated in the Chittagong Hill Tracts and the northern Bangladesh. Several analysts have argued that the population of ethnic minorities may be higher than the official figures. The linguistic minorities include the Biharis who opted in 1973 to go to Pakistan, who claim to be Urdu-speaking, and the Adivasis speak several different dialects. The proportion of the largest religious minority, the Hindus, in the country's population has been going down.

In 1941 they formed 28. 3 p. c. of the population. In 1947, when the territory became part of Pakistan, the figure came down to 25. c., and further down to 12. 6 p. c. in 1991. The head count shows that while the population of Muslims rose by 219. 5 per cent during 1941-91 that of Hindus increased only by 4. 5 per cent. The demographic change in the area of concentration of the ethno-linguistic minority has been most pronounced. In the Chittagong Hill Tracts the indigenous population was 97 per cent in 1947, by 1991 it had declined to

51. 5 per cent while the Bengali population had jumped from 2 p. c. to 48. 5 per cent. These demographic changes have had a wide-ranging impact on the rights and properties (especially land) of the minority communities.

In the Chittagong Hill Tracts, the British had made special laws that allowed the indigenous tribes considerable autonomy under their chiefs. This included some autonomy in land regulations and administration of justice and declaration of excluded (from government's control) areas. By 1937 the powers of the tribal chiefs had been reduced and, more importantly, in that year the safeguard against immigration was withdrawn. The special administrative status of the Hill tracts was ended in 1964. The government policy of setting Bengalis in the hill tracts deprived the indigenous tribes of substantial parts of their land and forests, and sparked an insurgency which continued for two decades and ended only with the signing of a peace accord with the government of Sheikh Hasina Wajid in December 1997.

Saleem Samad notes the view of Philip Jain, a widely respected research scholar, that "the principal causes of the political and economic disturbances in the Adivasi areas are attacks on its soil, forests and local resources. " And he quotes an indigenous community's leader who argued that "the nation-state, through the expansion of the market economy into the adivasi-inhabited areas, had seriously threatened their traditional rights. " Of late complaints of non-implementation of the peace accord have multiplied and the tribal people are reported to be up in arms against not only the government in Dhaka but also against their own leader who had signed the accord in good faith. The Hindus lost a large part of their lands during the communal riots at the time of partition of India in 1947, through the land reforms in the early fifties, and as a result of migrations to India during riots in fifties and the sixties.

While the territory formed part of Pakistan (1947-71), many Hindus also lost their lands and houses under the

Enemy Property Act, which empowered the government to seize the property of all those who had migrated or had been deemed to have abandoned their country in periods of conflict with India. The replacement of the Enemy Property Act with the Vested Property Act sustained the process of depriving the Hindus of their property. According to Mohammed Tajuddin, "the Vested Property Act is being rampantly misused to appropriate the properties of Hindus by declaring them as migrants to India before 1965. The Hindu owner might not have migrated to India and may be a citizen of Bangladesh. The act has become a tool in the hands of the rural elites to dispossess and displace the Hindus. "

According to Saleem Samad, the Bangladesh parliament was informed in July 1991 that 827, 705 acres of land was listed as vested property, and a Bengali daily reported in 1993 that 757, 704 acres of land was under the Ministry of land, 28, 768 houses were listed as vested property, and a few jute mills, textile mills and other industries were under the various ministries. Resistance by the Hindu community has brought some relief but the bulk of the loss to the minority is irreparable. The Awami League government did honour its pledge to repeal the Vested Property Act but left the matters of already seized properties undecided and the number of people seeking justice is quite large. The state of Bangladesh has for the last many years been moving towards a theocratic model.

For two centuries (mid-18th century to middle of the 20th century) they lived under the secular laws of England, first under the East India Company till 1858 and then under the British Crown till 1947, though during the latter period the communal safeguards increased. The position did not change materially between 1947 and 1956 while as citizens of Pakistan they were governed under the colonial basic law (the government of India Act of 1935). In 1956, when Pakistan's first post-independence constitution was adopted they became citizens of an Islamic Republic that had begun to take the critical first steps towards a religious polity. They gained independence after a brutal war which demarked enormous sacrifices at the end of 1971 and began their journey as a secular democracy. The constitution of the new state abolished communalism, state's recognition of the political role of religions, abuse of belief for political ends, and discrimination on religious grounds.

However, since the assassination of Bangladesh's founding father and President, Sheikh Mujibur Rehman, the state has been drifting away from its secular, democratic ideals. The changes made in the constitution over the past 27 years include: removal of the prohibition of communal political parties; deletion of the cultural and linguistic foundations of Bengali nationalism; replacement of a citizen's identity as a Bengali with Bangladeshi; replacement of the secular principle with absolute trust and faith in the Almighty Allah as the basis of all action; and declaration of Islam as the state religion. All these developments have adversely affected the minorities.

Ranabir Samaddar notes that 'the constitution of independent Bangladesh does not recognise minorities as groups distinct from the Bengalis; everyone is a Bangladeshi, " and adds that the obligation assumed by the state to "conserve cultural traditions and heritage of the people" has the objective of enriching the 'national culture'. And Saleem Samad accuses the state of "trying to establish a hegemony over the entire population on the basis of either a single dominating language, or a single dominating religion, or both. " These constitutional changes have increased societal intolerance of diversity and the hazards to minorities' rights. Soon after the last general election which brought Khaleda Zia back into power there were widespread reports of violence against religious minorities. The opposition alleged genocide though its protests sounded somewhat exaggerated. Nevertheless, few discount the view that life for the minorities has become much harsher than before. The situation is unlikely to change for the better, considering the course the state has adopted. Bangladesh may not be as conservative as Pakistan but it has also created many of the obstacles to the realisation of minorities' rights noticed in Pakistan.

Sri Lanka

All eyes across the globe are on the Sri Lanka peace process and hopes are being entertained that the 20-year-old bloody conflict between the Sri Lankan government and the Tamil Tigers will come to an end. But those who know the history of Sri Lanka over the past half century, especially of accords made and unmade in the past decades, are keeping their fingers crossed as some of the basic issues between the majority Sinhalese and the ethnic, linguistic and religious minorities remain unaddressed. Like India, Pakistan and Bangladesh, Sri Lanka inherited at independence in 1948 a British-made basic law that envisaged a centralised unitary state, did not pay adequate heed to the issues of diversity except for recognising and using it, and emphasised law and order more than political and economic justice. The Soulbery constitution of 1948 made little change and a combination of Sinhala nationalism (they constitute 74% of the population) and the Buddhist religious code (70%) of the Sinhalese are Buddhists) made for an even more aggressively majoritarian state. This State offered little accommodation to the minorities - Tamils 18%, Muslims 7%.

In 1957, Prime Minister Bandaranike tried to correct the anti-minority bias through an agreement with the Tamil Federal Party. The key was devolution of some powers to regional councils, as the Tamils were concentrated in the northern region. This agreement was unilaterally scrapped by the ruling coalition. Another accord was signed in 1965 and this too was abandoned. Instead, the constitutional changes in the early seventies aggravated the plight of minorities and led to armed conflict. Yet another accord was negotiated in 1987 through Indian good offices and it too failed to work. Mrs Chandranaike then drafted new devolution proposals and at the same time launched an all-out war with LTTE which continued till 2001, when the present ceasefire took effect.

During all this process, ethnic /religious identities have been further strengthened. The Tamils' hopes of a good bargain with Colombo have given them reason to be firm on their demands and the Sinhalese reaction to possible compromises on the unity of the state and primacy of Buddhism too appears to have hardened. Between the two sides, the Muslim minority is going through a phase of religious revival and also has its eyes on a piece of the political cake. Although caught in the web created by Sinhala-Buddhist politics of excluding all other elements in society, Sri Lanka has at the same time made considerable effort at developing mechanisms for minorities' protection. Its constitution guarantees basic freedoms and there is a Ministry of Ethnic Affairs and National Integrity. A National Human Rights Commission has also been functioning for some years.

It is too early to say whether the present peace process will lay the basis for constitutional changes that establish majority-minority relations on the basis of justice and mutual good. Even if this is possible both majorities and minorities will take time to purge their minds of notions that have provided them with war cries for a long time. At the same time it will be wrong to suspend discussion on minority rights in the future setup and it is necessary to stress the need for effective decentralisation of power, meaningful devolution of authority and giving minority protection provisions the support of workable enforcement mechanisms.

Nepal

Ethnic, linguistic and religious diversity in Nepal is far greater than one would expect in a small country. Official institutions have listed at least 61 indigenous ethnic groups and more than

70 linguistic groups. 86 per cent of the population is Hindu, the Buddhists account for 8% and the Muslims for about 4%. Nepal was a feudal monarchy and effectively controlled by a military dynasty till the democratic revolution of 1990 when a new constitution was drafted and the country stole the lead over its South Asian neighbours by ratifying a larger number of international human rights instruments than any one of them. However the promise of democracy remains unrealised and adherence to international covenants brought little relief to the disadvantaged. The Maoist insurgency has aggravated the conflics over division of state power and distribution of economic benefits and a massacre in the palace has resulted in the suspension of democratic governance.

The constitution declares Nepal as a "multi-ethnic, multilingual, democratic, independent, indivisible, sovereign, Hindu and a Constitutional Monarchical Kingdom". While religious diversity is not admitted, the basic law concedes basic rights and freedoms, of course, subject to law as in other South Asian states. All minorities have serious grievances about lack of political space that a democratic dispensation should offer them. The differences between the people living in the different regimes have led to demands for a federal structure and recognition of nationalities. Half the population has problems with the national language. The worst off minorities are the low-caste people, estimated at around a fifth of the population, and people of non-Napali origin and refugees. In the present situation the fate of the minorities depends on the country's return to democratic ways followed by the evolution of a new constitution based on devolution of power to the local communities and creation of appropriate judicial mechanisms.

Bhutan

As a full and equal member of the South Asian Association for Regional Cooperation (SAARC) since its inception in 1978, the independent Himalayan Kingdom of Bhutan cannot be left out of a discussion on minorities in the sub-region, especially in view of the diversity of its population. Although quite a few social and political changes have taken place during the three decades since the kingdom started opening up to foreigners, an objective analysis of the minorities' condition is made difficult by the existence of two conflicting sources of information. In one group fall observers who are enchanted by the pristine environment of the country and its strong adherence to the traditional culture. They focus less on the human rights situation in the kingdom than on its steps towards constitutional rule. One even detects a tendency to glamourise want and condone reservations on pluralism.

Likewise, little attention is paid to the state's repudiation of pluralism through a 1989 proclamation. Pluralism is only practical for a larger / country where a diversity of customs, traditions and cultures enriches the nation. A small country like Bhutan cannot afford the luxury of such diversity, which may impede the growth of social harmony and unity among its people. Such a proclamation points to the choice of a policy of assimilation. The second source of information is the fairly sizeable Bhutanese diaspora which is stridently critical of the state's treatment of its minorities and dismisses the king's proclamations on decentralisation and the promise of a new constitution as a eyewash. Even after making allowances for the subjective factors underlying the latter view, the problems faced by the Bhutana minorities are serious enough to merit attention.

Bhutan's population, estimated to be around 700, 000, comprises three main ethnic groups - the Sharchops (about 40 per cent), the Lhotshampas (also about 40 per cent), and the Ngalungs. The smaller tribes include the Khengs, the Brokpas, the Merak-Saten, the Doyas, the Totas, the Mangdeps, the Kurteops, Tibetans, and adivasis. The Buddhists from the largest religious group. However, they are divided into two sects - the Drukpas, whose faith is recognsied as the state religion, and the Nyingmapas, who are treated as a religious minority wlong with the Hindus and Christians. There is a small population of animists also. The ruling group, the Ngalungs, is smaller in size than both of the main ethnic groups, the Sharchops and the Lhotshampas, and Bhutan invites attention to the possibility of majority ethnic communities being treated as minorities.

The political system so far has depended on the will of the hereditary monarch. Between 1972 and 1998 he was not accountable to the Tshogdu (the National Assembly). In 1998 king Jigme Singye Wangchuk revived a previously suspended provision that he should receive approval of his policies from the Tshogdue every three years. Under the same order the choice of ministers was almost entirely limited to those elected by the Tshogdu. The Tshogdu has 154 members - 105 are directly elected by universal adult suffrage for three-year terms, 37 are nominated by the government and 12 seats are reserved for religious bodies. There is no system of general election as election is held for each seat in the assembly on the expiry of its holder's term. There is no opposition in the assembly as there are no political parties.

There are some signs of progress towards responsible government. Adult franchise has replaced the system of voting by household. Local government elections were held in 2002. The 1991 incident of the dismissal of 17 members of the national assembly for failure to control a crowd that had dared to remind the king of his promises seems to have been superseded by subsequent developments. In 1998 the king did sack the cabinet but he also imposed some restraints on himself and made the office of the Prime Minister subject to rotation. These features of the state order need to be borne in mind while assessing the new constitution drafted by a special committee and submitted to the king recently. The position of minorities under the new dispensation will also be judged in the context of their grievances voiced over the past decades.

The drafting of a constitution, the kingdom's first, itself has give rise to a minority grievance. The constitution committee did not include any representative of the large Lhotshampa community. It is asserted that this omission alone will make the constitution controversial. Perhaps the most serious grievance of the minorities stems from the citizenship law of 1985, which has deprived a large number of Lhotshampas of citizenship and obliged many of them to take refuge in Nepal. Their other grievances include denial of the rights to freedom of expression, association and assembly, discriminatory treatment by the police in matters of identification, the imposition of a dress code on the entire population, and lack of access to justice.

If after the promulgation of the constitution the citizenship issue is not resolved to the extent that the Bhutanese refugees can return home, discriminatory laws are not revised, basic freedoms are not guaranteed, and forced assimilation measures are not given up, the minorities will not be able to enjoy even their elementary rights. Nor will a constitutional order become stable and painless. Progress towards these objectives will demand not only specific measures to end discrimination but also, and more essentially, a realisation on the part of the government that acceptance of pluralism will bring peace and progress.

4
Communal Violence

One of the crucial issues affecting women in South Asia today has been the growth of state sponsored religious fundamentalism. Increasing evidence of violence against women - dowry murders, sexual harassments, rape often by the police and army, and the throwing of acid on women in the streets. As a result of campaigns and agitation by women's movements, these incidents have been highlighted and the governments have passed some preventive laws, albeit with many loopholes and limitations. However what is significant is that in recent years there has been a shift away from even the liberal rhetoric of equal rights for women and laws have been passed to withdraw the legal and political rights which women already had won. These developments are linked with the broader process of economic and political changes which have laid the basis for religious fundamentalist groups to grow, as well as for the support to these tendencies by the governments in these countries.

The emergence of fundamentalist groups is not specific to South Asia alone. Fundamentalist forces, often with state support have emerged in Sudan, Nigeria, Egypt, and Malaysia, with Iran offering the best example of what implications this phenomenon has for women. Iranian women took an active part in the anti-imperialist struggle against the Shah, making the veil into a symbol of resistance only to find themselves pushed afterwards into the restricted roles of mothers and wives. The "chador" became a legally binding requirement, the age of marriage was reduced to 13 years and divorce became nearly impossible.These trends with very specific injunctions for women can be seen also in developed capitalist countries, thus bellying any link of this phenomenon with backwardness and underdevelopment. In fact manu of these movements use the latest and most sophisticated technology in modern communications.

In the United States, the Moral Majority, with close links with the extreme right, have initiated a reign of "holy terror" with senators opposing the Equal Rights Amendment on the grounds that it undermines the family and "deprives men of their right to come home from work to a fresh martini, cooked dinner and a cheerful and compliant wife". Electronic evangelists fill the air waves with relentless exhortations attributing all of America's problems to the communist menace and the recent movements for racial, sexual and social emancipation. In South Asia in recent years a number of developments show the increasing hold of religious fundamentalist forces in the region. In 1986 the Indian Parliament passed a bill called the Muslim Women 's Protection of the right of Divorce Bill, which withdrew a right from Muslim women to appeal for maintenance under a special provision in the Criminal Procedure Code.

This bill was passed after a period of mass demonstrations, strikes and petitions presented by Muslims and Hindus all over the country, as a reaction to a Supreme Court judgement to grant a 73 year old woman, Shad Bano, the paltry sum of Rs. 179 per month as maintenance from her husband. A simple issue of women rights turned into an issue of minority vs. majority community interests and led to a withdrawal of legal rights for Muslim women. In Pakistan, the Hadood Ordinance of 1979 sanctioned flogging for adultery and rape, with little to distinguish the two, a Law of Evidence reduced a woman 's evidence to half that of a man, and a proposed Shariat Bill, now seeks to deprive women of even more political and social rights, including their participation in politics. In Bangladesh, while there have not been specific changes in the law as yet, attempts are being made to assert "Islamic" codes of dress and conduct for women.

Women announcers on television were told not to cover their heads and not to wear "bindis" on their foreheads. At the moment there is a bill being debated on making Islam the state religion. These attempts to reverse the status of women and withdraw the rights which earlier generations of women had won, all in the name of preserving traditions and the fundamental tenests of a religion needs to be understood in relation to the role of the state. While this is clear in countries where a religion is the state religion, even in countries which purport to be secular, there seems to be support if not outright sponsorship of fundamentalism. Interestingly these trends go alongside government policies and programmes to integrate women into development. These are not just part of the rhetoric of the International Women Decade which most governments have to project as part of their "modern and progressive image".

The apparent contradiction between special programmes for women's employment and skill training and the passing of restrictive laws which raise images of medievalism in the 20th Century, can be seen as two sides of the same imperative to control and direct women's labour, fertility and sexuality to suit both capitalist and patriarchal interests. Although significant work has been done on the implications of capitalist development on women's work and the fact that the needs of capital and the needs of patriarchy can either coincide or conflict with each other, more work need to be done at a theoretical and empirical level on the relation between the state and women's subordination.

Religious Fundamentalism

Post colonial states in South Asia have followed a capitalist path of development, notwithstanding the rhetoric of socialism, whether of the Indian or Islamic variety. There exist differences in the nature of the state, for instance, the specific constellation of class forces, the degree of dependence or independence from foreign capital, or the degree of repression and the right to assert democratic rights. However, development programmes in all these countries for agricultural and industrial growth, have resulted in structural changes in the ownership and control over productive assets, especially land which have furthered the process of class and sexual differentiation. One contribution the decade has made is the challenging of the notion that development policies are sexneutral; today there is a wealth of empirical material which documents the differential effect of development policies on women and men.

Technological changes, legislation, etc., interact with a preexisting class and sexual division of labour, both within the community and within the household. This has resulted in a deepening of inequalities between women and men, in terms of their access and control over food, education, health care and productive resources. State intervention is today, explicitly restructuring not just the arena of the economic but also other arenas of civil society, those which concern the most "private" areas of religious beliefs, reproductive choices and man-woman relationships. Given this pattern of development, the continuous aggravation of inequalities of wealth, income distribution and uneven regional growth, have resulted in various formes of oppositional movements for land-rights, higher wages, regional autonomy and implementation of legal rights.

These movements have usually been repressed by governments and power wielding groups, resulting in a tremendous increase in class, caste, communal and sexual violence since the mid-sixties. The inability of the governments to tackle the roots of these problems has resulted in a crippling crisis of legitimacy. The ruling parties in all these countries are seeking to create an ideological unity through the sponsoring of religious fundamentalism. This is expressed openly in General Zia 's Islamisation drives and in a more covert form in India and Bangladesh. In 1977, the secular principles of the Bangladesh constitution were reversed and since then, the government has been supporting the growth of Islamic institutions and linking up with Islamic state. At the moment there is a bill introduced in parliament to make Islam into a state religion.

In India, the complicity of the ruling party in the attacks on Sikh families in Delhi in November 1984, the succumbing to Muslim and Hindu fundamentalist pressures and the total lack of political will to solve the increasing communal tension in the country, have shattered the illusions of the secular ideology of the Indian state. The trend is towards a communal state ideology with majority Hindu fundamentalism as a dominant component. There are differences in the specific factors necessitating the use of religious fundamentalism to create an ideology unity. In Pakistan, the nationality question is the most important. The only way by which Punjabi domination in the economy, bureaucracy and military could be preserved by the ruling party was by stressing that there were Muslims.

A homogenous "Muslim" identity had to be stressed to avoid confrontation with the very real structural inequalities between the provinces, each with their own distinctive culture and language. General Zia himself, is said to have stated that without Islam, Pakistan, would disintegrate overnight. In Bangladesh whose creation, in fact, is the best expression of the fragility of religion as the basis of national identity, the upsurge in Islamic activities is linked to other factors. The dependence for foreign aid on the oil-rich-Middle East, and the co-option of right wing fundamentalist forces in the ruling party, are some of the factors pushing towards the Islaminsation of Bangladesh. In India, the situation is more complex since it continues theoretically at least, to be a secular state. Rather than a direct projection of religious fundamentalism as a state ideology, there is a more indirect sponsorship of fundamentalist forces.

The emergence of state sponsored religious fundamentalism has to be seen in the broader context of the communalisation of Indian Society "Communalism" as an ideology projects the "belief that because a group of people follow a particular religion, they have as a result, common social, political and economic interests. "Analysis has shown that this assumption of a homogenous identity ignores the real divisions of caste and class and that in fact, a "communal identity" has no natural basis but has to be created. Inspite of the production of historical and contemporary studies which provide evidence of the above mentioned processes, many commentators continue to see the South Asian region as one torn by inherently antagonistic religious communities, with the roots of this antagonism traced to the medieval past.

The demands put forward by the regional opposition party in Punjab (Akali Dal) i.e. for water, territorial redivision with neighbouring states and Chandigarh as the state capital for Punjab, which were secular demands, were continuously ignored by the ruling party till they became linked with the communal demand for a seperate nation i.e. Khalistan. The emergence of communalism as an ideology which leads to violence between groups who coexisted peacefully before has to be situated historically and in relation to the specific socioeconomic and political factors leading to such developments.

Communalism

Historians have established that communalism in the Indian subcontinent, was a product of colonial underdevelopment, located most specifically amongst the middle classes. The breakdown of existing class identities and status systems, along with economic stagnation forced middle class Indians to compete with each other for the scarce resources. The ensuing frustration, combined with a sense of deprivation and fears of the loss of identity, created a volatile situation in which a religious issue could trigger off immediate violence and extreme brutality.

Given a crisis of identity, the protection of cows, or music before a mosque became crucial issues, issues of life and death, because these religious symbols came to represent symbolically, the preservation or destruction of these middle classes themselves. It is therefore, not accidental that communal struggles during the colonial period occurred mostly over government jobs, educational concessions and the political positions in the legislative councils and municipal bodies which enabled control over them. Communal struggles were therefore over secular issues. In fact, the "purely religious or theological content of communalism has tended to be meagre "In addition, from the end of the 19th Century, communalism became an important instrument of colonial policy in the effort to thwart the rising national movement. Communalists, especially the Muslim League were encouraged through the ready acceptance of their demands, official patronage etc.

The Indian national movement itself, though secular in its objectives, also used communal consciousness. There was a distinct Hindu tinge in the leadership's work and thought. Many nationalist identified nationalism with the revival of Hinduism. Modern literature in Bengali, Hindi and Urdu was partly communal in tone, portraying Muslims as foreigners and oppressive lecherous tyrants, while Hindus were portrayed as heroes struggling for positive values. Many leaders used Hindu symbols, idioms and myths in their political speeches and writings. India was often referred to as the Mother Goddess or compared to Durga, Kali, and other Hindu goddesses. Gandhi too, appealed to people in the language of religiousity, for e.g. his interpretation of independence as Ram Rajya.

The same divisions affected women in the early women's movement and national movements. In their struggle for suffrage, education and legal rights, both Hindu and Muslim women attacked the system of seclusion. However, as communal divisions intensified, Hindu feminists began to see purdah (seclusion) as a custom bought to India by Muslim invaders and a cause for the fall in women's high status in the Golden Age, and Muslim women, fearing that they would be swamped as a minority in a India ruled by a Hindu majority, began to defend passages in the Quran about female modesty. This Hindu tinge in the national movement and the subsequent failure in fostering the development of a national consciousness in the post independence period, left the space for communalism and casteism to grow inspite of a secular Constitution. While communalism in the present period does not have the same causes as under colonialism, at level of ideology, it does find an echo in past memories of communal violence.

In the decade between 1950-1960 communal incidents were few but since the 1960's there has been a tremendous increase in communal violence involving many more communities and creating new divisions as for instance, between Hindus and Sikhs. These incidents occured mainly in urban areas, though recently, communal violence has spread to rural hinterland as well. Analysis of these incidents have shown that they were systematically planned with selective targets and were a disguised from of economic competition between the two communities. In many cases, the targets were Muslim artisans and small entrepreneurs who had achieved a degree of relative prosperity and were cutting out the traders who happened, to be Hindus. This competition for scarce resources - markets or jobs has even led to the old caste conflicts being converted into communal struggles today.

Another significant factor behind these incidents of violence was the evidence of the complicity of the ruling party in either engineering these riots or not acting swiftly to prevent their occurence. Fact after fact in Punjab, Delhi, Meerut, Bhiwandi, all point out the complicity of the ruling party and the state apparatus. Behind the specific "riot" however, is the much more disturbing growth of communal ideology amongst large sections of people. Over the years there has occured a consolidation of Hindu sentiments, a process which escalated when some dalits converted to Islam in South India. Hindu organisations held conferences, and went on all India pilgrimages carrying holy water from the Ganges. Organisations like the Hindu Manch, Vishwa Hindu Parishad, Hindu Ekta Manch, along the older Rashtriya Swayemsewak Sangh, have initiated militant programmes to counter what they perceive as a threat to Hinduism. These organisations are highly authoritarian in structure, have paramilitary wings and an ideology of Hindu expansionism.

For instance, the Vishwa Hindu Parishad has openly declared that Hindus are the only people who accept India as their motherland and that national integration is synonymous with Hindu consolidation. This includes the recovery of Pakistan, Bangladesh and Afghanistan as part of Greater India. Like fascist organisations elsewhere, these are all male dominated, if not exlusively male organisations. These organisations have been given state patronage, are allowed to function freely with members of the ruling party publicly supporting and attending their conferences and meetings. This phase of communalism in India is significant in that it emerges in a context of rising religious fundamentalism. Communal tensions in earlier periods have not neccesarily been accompanied by fundamentalist movements. The other significant factor is the role of the ruling party in supporting these religious fundamentalist forces, especially Hindu fundamentalists.

In sharp contrast to its positions in the late 1960's and 70's, the ruling Congress Party has now shifted from its earlier public condemnation of communalism and of Hindu organisations and support to the victims of minority communities to a more generalised condemnation of communalism and the foreign hand in public pronouncements along with a series of concessions to communal demands, a refusal to indict individuals identified as being responsible for the violence, and a stifling of secular opinion, both, within, and outside the ruling party. This shift in the stand of the ruling party on communalism was partly due to an electoral strategy to cash in on the "Hindu vote", especially in North India. When this strategy did not result in large scale support in the 1986 by elections, there was a shift back to and a succumbing to Muslim fundamentalist demands by pushing through the Muslim Women Bill.

The ruling party played one communalism off another in the electoral numbers game. However, it would be a mistake to see the consolidation of communalism today only as the backlash of a short sighted electoral strategy. There are far deeper factors at work which need further research and exploitation, to enable us to understand the reasons for people's responses to communal propaganda and the increasing crisis of the ideological legitimacy of the Indian State and its need for a new hegemonizing ideology. An area for further exploration would be to see how far the attempt to forge a national identity after the collapse of anticolonial nationalism would take the form of a projection of a Hindu nationalism. Such an ideology has today ready recipients in the products of the peculiarly Indian pattern of industrialisation i.e. the sections of the population who live off rentier and trading profits, the bulk of whom come from the "intermediate" or backward castes which form the Hindu majority.

It is these sections, along with the newly emerging rural kulaks, who today seem to be supporting the fundamentalist movements. Whether India becomes a Hindu fundamentalist state or not is an open question but the fact is that it is today a communal state with government support and even sponsoring of religious fundamentalism. These developments are occuring in the context of a growing authoritarian state structure. Over the years there has been increased investment in the police, paramilitary forces and the army, along with the passing of laws like the National Security Ordinance, Terrorist Affected Areas etc. which give wide powers to the police and the state apparatus over the lives of citizens.

State sponsorship and the emergence of fundamentalist organisations among Hindus, Sikhs, Muslims, and Christians along with an increasingly authoritarian state structure, has serious implications for the future of democracy in India. These trends in the South Asian region have also very specific and disturbing implications for women. Processes of class formation and the construction of nationhood are not seperate from the particular forms of women's subjugation in these countries. Religious fundamentalism as a crucial component of communalism provides a lethal combination to prop up or resurrect patriarchal controls over women. The terms fundamentalism, revivalism, obscurantism, are often used interchangeably and loosely.

There is considerable controversy over the use of these terms. Religious fundamentalism is used rather than revivalism. Revivalism implies a "renewed attention to" or "interest in" while fundamentalism implies an adherence - often a strict and literal adherence to a set of basic principles. Thus there could be movements of religious revivalism which could over time become fundamentalist i.e. focussing on only one set of principles can vary, as studies on Islamic Fundamentalism have pointed out. Fundamentalism is the "return to..., the rereading, the quest for origins". This rereading, return to the origins can take many different forms and therefore is not in itself a political position. A purely textual definition would equate the proponents of liberation theology in Latin America, who base their work on the original Christian communities of Christ, with the ravings of right wing tele-evangelists like Jerry Falwell and Oral Roberts in the United States.

Movements inspired by religion - revivalist or fundamentalist have played a revolutionary anti-imperialist role in the national movements of the 19th and 20th centuries, and have also expressed the needs and aspirations of working people. Religious movements therefore are not necessarily conservative. Similary, religious fundamentalism does not always refer to the past - in fact what is being asserted as a basic tenet is often a totally modern practise. This is why it is problematic to call the recent occurence of sati as a revival. In addition, the meanings that people give to these principles can also vary. For example, Iranian women who supported Khomeini, and marched in thousands, as organised militant contingents turning the veil into a symbol of solidarity and struggle, were not simply retreating to the past, but were asserting a certain positive conception of the future. Islam offered an alternative to the "consumerism and the modern consumer woman" projected by the Shah's economic and social policies. Similarly, attempts by disadvantaged groups to rise in ritual status by strict adherence to "tradition" or the Shariat are not seen by them as a return to medievalism but in fact as symbols of achievement.

Fundamentalism then, can only be understood in relation to a specific historical context. It is crucial to identify when it emerges, which are the social groups initiating as well as consituting the support base of this phenomenon and what exactly is being projected as the basic principles of adherence. One feature of fundamentalism is its selectivity in choosing what is the true and original teaching. In the sense fundamentalism constructs a particular version of Islam/ Hinduism/Sikhism/ Chritianity as the only valid representation of that religion. This construction makes little distinction between what is textual and what may be local specific cultural practices. Most significantly it abstracts from history and projects that particular amalgam of belief, ritual and practice with a transcedental validity. In Pakistan for instance, the islamisation process selects elements from 19 schools of jurisprudence as well as customs and practises which existed in the 8th and 9th centuries in what is Saudi Arabia, Iran and Syria of today.

Similary, the "Hinduism" being projected by various Hindu organisations as the only true Hinduism denies the historical existence of two seperate and anatgonistic religious traditions amongst people designated as Hindus. One tradition was Brahmanism which was based on Vedic texts and the Dharmashastras, restricted to the upper castes, buttressed by royal patronage and the creation of a priestly caste. The Shramanic tradition was popular amongst lower castes, had a universalistic ethic and exhibited a wide diversity in ritual and belief. Historically one cannot speak of Hinduism as such but a variety of 'Hindu' religions. The Hinduism being claimed by fundamentalist organisations draws on the first tradition but here too it incorporates elements from caste customs, particularly Kshatriya notions of honour, as well. Social scientists have labelled this very modern Hinduism - "syndicated Hinduism"

That this contemporay construction of Hinduism has no need of either textual or historical verification was brought out very clearly in an interview with Ramanand Sagar, the producer of a television serial on the Ramayan recently. When asked about the historical sources for the film, he mentioned how during that period women did not cover their torsos but it was impossible for him to allow that on the screen since the image of Sita as a pure, chaste and ideal wife was so strong and important that showing her without a blouse would violate the moral message of the serial!. Similarly when the Council of Islamic Ideology in Pakistan was discussing whether women should have the right to vote, whether blood money or compensation paid to a female victim should be half that of a male and whether women's evidence should be half that of a man's evidence in court, there was no discussion of "khula" which is the Quranic equivalent available to women, of men's right to the "talaq" form of divorce.

Since then the Hadood Ordinance and the Law of Evidence have been passed and there is now the proposal for a Shariat Bill which will extend the jurisdiction of the Shariat

Court to all areas of life. However, even here there is the process of selectivity - while the Federal Shariat Court is seen as having only an advisory role regarding fiscal matters, in matters, of Muslim personal law, anu judgement passed by the court will be binding. Almost all the issues concerning women's rights fall under personal law. It seems that the criteria for selection and implementation of true Islam is the crucial area of man-woman relations rather than more general theological issues. A similar process of selectivity can be seen in the codification and implementation of personal laws in India. While a common criminal code exists for every Indian citizen, areas of marriage, inheritance, divorce etc. are governed by separate personal laws for Muslims, Christians, and Hindus. More studies need to be done one on the process by which these personal laws were codified involving not only a specific interpretation of each religion but also the incorporation of the assumptions of colonial administrators and native representatives.

Hindu personal law for instance, was interpreted initially in 1772 when Warren Hastings appointed ten Brahmin pandits from Bengal to compile a digest of Hindu scriptural law in civil matters - marriage, divorce, inheritance, succession. These interpretations, however were only codified into one uniform law in 1941. Prior to this, there had been separate laws for different castes and communities i.e. separate customary laws existed for Nairs, Nambudris, Kulins, Jats etc. The Draft Hindu Code was thus based on specifically Brahmanical interpretations of Hinduism. Changes were introduced into this as a result of the struggles of women and men in the early women's movement and hence contained some rights for Hindu women. It is significant, however, that the Hindu Code Bill was only passed after Independence after a great deal of opposition. A process of secular reform to abolish all personal laws for a uniform civil code prior to indenpendence was scuttled on the grounds of political expediency and although the ideal of a uniform civil code is enshrined in the Directive

Principles of the Constitution, till today, seperate personal laws continue to operate.

It is not accidental that issues of religious identity are tied so closely with the regulation of relations between men and women. All personal laws, including the reformed Hindu law have certain common features which reinforce the patriarchal, patrilineal and patrilocal family. This is the main family form in India, especially in the north, central and eastern parts of the country. Even where matrilineal forms have existed, as in the taravad of Kerala, economic changes and colonial policy have invested defacto rights over property in the hands of men. Government intervention through changes for example, in laws on inheritance have tended to maintain this patriarchal authority. In situations of the breakdown and emergence of new class / caste / communal identities it is these elements of man - woman relations which become crucial markers of identity. It is significant that during the agitation in Punjab, a demand was put forward for a seperate personal law for Sikhs as well.

This customary law deprives women of the right to property, and to divorce and contains the provision for a widow to marry her husband's brother all these features link patriarchal control to newly emerging class interests particulary the need to maintain and keep control over landed property by sections of the Punjab peasantry. It is also not accidental that while the ruling party ignored the other secular demands for water, territory and Chandigarh as the capital city, this communal demand was being considered. It is this linkage which needs to be explored to understand why religious fundamentalism has very specific implications for women.

Challenges of traditional structures

There are two processes occuring within the South Asian which are leading women to "take off the veil "- the changing demand for women's labour as a result of capitalist developments in agriculture and industry and the challenge of a newly developed consciousness about the rights of women. In India, since the 1960's agricultural development has been based on a technological package to increase agricultural productivity, marking a shift away from the earlier focus on land reforms. The effects of the Green Revolution have been extensively documented. Although there are regional differences, depending on prior patterns of landholding and landlessness, as well as technological contraints imposed by the kind of crop, there have been considerable changes in women's participation in wage labour and their position relative to men in the rural areas. Capitalist development has resulted in many peasants and marginal farmers losing their landholdings at the same time as there has been the crystalisation of a new layer of rural kulaks.

There has been a dramatic increase in the number of agricultural workers, within which section the number of women is higher and increasing faster than the number of men. The 1981 Census showed that half of all rural female workers (as against a quarter of all women is more seasonal and as a result, most women are casual workers. The numbers of female cultivators has declined relative to men, highlighting women's lack of independent access to land. In addition, in 15 states, surveys reveal an increase in the differential between male and female wages, with women's earnings being close to half or less than half of men's earnings. On other hand, the emergence of a rich peasant class had led to the withdrawal of women of this section from work in the fields. However, this has not meant an improvement in the status of these women. Seclusion only serves to hide the labour women perform within the household, which sometimes increases as a result of hiring in wage labour.

In any case, this process does not result in any increase in women's economic control over resources and property or decision making. In Bangladesh, there has been an increasing trend of landlessness documented along with an increase in the number of poor female headed households. Female headed households are estimated to range from 6.4% to 16% of all rural households. Around 40% of all rural women are today seeking wage employment. Studies done on rural areas in Pakistan especially in the Punjab point out the high degree of male out-migration and the importance of foreign remittances in changing the rural setting. Although men do return home for crucial production periods, women have begun to enter areas of work and take over desicion making in spheres previously the prerogative of men. One study notes the contradictory implications of these changes. While some women are wearing modern clothes and cosmetics, for many others there is now the introduction of seclusion as women are withdrawn from work in the fields. The same study also points out to the increase in social networking between women in different households and the issues which are discussed together range from marriage alliances, problems with family members to monetary matters.

There are also variations in the effects of industrialisation strategies, but certain broad trends can be identified. In India, women were mainly employed in textiles, mines and plantations. In all these sectors there has been a decline in women's employment, especially in textiles and coal mines. Of all nonagricultural jobs that women lost during the period of 1911 and 1961, only 8% were due to these jobs becoming obsolete and in the remaining cases (92%) women were simply replaced in their past occupations by men. However it is important to note that women are still employed by these industries either as contract labour or through the decentralisation of production to sall sweatshops or home based units, especially in the textile industry.

The decline in the relative and absolute employment of women in the traditional sectors is also a part of the general crisis of these sectors of the economy in modern sub-sectors like pharmaceuticals, electrical appliances, motor vehicles, machine production, heavy chemicals, which anyway have a low labour absorption, women are concentrated in certain industries like garments, food processing, electronics i.e. the new export oriented factories, many of which fragment production to household units, as well as in the unorganised sector. A study on the unorganised sector in Calcutta points out that not only is women employment in this sector increasing faster than men employment but that men and women are now, competing for these scarce jobs. Census figures with all their limitations, have also registered an increase in the work force participation rate of urban women i.e. from 11% en 1961 to 14% in 1971. Since women employment in the organised sector is less than 33% of the urban female employment, this increase of registered employment seems to be in the unorganised hence low waged sector.

In Bangladesh, given the low level of industrial development, women are only rencently being employed in the new export industries set up in and around Dhaka. 80 to 90% of the garment workers are young, unmarried women, mainly from the urban areas. In Pakistan, data based on the 1975/76 CMIU shows that the total non-farm employment for women was less than 3% of the total. In the manufacturing sector women again are concentrated in the food processing, textiles, cotton ginning, pharmaceuticals, garments and electronics factories. The CMI date clearly does not reflect the level of women's employment since it does not include the category of casual contract labour or subcontracted home based production. Various case studies have revealed high rates of female employment in the unorganised sector. Contrary to the general impression, there are quite a few single women working in urban based industries, i.e. not necessarily only widowed or divorced women.

Broadly then one can see that capitalist development, in agriculture and industry, has resulted in an increase in landlessness, increased dependence of women on wage work which is seasonal, low earnings and the increase as well as invisibilisation of their work in the unorganised sector. In broad terms then more women are being forced into looking for work and the work that is available is in the unorganised sector, with a large section engaged in subcontracted home based production. The new export oriented industries are drawing in a new layer of younger women. Although studies of these industries show variations of age and marital status thus showing a deviation from the South East Asian model, many of these young girls are having to take over the traditional obligations of fathers and brothers for instance, to provide a dowry for their marriage and are now earning their own dowries.

Studies of young women workers in the garment and electronic factories show a sizeable number who come, from disintegrating middle class to lower middle class families, who hope to earn enough to have a large dowry which is seen as the passport to marriage and an escape from factory work. However the bulk of their earnings were in fact going towards household expenses, as the families struggled to maintain a increasingly threatened middle class status. In these families, the traditional structure of male provisioning could be maintained in practice. The pressures of increasing poverty in the countryside as well is forcing a renegotiation of structures of authority. As women are moving out of the homestead in search of work and therefore away from the direct control of family patriarchs, they are entering "male space" in search of wage labour in addition there is the attempt to reassert control by regulating women's mobility and access to wage labour and product markets.

Marty Chen describes such a process in rural Bangladesh, Patriarchal control over poor women's labour is operated not by the family patriarchs but by the village patriarchs The Village patriarchs, men from rich households, control the paid labour opportunities within the village and dictate the norms of purdah and status that discourage women from seeking wage employment or engaging in trade outside the village.

Indeed to show their disapproval of women who break these norms, village patriarchs have been known to stop hiring those women to work in their households and to stop extending them credit or other forms of patron-client service. These material processes which are threatening traditional patriarchal structures, can create conditions for the emergence and support for ideologies that stress women's traditional roles. In Iran, this took the form of a move to drive women out of office jobs, the closure of workplace nurseries, and the restoration of the husband's right to bar wives from paid employment.

There has been extensive documentation of the link between the demands of the capitalist economy and the emergence of ideologies which justify the exlusion or incorporation of women into the labour force. The best example, is of course pro-natalism in Nazi Germany in the early thirties and its reversal in 1937 when women were exhorted to contribute to the war industry. These ideologies do not always functionally respond to the needs of capital in a purely economic sense. Ideologies of domesticity for women are being forced to seek work. Religious fundamentalism as a state supported ideology in the given economic and cultural. Already communal organisations have started issuing aggressive statements about the right place of women. In the communal violence recently in Ahmedabad, Hindu fundamentalists put forward what they called a "theory of truth" (satyawad), in which they condemned abortion as murder and advocated that women return to the home and give up their jobs in favour of unemployed men.

Apart from the changing structures of women's work, the other factor which could lay the basis for support to fundamentalist ideas is the growing strength of the women's movement and a generalised awareness about women's rights in the region. There has been a rich tradition of women's struggle against patriarchal structures in the history of South Asia. The nature of these struggles has depended on the specific historical circumstances and options available for women during these periods. The early 20th century women's movement for example, did not question the sexual division of labour within the family, but did build independent organisations and fought militantly for equal rights, whether for the right to property which benefited few women, or for the vote, which (at least potentially) benefited all women, as well as for higher wages, food and the right to organise which benefited working class and peasant women.

After independence there was a lull but in the late 1960's and early 1970's in India a new women movement emerged. The economic crisis of the sixties led to numerous working class and peasant movements all over the country, and in the early seventies, women's issue bagan to be taken up in the context of these general struggles. In urban areas, small women's groups emerged, constitued by women who were or had been linked with radical left groups as well as activists involved in development work. After the lifting of the Emergency in 1977, women's groups mushroomed in the larger cities of Bombay, Delhi, Hyderabad, Bangalore. What was new about these groups was the fact that they autonomous organisations, used different forms of organising based more on the consciousness raising model rather than the mass recruitment strategy followed by the party linked women organisations, with a stress on non-hierachical internal organisation structures.

Since the seventies, the new women's movement has grown tremendously and has taken up the issues of dowry murders, police rape, domestic violence, reproductive rights and recently the issues of rights for Muslim women and sati. There are two levels at which the issues of patriarchal control are being challenged. The first, and the dominant trend is to expose and agiate around the most extreme manifestations of women's subordination in India - dowry murders, police rape, abortion of female foetuses after amniocentesis, sati etc. This is done often within the terms of the argument of the early social reform and 20th century movements of condemning these as social evils and therefore mobilising a much wider layer of public support.

The second level is the less publicised work that women's groups particulary the women's centres in Bombay, Delhi and Bangalore are doing in connecting these extreme forms to the structural violence against women within the existing patriarchal family system. The issue of dowry murders is linked to the much more hidden and more widespread issue of violence within the family and the fact that women do not assert their right to property. Such issues provide a far greater challenge to patriarchal authority and as a result provoke a more violent reaction from conservative sections of society. A case which has not received that much publicity but this second level of the women movement's struggles is that of a 21 year old girl Asha who wanted to study and work rather than get married.

A women's center took up her case, found her a room in the hostel and informed her family of her decision to study and live in a women hostel. The men of her family arrived at the centre ; manhandled the volunteers and then filed a case of Habeus Corpus in the Supreme Court accusing the centre of kidnapping and running a prostitution racket! After many dramatic incidents, the Supreme Court finally passed a judgement stating that a 21 year old was mature enough to make up her own mind and decide what to do with her life. Such a simple judgement yet it was the first issues where centre volunteers were attacked physically as well as slandered in the press. This violent reaction which agitation against dowry murders have rarely provoked, was due to the recognition that this simple judgement was in fact eroding one of the pillars of patriarchal authority within the family and therefore had radical long term consequences.

In fact, after judgement the centre received numerous letters from young girls requesting support to leave their families and work, requests which the centre with its limited resources could in no way handle. Although many of these struggles are occuring in big cities and movement has yet to extend to the larger number of women in rural India, there has been the emergence of a generalised awareness of women rights and women are becoming aware of options that are available to them. This implies that they are no longer willing to submissively accept traditional patriarchal controls. Even if they may not directly challenge men's authority, in every family which has access to the radio, T.V. and newspaper there is a process of questioning, a shaking of the grounds of legitimacy. Such a process is extremely threatening and it is natural that attempts will be made to reassert traditional controls.

Religious fundamentalism could provide a ready ideology specially since the preexisting structures of the patriarchal household with intra-household discrimination between male and female access to food, health care and other resources has often been justified in the name of religious traditions. The preexisting culture of son-preference has already made the South Asain region significant in having a declining sex radio i.e. the decline in the number of women relative to men in the population. While in most countries, developed and developing, women outnumber men, the populations of India, Bangladesh, Pakistan, and Nepal are exceptional in having an adverse sex ratio. In Bangladesh in 1981, there were 94 females of 100 males, in Pakistan there were 87 females to 100 males and in India there has been a long term decline in the proportion of women to men in the country's population. According to the 1901 census there were 972 females per 1000 males while in 1981 there were 935 females per 1000 males.

The recent rise in the latest census is restricted to certain regions and does not seem to project a reversal of the earlier trend. Although there are regional variations, studies have now established that this unusual sex radio is due to higher female death rates which are a result of unequal access to food and health care within the household. Numerous studies have by now established that son-preference is not linked to religion but has a close correlation with labour force participation of women. The practise of dowry for instance has spread in the last 30 years in India to entire communities and castes who had no tradition of this form of marriage payment. Even in the predominantly Muslim countries of Pakistan and Bangladesh, the practise of dowry has increased and both countries have a Dowry Prohibition Law. While labour participation is an important variable, the increase in dowry practises do not always relate to the withdrawal of women from work outside the home. 'Cost-benefit ratio' analysis is not only narrowly economistic, but cannot account for the fact that large numbers of women have been earning their own dowries and continue to work after their marriage.

The increase in dowry has to be seen in the context of rising consumerism (commodities and bank loans openly for dowry), the competition to get men with jobs in the organised sector (a new form of hypergamy), which is also a form by which certain men are accumulating seed capital to set up new businesses or investments. There have been quite a few cases of men marrying two or three times, each time collecting a dowry and murdering the wife. While further research has to be done in this area, it is also important to look at what kind of ideological belief system legitimises these practices and its violent effects in dowry murders. If we are not to fall into the biological trap of seeing inherent evil in these acts of violence, then it is necessary to look not only at the material basis but also the legitimising belief systems which sanction such practices. The recent incidents of sati, where large crowds gathered to watch a woman being burned, and the subsequent defence of this in the vernacular press and by sections of the intelligentsia can only be understood by examining the ideological systems which legitimise this.

Specific cultural practices can acquire a more widely embracing religious sanction and in a context of preexisting son preference, religious fundamentalists could find support for asserting 'traditional' roles for women. It is significant that Hindu fundamentalists have not condemned the burning of Hindu brides though they have been vociferous over the issues of Muslim women's rights ! The challenges to patriarchal structures of authority, arising from the demands of the capitalist labour market and as a result of the confrontations by the women's movement, leads to attempts to reassert control and reimpose systems of domination. Religious fundamentalism with its emphasis on circumscribed roles for women can find ready support.

Communal identity

Some tentative links between notions of masculinity / feminity and the construction of communal identities are explored. This is an area which needs a lot of research as well as conceptual reflection since there is always the danger of a crude psychological reductionism. It is only possible to make some connections which would have to be developed much further. Communal identities do not exist as fixed primordial essences but as we have seen emerge in particular socioeconomic contexts and are created identities, which attempts to homogenise other differences within the community. In this process of identity creation women figure in crucial ways at a symbolic level they become symbols of culture and tradition, i.e. identity markers while at the material level their particularised feminine identity forms the complementary role to enhancing a particularised masculine identity.

The crux of the fundamentalist rhetoric a call for a return to culture and tradition, is almost always a call first addressed to women. When western dress is rejected, no one demands that men stop wearing suits and ties. Once again the sex-selectivity of fundamentalism becomes obvious as women who "cut their hair, speak English, wear national dress without the chador..." are attacked for being western while "men do all these without their national or Muslim identity being challenged. "Women are neither acknowledged nor allowed to be producers of theology, although they are the main practitioners of religion and hence the reproducers of culture and tradition. 'The culture and tradition that is resurrected is, of course, a particular one. Along with the myth of a "Golden Age" another common feature of fundamentalism seems to be the stress on a martial tradition.

The Rashtriya Swayam Sewak Sangh from its inception built its ideological and organisation structure around the "akhara" (traditional gymnasium) with "lathi" (a five foot stick used as a weapon) training by former army officers, uniforms and strict military discipline. This "kshatriya (warrior) model which combined elements of militancy, vigour, and domination, was called upon to overcome the perceived cowardice of Hindus." This emphasis on virility occurs as a constant theme for instance in the reminicences of older RSS members who attributed the popularity of the paramilitary training among young middle class Hindu men in Nagpur to the fact that it proved that these young men were equal in manliness to the British soldier. Its ultimate expression is conveyed by the statement made by Gopal Godse, the brother of Nathuram Godse, an ex-RSS memeber who assasinated Gandhi

> "Our motive was not to achieve control of the government ;... we were simply trying to rid the nation of someone who had done and was doing great harm to it. He had constituently insulted the Hindu nation and had wickedness it by his doctrine of ahimsa. On his many fasts, he always attached all sorts of pro-Muslim conditions... He never did anything about the Muslim fanatics. We wanted to show the Indians that there were Indians who would not suffer humiliation-that there were still men left among the Hindus."

An area that needs further investigation is how the "traditions" that were resurrected by different groups -social reformers, cultural critics and fundamentalists -during the anti colonial struggle in India, were in many ways based on core values of colonial ideology. Colonial ideology itself was based on changes in man-woman relations and cultural models in Britain an its incorporation into oppositional nationalist ideology in India, simultaneously created a model of "hypermasculinity" for men. In the present period one can see a similar emphasis on the military model amongst fundamentalist groups. In Punjab, for instance the Sikh fundamentalists have drawn on the Jat culture and the warrior legacy of the tenth Guru Gobind Singh rather than the tradition of the first and earlier Gurus who emphasised peace and reflection. The same process of selectivity occurs in the choice of the female symbol.

The ideal of "Indian womanhood" -Sita- as the passive, chaste, faithful wife who worships her husband, is based not only on a choice between other known female figures like Draupadi or Radha, but is also a choice of a popular version of the epic Ramayana written by Valmiki and Tulsidas as against other versions which show Sita as a more assertive person. The reiteration of the "pati-parameshwar" (husband as god) model through the yearly performances of the Ramayana, in films and television has a clear function in ensuring that women had to be confined within the household and that "tradition "sanctioned violence to ensure that women remained within these boundaries. It is this alternative tradition, especially amongst the adivasis (tribals) where women were independent and sexually uninhibited.

These symbolic representations of masulinity and feminity are crucial to the process of identity creation. Communal consciousness arises as we have seen in situations of insecurity and fear of the loss of social or economic status. Notions of "izzat" (honour) and "biradari" (brotherhood) are the main elements which link a family's honour with the conduct of women. A family's public position is lost if the honour of a family's woman is lost. These notions get generalised to the community having total control over their "own women". Communal propaganda is full of the fall from greatness in the past, challenge of foreign domination today, the need to prove strength, courage and manliness. What better way to prove manliness than by showing that your women are under your control.

If the community is losing its economic status, its social status, at least it still has one form of property within its reach. The fact that women are raped during communal riots is an expression of the same principle. Rape of the other man's woman is a way to humiliate him and show access to his property. Many riots are sparked off by alleged acts of harassment of women of one community by men of the other community. Threats to or the loss of their women, in a situation of economic competitiveness, is seen as a direct threat to manhood. In the Jabalpur riots of 1961 for instance, the cause of the riot was the economic competition between a local Muslim bidi (cigarette) magnate and his Hindu competitors, but what sparked off the riot was the fact that the son of the Muslim owner had eloped with a Hindu girl.

In the communal image, a Muslim was/is a man of low morals and uncontrolled lust, who was/is never ready to seduce, abduct, and assault Hindu women. The Hindus were seen as mild, docile and emasculated. These stereotypes have often been transferred to other communities without much change. The same stereotype as the Muslim now exists for the Sikh, or the adivasi or the dalits. During the caste riots in Ahmedabad in 1981, it was said - "... the harijans do not really want reservations, they want our women. Once they could only come as far as our toilets. Then we felt sorry for them and let them come into our homes. But now they want our women. We must beat them and teach them a lesson."

The speeches of communalists are similary peppered with references to the "violation of our sisters and mothers" and exhortations to take revenge and prove that the men of that particular community are still men. Whether it is an attempt to reassert traditional authority, or to create a certain identity in the context of economic dislocation, the symbolism of the community gets tied closely with a particular meaning of femininity and masculinity. This process of identity construction results in a series of measures which leads to increasing patriarchal control over women. The rhetoric of communalism is full of the increase in numbers of the other community, the excessive breeding of the Muslims, etc.

For instance, the Vishwa Hindu Parishad has published a pamphlet which argues that due to polygamy, by the year 2000, Muslims will outnumber Hindus. In fact, studies reveal that the fertility rate of Muslims has been declining and anyway has no relation to polygamy. It is not too far fetched to imagine that population policy, in a context of state - supported fundamentalism, could be directed not just on a class basis, as it has been so far, but also on a community basis like other countries in South-East Asia. On the other hand, the fears of a minority community can mean additional pressure to produce more and more children. In either case, women increasingly loose control over their own bodies. Control over woman and the exercise of patriarchal authority has to be differentiated across classes as well as decomposed to allow for the variations that emerge if the control is over women's labour, or sexuality or fertility.

Given these differences, however, in south Asia today, this control is exercised by particular men i.e. it is fathers, brothers, maternal uncle or husbands who have rights over their daughters, sisters, nieces and wives. What is significant about state sponsored religious fundamentalism is that it not only gives further legitimacy to this control but, more importantly, shifts the right of control to all men. The legitimacy given by the state to follow and enforce a particular interpretation of a religion means that any man on the street can stop any woman who does not conform to the "traditional" and "proper" role assigned to her. This can be seen clearly in the countries where the State is declared a mono religious state. In Iran, the "Hezbolahis" attack women on the streets with guns or knives if they are not wearing the chador.

Recent press reports from Punjab mention that in the campaign by the extremists against liquor, meat and tobacco shops, women who wear saris, pluck their eyebrows and put on lipstick will face dire consequences"! There were reports of such control by Muslim fundamentalists when they shaved the head of Shabana of Perunthura and Zulaikha Bibi from Kerala who was given 101 lashes as punishment for the violation of Muslim personal law. At the moment such incidents are few in South Asia but continued state sponsorship of fundamentalism would intensify and sanction such acts of violence. The contradictory tendencies at the level of government policies for women and development with the aim of drawing women into the labour market, and the attempts through legislation to restrict women access to the public world are part of one process by which the interests of patriarchy and capital are ensured.

Religious fundamentalism as a state ideology thus provides the possibility of a coincidence of interests between patriachy and the demands of the capitalist economy. This remains of course an uneasy coincidence but it would be a mistake to continue seeing the logic of the market as necessarily leading to a liberal ideology of women work. An ideology of restriction even though large numbers of women are being drawn into work outside the home and therefore competing with men, can be a viable ideology of legitimation. There are however, other countervailing tendencies within South Asia which could reverse these trends. One of these are the growing social movements which are challenging and questioning the overall paths of development as well as specific issues of patriarchal control. In India, for instance, feminists from the women's movement and the democratic rights movements have entered the arena of general politics.

Women's groups have been one of the first to condemn communalism, have been actively involved in supporting victims of communal violence, and held special investigations into the situation of women during communal clashes. Most significantly, feminists have taken initiatives in supporting proposals for political solutions for instance in Punjab and are engaged in a national discussion on the dangers of rising fundamentalism. At present, there is a debate on the issues of the demand for a uniform civil code. While all sections of the movement agree in principle to the demand for a uniform civil code, there are differences on strategies and implications, since this demand has also been put forward by Hindu communal groups, and as a result creates fear in the minds of minority groups. Some sections of the movement support a strategy of reform within separate personal laws while others have pushed for a uniform civil code.

In Pakistan, women groups have been fighting on the terrain of religion itself and have argued for improving the conditions for women within the Islamic structure. In Bangladesh, there are strong representations being made by minority groups and women's groups against the proposed bill to make Islam the State religion. These developments have led women groups to directly confront the ruling parties in their countries. This is a significant development since inspite of militant struggles and anti-government and anti-patriarchal slogans, most of the campaigns were directed towards changes in the laws and often demanded more intervention by state authorities in implementing these laws. In practice, the movement has operated with the assumption of a liberal state.

Today, it is clear that even demands for legal changes are not going to be granted easily. This implies that women groups will have to develop a fuller understanding of the State and State ideologies and evolve strategies which go beyond reflex actions. It would mean tackling the wider questions, not just of the relationship between patriarchal control and the socioeconomic changes in the region, but also the problematic issue of cultural identity creation. Although the present constitution of communal identities is repressive for women, there are positive elements which lie behind the need for cultural identity, This has to do with the broader process of the failure of the creation of a national identity in post colonial states as well as the restrictions in a identity based on caste, community or the family, especially for women.

In the discussions on what constitutes the a basis for an alternative cultural identity, feminists in South Asia have taken different stands. Some have argued for religious, or on the basis of tactical reasons to reach out to the vast majority of women who are believers. Another view is to draw on the anti-brahmanical culture of the dalits and adivasis in India, to build an oppositional culture. All this requires a reassessment from a feminist perspective, of what has been the content of nationalism and the process by which each "nation state" was constituted in the region, the limitations of the present definition of secularism, the problems in trying to seperate religion from culture and finally whether the women movement, given its internal differentiation, can project an alternative culture for women in each country.

While these are crucial questions for future strategising, at a practical level a significant development in the last few years is the linkage and exchange between feminists in South Asia. These exchanges have had a tremendous emotional impact as women shared their common problems even as their governments prepared for war against each other. This process of the sharing of common experiental situation, the questioning of "national" borders and restrictions on travel and visits and the identification of similar issues and struggles is creating the basis for the emergence of a regional perspective. Such a perspective is crucial since the link between the state and religious fundamentalism in each country is closely tied to the political dynamics of the South Asian region as a whole. The strengthening of such initiatives provides hope for a process of democratisation and a redefinition of man-woman relations within the region.

Problems in Fundamentalism

The problem of fundamentalism knows no borders, and it is

a common enemy of humanity. In cases in which the state is fundamentalist or has been influenced by fundamentalist sociopolitical agendas, the fundamentalism of the enclave is encouraged or even empowered to spill over its natural boundaries and permeate the larger society. The impact in these instances is of a different order than in a society that successfully marginalizes fundamentalists within it, as does the scientific establishment in the United States or the political establishment in Japan. Among the many dreams of both the British masters who quit the Indian subcontinent in 1947, and Mahatma Gandhi and his followers who forced the colonial power out, none was perhaps dearer to their hearts than the desire for the foundation of secular democracies in South Asia that were free from the turmoil of caste and religious violence.

But from the very dawn of independence, sectarian rivalries have undermined that aspiration. Partition was followed by the two-way exodus of Hindus and Muslims and the communal carnage that took the lives of thousands of innocent victims. Since then, most nations of South Asia have constantly been plagued by increasingly violent political turmoil due to a growing intolerance toward their minorities. Religious fundamentalism and militancy are not only destroying South Asia's ethnic diversity, but also are putting the region's political secularism in danger of collapse. Hindu extremists in India, Tamil militants in Sri Lanka, and Islamic fundamentalists in Afghanistan, Pakistan, and Bangladesh pose a threat to the region's secular fabric. Indian experience with fundamentalism has been bloody and traumatic.

Mahatma Gandhi, before he could fully savour the fresh air of independent India, fell victim to a Hindu fundamentalist's bullets. Prime Minister Indira Gandhi was gunned down by her own Sikh bodyguard in the aftermath of the Sikh fundamentalist movement that swept through the vibrant state of Punjab in the early 1980s. And a female suicide bomber of the Tamil fundamentalist group from Sri Lanka blew up Indira's son Rajiv Gandhi, who had succeeded her as

Prime Minister. The assassinations of the Mahatma, Indira, and Rajiv serve as stark reminders of what happens when contractual bonds holding together the complex social elements composing the body politic are broken and when political affiliations are weakened.

John Mearsheimer's thesis that the end of Cold War would lead Europe to factionalism, violent ethnic conflicts, and civil wars seems applicable beyond Europe. Until the mid-1980s, the impact of Hinduism on the political landscape of India, where more than 80 percent of the people are adherents of this faith, was moderated by the political parties in power to maintain a secular democracy. But since the late 1980s, there has been increasing popular support for Hindu nationalist parties among the people of India. Tension and distrust between Hindus and Muslims have long been a normal facet of life in India. The 1992 destruction of a disputed Muslim shrine in Ayodhya (in the Northern Indian state of Uttar Pradesh) and the subsequent anti-Muslim riots in Bombay are among the events that have heightened Hindu-Muslim tensions.

Surging populations, environmental degradation, and ethnic conflict · all of which are deeply related-are sowing the seeds of discontent across the globe. Or is the disenchantment with existing conditions which these movements express normal and to be expected? Unfortunately there is no good way to measure the levels of discontent that prevailed in times past. Hence historical comparisons with today's occurrences become merely impressionistic. Selecting the elements of tradition and modernity, fundamentalists seek to remake the world in the service of a dual commitment to the unfolding eschatological drama (by returning all things in submission to the divine) and to self-preservation. Boundaries are set, the enemy identified, converts sought, and institutions created and sustained in pursuit of a comprehensive reconstruction of society.

The term "fundamentalist" was first used with reference to a group of US Protestant churches that arose in the 1920s. For many liberal or mainline Christians, the term "fundamentalist" is pejorative. It is applied rather indiscriminately to all those who advocate a literalist Biblical position. Generally, fundamentalists are regarded by their opponents as static, retrospective, and extremist. Three decades ago, the Encyclopedia Britannica described them as "a motley group of theologically conservative communities which emphasize total and even literal inspiration from the Holy Scriptures and their absolute authority in matters of faith and works. "The term eventually came to be used for all religious movements that seek to return to "fundamentals" and to any movement seeking political power for the purpose of governing according to religious values. In his book, Defenders of God, Bruce Lawrence defines "fundamentalism".

The affirmation of religious authority as holistic and absolute, admitting of neither criticism nor reduction; it is expressed through the collective demand that specific creedal and ethical dictates derived from the scriptures be publicly recognized and legally enforced. Scott R. Appleby, Emmanuel Sivan, and Gabriel Almond list the following five ideological characteristics linked to fundamentalists and fundamentalism:

— Fundamentalists are concerned first with the erosion of religion and its proper role in society;

— Fundamentalists are selective of their tradition and what part of modernity they accept or choose to act against;

— They embrace some form of Manicheanism (dualism);

— Fundamentalists stress absolutism and inerrancy in their source of revelation; and

— They opt for some form of Millennialism or Messianism.

Fundamentalists in various traditions teach that there was a perfect moment, and they endeavour to recover that moment. This often involves reacting to that which is seen as a threat to realizing the ideal, even if the ideal never actually existed. It should be emphasized that there is a very thin line between fundamentalism and religious orthodoxy.

The fundamentalists go a step further by being radical and in some cases spreading terrorism and violence as part of their zeal to spread their religion. "Fundamentalist" connotes a certain kind of believer who wishes to form or defend a state or society based in some explicit way upon sacred history, customs, traditions, and moral obligations. Yet there are both moderate fundamentalists, who work within the law to achieve these ends, and radical fundamentalists, who adopt extralegal means and resort to violence. From the perspective of a non-fundamentalist, fundamentalisms are often scandalous.

They appear to stand in the way of individual self-determination, to violate basic human rights, and to impede material advancement, progress, and prosperity. But this is precisely the point of fundamentalisms: they and their gods are not to be judged according to human standards. In their view, one cannot evaluate social behaviour along strictly humanistic lines; behaviour is good if it conforms to God's will. In contemporary political discourse in India, a "fundamentalist" is a person who resorts to selective retrieval, picking out from his religious tradition certain elements of high symbolic significance with a view to mobilizing his co-religionists for action. The goals of such action are usually a mixture of religious objectives and the politico-economic interests of one's own community as against those of similarly defined other communities.

n the near contemporary religious history of South Asia, with its diverse religious and ethnic divisions, fundamentalist movements that have affected the events in the subcontinent are primarily the fundamentalist Jamaati-Islami, Hindu Nationalism, and Sikh Fundamentalism. Although the Sikh Fundamentalist Movement led to tragic events in the 1980s and 1990s, its impact has largely been contained, as its contours of influence were limited to the state of Punjab alone. However, the rise in popularity of the other two religious movements and their adverse effect on the internal stability of the subcontinent warrant detailed study to clearly assess the threat they pose.

Jamaati-Islami

Mawlana Mawdudi was born in 1903 to a very religious family in Aurangabad, in Central India. His father, an austere and devout Muslim, educated his children at home in order to protect them from the social customs of the West that were invading Indian society. He was 16 when Gandhi started his nationalist movement for home rule. He cooperated with the Hindus for independence for some time, but eventually separated himself from the cause. He devoted his time to studying the Koran and to developing his ideas on an Islamic society apart from India. His writings indicated how to stem the flood of Western influences, claiming the superiority of Islam over non-Islamic ideas. In the mid-1930s, when the Muslim League of India started to propagate its idea that the Muslims of India constitute a separate and distinct nation, Mawdudi was incensed. He feared that Muslims would stray from Islam toward nationalism. Nationalism, in his view, was a Western idea that rested on non-Islamic concepts.

In 1941, he created his own fundamentalist group, the Jamaati-Islami (the Islamic association). In his view, the best way to transform society was to create a small group of dedicated followers in order to capture political leadership. He cited the Fascists in Italy and the Nazis in Germany as examples. His intention was to restructure the whole of Indian society on an Islamic pattern. After partition of the subcontinent in 1947, Mawdudi went over to Pakistan like scores of other Indian Muslims. There he sent preachers to the villages of the new state. Very soon the number of his supporters swelled and the Jamaati-Islami (JI) emerged as a genuine political party which continued to develop and strengthen. But JI's attacks on the military dictatorship of General Ayub Khan, who took power in Pakistan in 1958, prompted its dissolution and the imprisonment of its leaders, including Mawdudi.

On his release in 1962, Mawdudi resumed his activities. Despite the fact that his association had lost its political clout, his ideas gained wide publicity in fundamentalist circles both in Pakistan and in the Muslim world at large. His concept of an Islamic state was used in 1978 by General Zia-Ul-Haq to justify his coup against the elected government of Zulfikar Ali Bhutto. The General declared that he was a soldier of Islam dedicated to creating an Islamic state in Pakistan based on Mawdudi's ideas. Although the founder of JI was not there to give his opinion, his supporters denounced Zia's usurpation.

Despite the fact that the JI lost its importance as a fundamentalist group in Pakistan, the writings of Mawdudi, especially his concepts of an Islamic state, had started to penetrate every corner of the Muslim world. One of the most important contributions of Mawdudi in 20th-century Islam has been his presentation of Islam as a system of life, a complete code of conduct that governs all aspects of human existence. The basic proposition in Mawdudi's theory is God's exclusive sovereignty. According to him, God's sovereignty covers all aspects of political and legal sovereignty also, and in these too no one other than God has any share. No monarch, no royal family, no elite class, no leader of any religious group, no democracy vested in the sovereignty of the people can participate in God's sovereignty. Whosoever claims such a position is a rebel.

Similarly, any institution or individual attempting to assume political and legal sovereignty and seeking thereby to restrict the jurisdiction of God to spheres of personal law or religious duties is a usurper and a rebel. The truth is that no one can claim to be a lawgiver, save under the dispensation of God. No one can challenge the supreme authority of God Almighty in any sphere. Mawdudi's concepts of an Islamic state reject any Western model. In his view, everything about Western civilization is wrong and harmful because it is not God-given but elaborated by political leaders on the basis of false beliefs. To him and his followers, the West long ago denied the sovereignty of God. Therefore all things its people have constructed are unacceptable. The works of Mawdudi were translated into Arabic and other languages as early as 1940. They exerted a profound influence on the Muslim Brotherhood in Egypt and in other Muslim countries.

They helped shape contemporary military fundamentalist movements. Mawlana Mawdudi, although not a classical Muslim cleric and scholar, played a key role in the spread of militant Islamic fundamentalism. As early as 1926, when he was a journalist in India, he wrote, "Islam [is] a revolutionary ideology aimed at destroying the social order of the world, totally rebuilding it from scratch. "At the same time, he wrote that "Jihad [is] a revolutionary struggle and... the pristine struggle between good and evil [has] evolved into a conflict between Islam and non-Islam. "Mawdudi's ideas epitomize the views of today's militant Islamic fundamentalists who believe that contemporary Muslim societies have returned to Jahilya.

The Jamaat views Islam as a comprehensive way of life that covers the entire spectrum of human activity (individual, social, economic, or political). For the JI, Islam means the total commitment and subordination of all aspects of human life to the will of God. The JI has traced different paths in different regions of South Asia. At the level of ideas and political strategy, the South Asian Islamic scene offers an interesting example of how a religio-political movement tends to articulate its ideology in different political contexts.

When the Jamaati-Islami became formally organized into two separate entities at the time of partition, the Pakistan Jamaat launched a campaign for the establishment of an Islamic state as the most important means for creating the order envisaged by Islam, while the Indian Jamaat deleted all references to the goal of establishing an Islamic state from its program of action. According to the Jamaat of India, there is nothing wrong with the formulation of secularism that states, "Secularism as a state policy implies that there should be no discrimination or partiality on the basis of religious belief. "

In fact, the Jamaat has categorically affirmed that in the present circumstances it wants the secular form of government to continue. The Jamaat seems to believe that "the state must remain secular, but the Muslims should be saved from secularism. "The Jamaat of erstwhile East Pakistan (present-day Bangladesh) followed a different path. During the 1971 civil war, the Jamaat was the only political party in East Pakistan that openly collaborated with the central government. With arms and weapons supplied by the Pakistan army, the Jamaat organized the Al-Badr Paramilitary Student Wing and fought pitched battles against the secessionist Mukhti Bahini (freedom-fighter) guerrillas. The Jamaat of Kashmir follows a different path altogether. Though it lacks the political clout to influence the people or polity of the troubled state, it raises its voice for separation from India and covertly supports and coordinates militant activities in the Kashmir Valley.

Islamic fundamentalism

Several forms of fundamentalism promote revivalist movements of various religions, but internationally, Islamic fundamentalism is the most pronounced and widespread. The entire Muslim world turned fundamentalist around the 12th century, when the ultraconservative interpretations of the Koran triumphed. Since that time, whenever Islamic ways of life have "softened, " ultra fundamentalists have reacted against the laxity of leaders who failed to implement the Shariah, the revealed laws of the religion of Islam. In the Indian subcontinent fundamentalism has surfaced in the chronic national and ethnic conflicts which have marred this ancient land. The rise of fundamentalist forces in other countries certainly helped revivalists in India gain popular sanction in the 1980s. Islamic fundamentalism in Pakistan and the Middle East made a definite impression on Indian Muslim leaders, and this in turn further strengthened the morale of religious revivalists. Fundamentalisms seem closely aligned with nationalism and popular reaction against what are felt to be foreign cultural and religious traditions.

This is especially clear among the Muslims. According to Dilip Hiro, "It is in the nature of any major religion to revitalize itself periodically. But Islam is special, because it is more than a religion. "More than anything else, reaffirmation of Islam, whatever its specific sectarian form, means the repudiation of European and American influence upon local society, politics, and morals. For many centuries Muslims have lived with a sense that their world is superior to the non-Muslim world. They believe that Islam is the "last" religion, the final message sent by God to humans. In the 19th century, when Muslims began to discover that the West had advanced ahead of them in technology and in military power, a feeling of humiliation stirred in them. They had lost their dominant place in the world to the more advanced Christians. The feeling of humiliation reached its peak when tiny Israel defeated the Arabs in the 1967 war. Nationalism, which had soothed Muslims for some decades, lost its attraction.

At that point, militant fundamentalism came into the picture. Only God could help Muslims in their adversity. For that to happen, they had to return to the strict implementation of divine law. Militant fundamentalism helped Muslims restore their sense of superiority. Fundamentalism has given Muslims confidence in their future. Slogans such as "Islam is the solution, " "Everything is in the Koran, " "Islam is superior to other religions, " and "Let's start a new Jihad, " and so on, have renewed the pride of Muslims. If we speak of fundamentalism as a return to the foundations of Islam, the Koran, and the example of the Prophet in order to renew the community, then these movements are neo-fundamentalist or neo-revivalist, for they look to the sources of Islam not simply to replicate the past but to respond to a new age.

Modern Islamic organizations have been the driving force behind the dynamic spread of the Islamic resurgence. The Iranian revolution of 1978-79 focused attention on Islamic fundamentalism and with it the spread and vitality of political Islam in other parts of the Muslim world. Mawlana Mawdudi noted, "Be it in the sphere of economics or politics, or civics or legal rights and duties, those who accept the principles of Islam are not divided by any distinction or nationality of class or country. "Islam divides the human family into two factions the believers and the infidels. It divides human history into two periods the age of ignorance (jahilya) and the age of enlightenment. And it divides the inhabited earth into two camps the land of the believers (Dar-ul-Islam) and the lands of the infidels (Dar-ul-Harb). Further, it postulates a permanent war between these divisions.

The believers are called upon to wage an unceasing war (Jihad) on the infidels until the latter are converted or killed off. The age of enlightenment should strive in the same way, until everything belonging to the age of ignorance is remolded or replaced. And the Dar-ul-Islam should continue to send faithful followers of Islam to the Dar-ul-Harb until it is converted into Dar-ul-Islam. This is the behavior pattern of Islamic fundamentalists. They cannot but look upon their non-Muslim neighbors as subjects to be converted by all means. In his "Clash of Civilizations, " written almost a decade ago, Samuel Huntington talks about Muslims involved with all other religions in most parts of the world when he says, In Eurasia the great historical fault lines between civilizations are once more aflame. This is particularly true along the boundaries of the crescent-shaped Islamic bloc of nations from the bulge of Africa to Central Asia.

Violence also occurs between Muslims, on the one hand, and Orthodox Serbs in the Balkans, Jews in Is-rael, Hindus in India, Buddhists in Burma, and Catholics in the Philippines. Islam has bloody borders. In The Broken Crescent, Fereydoun Hoveyda makes a clear distinction between militant Islamic fundamentalism and mainstream Islam (or Islams). He believes there is not one single Islam, but different ways of expressing and practicing it. Muslim fundamentalism in India shares some of the abiding concerns of Islamic fundamentalism elsewhere in the world but also has some distinct local aspects. Besides the economic and social problems which Muslims share with non-Muslims in India, there are issues that specifically affect Muslims as a group. Muslims are convinced that there is a pattern of discrimination against them. They believe that they are considerably worse off than many other Muslim communities in non-Muslim countries and that their situation is deteriorating as a result of Hindu activism.

Hindu nationalism

Islam has always been considered a threat to the complacency of Hinduism. It threatens Hindus spiritually, socially, and ultimately politically, as well as in terms of classical Hindu values of tolerance, freedom of expression, and individualism. North Indian Hindus have been on the defensive since the end of the 19th century. The decennial census introduced by the British made the different communities aware of their own numerical strength, and showed the Hindus as losing ground in terms of population. Without drastic action, it appeared, the decline could be irreversible. Christianity, Islam, and Sikhism were all proselytizing religions, with active mechanisms for conversion; Hinduism was not. As things stood, the traffic in conversion was flowing only one way, and those lost to Hinduism were gone forever.

Hindu Nationalists strongly feel that three elements are most essential for the progress of the Hindu Jati that its members share a common language, that religion is held in common by them, and that members are in unity and share a common origin. "Hindi, Hindu, Hindustan, " thus became a slogan coined to awaken Nationalist feelings. The evolution and resurgence of Hindu Nationalism at the state level is not very old. Although the Hindus were the majority community ruled by minority rulers since the 12th century A. D., there was no major uprising in any part of the subcontinent against any of the foreign rulers. Despite forceful conversions to Islam and other deprivations imposed on the Hindus during the reign of Mughals in general and Aurangazeb in particular, the only forces that rose or stood up against these harsh treatments were a handful like Shivaji, the Maratha warlord, and the Sikhs.

Even the 1857 uprising against the British was more a military rebellion than one that was either a national or religious movement against the rulers. Later, with the growth of the Indian National Congress, aspirations for self-rule and independence were channeled along a nonviolent path. With the ascension of Gandhi, the manner in which the political goals were to be realized was clearly defined and meticulously followed. It was only after the Muslim League came into the political arena and advocated a separate homeland for the Muslims that the Hindus were awakened and rose up against this idea. The events that led to partition of the subcontinent as a consequence of independence, the Hindu-Muslim riots and trans-border movement that followed, and the assassination of Gandhi by a Hindu fundamentalist were the catalysts that really molded Hindu Nationalism into concrete shape.

The belief that Gandhi was inclined more toward the minority Muslims was something not very palatable to the Hindu Nationalists' psyche. To them, being the majority community meant automatic elevation to the prime position, especially after having been under subjugation by foreign rulers for centuries without any respite. Although Hindu Nationalist organizations were active in some parts of India since independence, their growth and rising popularity has been closely linked to the rise and increased activities of Islamic fundamentalists and vice versa. While occasional Hindu-Muslim riots did occur at a few places at irregular intervals, these were a result of localized frictions and often perpetrated by narrow-minded individuals out to gain some petty dividends. What gave direction and purpose to this movement was a chain of events linked to the liberation of Bangladesh.

The first among these was the influx of Muslim refugees from this newly formed state beginning in 1971. This led to changes in the demography of some eastern states of the nation, especially in the state of Assam. The majority community suddenly became the minority, and this changed status made them feel threatened. The next event that fueled the Hindu Nationalist movement is not linked to Islam directly but is worth mentioning. This was the traumatic experience of the Hindus during the brief period of the Sikh extremist movement in Punjab. Between 1980 and 1984, when the movement was contained, it was mostly Hindus who bore the brunt of Sikh militancy in the state.

The trust and brotherhood that had existed between the Hindus and Sikhs and which was the fabric of Punjabi rural life was suddenly shattered. Even after the situation was contained and normalcy returned, the Hindus remained shell-shocked by their traumatic experience. The ethnic cleansing of Hindus in Kashmir and the violence perpetrated there affected the Hindu Nationalists profoundly. For them, now the threat was real and violent. They had to act to heal their wounds and prove to the other side that they were not powerless. And so in 1992, the long-disputed structure in Ayodhya was brought down, leading to widespread riots in Bombay and many other parts and accounting for scores of deaths.

Coinciding with the turn of events in Kashmir, especially the proliferation of Madrassas in that state, there has been a discernible increase in the number of these Islamic religious schools in many parts of North India. The pretext to open these institutions was the plea that Urdu, the language of the Muslims, was not being taught in normal schools. But instead of knowledge to enlarge the mind with logic and analytical reasoning, what is being imparted to the pupils is religious indoctrination and narrow fundamentalist philosophy. Along with the mushrooming of Madrassas, there has been a discernible demographic change. The Muslim population that had stood at less than 10 percent at the time of independence has enlarged to over 14 percent and is continuing to grow.

Today there is a new Hindu identity under construction in many parts of India, especially in the northern and central states. It is a process which is undoubtedly propelled by the fact that this identity is also the basis of the political growth of some contemporary parties. Political scientist Gabriel Almond has stated, "It is not unusual for ethnicity and religion to combine, as in Hinduism. Hindu Fundamentalism is ethno-nationalist as well as religious. The two spheres are not neatly separated. The rise of Hindu Nationalism in a country with a very significant number of minorities means that India, for a very long time to come, will be embroiled in recurring crises like the many it faces now. This could impede the positive growth and development of its reviving but still shaky economy. Fanaticism and the chaos it could bring within India are not healthy for the growth and prosperity of the nation.

To live in India is to become aware that the psychological space occupied by religion, the context and inspiration it provides for individual lives, and its role in fostering the cultural identity and survival of different groups is very different from the situation in a country such as the United States. An Indian atheist cannot go along with an American counterpart's casual dismissal of religion as "important, if true. " In India, religion is visibly "important, even if not true. "Communalism in the contemporary Indian context is a deep, almost visceral form of antagonism and antipathy between communities of different cultural, linguistic, and religious identities. Based in part on fear and ignorance of the other, communalism often gives rise to conflict and violence between communities. But no single form of communalist conflict has cost so many lives as that between Hindus and Muslims.

Fundamentalism thrives within this system as a distinctively extreme reaction to threats to communal identity. It is a militant form of religious separatism. If we look closely, however, we will find that the much-touted revival is less one of religiosity than one of cultural identities based on religious affiliation. There is no great ferment taking place in the world of religious ideas, beliefs, and rituals, or any marked increase in the sum of human spirituality. What we are witnessing today is less the resurgence of religion than of communalism, where a community of believers has not only a religious affiliation but also social, economic, and political interests in common. These may conflict with the corresponding interests of another community of believers sharing the same geographical space.

The basic reason for supposing that religiously inspired reform movements may be gaining momentum in our time is that perceptions of inequity in human affairs and the tangible realities that provoke those perceptions are on the increase. Population growth on the one hand, and advanced means of communications on the other, more often than not disrupt accustomed ways of life. They help to create personal uncertainty, isolation, and disappointment. The resulting distress can and often does find expression in fundamentalist movements that attempt to counteract uncertainty, isolation, and disappointment by forming supportive communities of fellow believers. It is no accident that these movements are based in countries where the continuation of old village ways is becoming impossible for a majority of the population, where urban-based mass communications, by penetrating the villages, have begun to erode an age-old framework of peasant life.

The problem in India is that the nation continues to keep religion and the state intertwined. In a country that has many religions, the government and the people must realize that religion and the state have to be separate. Mixing the two has never worked, and it never will. The stability of the state system depends critically on the state's role in balancing and mediating relationships between thousands of separate communities. Such balancing requires careful and measured degrees of impartiality, neutrality, syncretism, and tolerance. What has bound communities to each other has been the manufactured mechanisms and symbols of the secular state. These structures, while supportive of local religious and sectarian institutions, had to remain impartial, neutral, or secular. Future conflicts will be those of communal survival, aggravated, or in many cases caused by, environmental scarcity. These conflicts will be subnational, meaning that it will be hard for states and local governments to protect their own citizens physically. This is how many states may ultimately die.

As state power fades, peoples and cultures around the world will be thrown back upon their own strengths and weaknesses, with fewer equalizing mechanisms to protect them. The coming decades will see us more aware of our differences than our similarities. To the average person, political values will mean less and personal security more. The story of Hindu-Muslim relations takes on different hues depending upon the color of one's ideological lenses. To the conservative Hindu Nationalists for whom the Hindu saffron and the Muslim green do not mix, the rift between the two communities is a fundamental fact of Indian history. To them, it is a thousand-year-old "civilizational" conflict in which Muslims, militarily victorious and politically ascendant for centuries, have tried to impose Islamic civilization on their Hindu subjects through all means, and yet had only limited success.

How non-Muslims think of Islam conditions the manner in which they deal with Muslims, which in turn conditions how Muslims think of and deal with non-Muslims. There is the opposite in everything between Hindus and Muslims. The Hindu faces the east to the rising sun to pray; the Muslim to the setting sun, toward Mecca, in the west. The Hindu writes from left to right; the Muslim from right to left. The Hindu eats with the right hand; the Muslim with the left. The Hindu worships the cow; the Muslim attains paradise by eating beef. The Hindu man keeps a mustache; the Muslim man always shaves his upper lip. Whatever one does, it is the other's religion to do the opposite. Violence is present in all religions, and has been seen as necessary for the realization of religious goals. Religious violence has taken many forms, some as extreme as the practice of animal or human sacrifice, the righteous and often excruciatingly cruel punishment envisaged for sinners, the exorcism of spirits and demons, the killing of witches or apostates, and in ascetic violence against the self.

More broadly, every religion has a vision of divinely legitimized violence under certain circumstances the holy war of the Christians, the just war of the Jews, and the jihad of the Muslims. As India's religious traditions developed, images of warfare persisted. The great epics (the Mahabharata and the Ramayana) contain grand accounts of wars and battles, and the enduring sermon of Lord Krishna, the Bhagawad Gita, was recorded in the Mahabharata as being delivered on the battlefield. The Gita gave several reasons why killing in warfare is permissible, among them the argument that the soul can never be killed "He who slays, slays not; he who is slain is not slain. "Another reason is based in Dharma (moral obligation) the duties of a member of the Kshatriya (warrior) caste by definition involve killing, so violence has been justified in the very maintenance of social order. Islam is ambiguous about violence.

Like all religions, Islam occasionally allows for force, while stressing that the main spiritual goal is one of nonviolence and peace. The Koran contains a proscription very much like the Biblical injunction, "Thou shall not kill. " The Koran commands the faithful, "Slay not the life that God has made sacred. " The very name Islam is cognate to Salaam, the word for peace, and like the Hebrew word Shalom, it implies a vision of social harmony and spiritual repose. It is time for us to lower the religious barricades and begin to set our houses in order. Having said that, is it ever possible to find answers to all the haunting questions related to the prevailing and growing fundamentalisms and arrive at possible solutions so as to steer India in particular, South Asia in general, and even the world community clear of the frictions generated by fundamentalist movements.

Since religious bigotry and fanaticism are at the heart of many of the crises confronting us, perhaps the scriptures can provide a way out of the violence, clashes, and conflicts that are perpetrated in the name of religion. All scriptures agree on the fundamentals of the equality of people in the eyes of the Divine. The injunction to free, spirited inquiry and the cultivation of a high personal standard of conduct in one's relationship with fellow humans and with society at large is a common feature of all religious tradition. A return to these fundamentals could be the bedrock of a true religious resurgence. The strongest fortress and protection that Hindu and Muslim societies and the nation states of South Asia have against the satanic fires raging within the belly of the Indian subcontinent is the investigation, recognition, understanding, and application of the true fundamentals of Hinduism and Islam.

Most people feel that religion should provide tranquility and peace, not terror. The challenge today is to appreciate the diversity of religions, ascertain the reasons behind confrontations and conflicts, and react to specific events and situations with informed, reasoned responses rather than predetermined presumptions and reactions. As long as religion is used to batter people into political submission, the poor and uneducated masses will remain in their shackles. True religion cares for the poor and acts as the servant of a God who needs no defenders with guns in their hands and hatred in their minds. To the religious person who seeks to understand the fundamentals of scriptures, it seems clear that the right to just treatment by the state, protection of cultures and diversities as expressions of the Divine, the right to worship freely, and the protection of intellectual inquiry are all sanctioned and safeguarded both by the Bhagawad Gita as well as the Holy Koran.

In fact, both texts define in clear terms what Dharma (moral obligation) is, and when and how a battle may and should be joined as a Dharmic (morally correct) battle or Jihad (holy war) carried out in submission to the will of God. This is the true fundamentalism. Islam began as a revolution against ignorance; yet today, 1, 400 years from its founding, the freshness of the youngest world faith is debilitated by ignorance. The fault lies not with the disenfranchised Muslim masses, but with dishonest leaders whose interests are served and strengthened by keeping the people as ill-informed as possible. Mass illiteracy guarantees that Islam will be used more to impede progress and less to aid it. The challenge Muslims face, therefore, is to realize the Holy Prophet's revolutionary message by identifying Islam as an ally of progress instead of its foe. In that realization could be the beginnings of a true Islamic renaissance.

In India, what Muslims need is the preservation and strengthening of their religio-cultural identity. The only solution to the problem faced by the Indian Muslims is to look inward to their own weaknesses, rectify the moral lapses in their personal behavior and realize their potential as bearers of the universal message of Islam. They should raise themselves above the petty concerns of material injustices and should not entertain any bitterness, envy, or anger against the majority community. At the same time, the majority community must always provide constitutional guarantees that the minority's rights will be respected, not trampled. Let Hindus in India choose their way of life freely. But if they attempt to impose it upon any other groups, then they are clearly in the wrong.

5

Caste Politics in India

Uttar Pradesh, Bihar, Madhya Pradesh and Rajasthan is often considered as the heart of India, not only because of its relative weight -which has no equivalent - but also because it is often seen as the cradle of the Hindu civilisation, where the spoken language is the nearest to Sanskrit and the caste system the closest to the varna model. This model is more deeply established than in the South where the twice-born are seldom 'complete': if the Brahmins are present, the warrior and merchant castes are often absent, like in Maharashtra and Bengal by the way. By contrast, in the North all the varnas are there and the system is all the more strict as the upper varnas are in larger number than elsewhere in India : they represent from 13,6% (Bihar) up to 24,2% (Rajasthan) of the population.

In Uttar Pradesh, the largest state of the Indian Union, the upper castes represented in 1931 one fifth of the population, from whom 9,2% were Brahmins - the highest percentage in India. In this area the Rajputs, 7,2% of the population, were traditionally zamindars alongside members of the Muslim aristocracy. However, during the 19century the tribute claimed by the British was such that many of them were obliged to hand over all or part of their zamindari to merchants they were heavily in debt with, Brahmins, or even Kayasths (scribe castes). The peasants, often tenants who could be expulsed at any moment, mostly belonged to lower and intermediate castes.

Amongst the intermediate castes, the Jats stood prominent. They represented only 1,6% of the state population but were concentrated in the west of the state where they competed with the Rajputs. Well considered for their warrior qualities number of them were sent to the front during the two world wars. The Jats were also active farmers, hard workers when cultivating their plots of land was concerned. Among the Shudras they were followed by a series of lower castes responsible for services farmers (Kurmis, Lodhis, Koeris, Gujjars) or ox- and shepherds, the Yadavs, the largest Shudra caste, with 8,7% of the population. No other Shudra caste exceeded 3,5% of the state's population.

The Chamars (leather workers), certainly, constituted the largest caste with 12,7% of the state's population but as Untouchables they held a marginal position. The socio-economic conditions of Bihar, Rajasthan and Madhya Pradesh had much in common with Uttar Pradesh. In Bihar, the upper castes represented 13,6% of the population including 4,2% Rajputs, 4,7% Brahmins and 2,9% Bhumihars - an upper caste controlling a vast superficy of land which claim that they are Brahmins. During the British Raj, most of the zamindars were Rajputs, Bhumihars and Brahmins. While the province was mainly subjected to direct administration, the British allowed the zamindars wide-ranging prerogatives. They could go as far as seizing a tenant's personal possessions and crop in repayment of debts.

After in 1857 having resisted to the insurrection thanks to the support of zamindari, the British increased the links with the landowners and accorded them a higher autonomy.Like in Uttar Pradesh, they mostly belonged to Shudra castes (Yadav, Kurmi, and Koeri etc.), among them the Yadavs again represented the highest number, 11% of the population. As for agricultural labourers and/or landless peasants, they were principally Untouchables (and more specially the Chamars).

Rajasthan is the North Indian state where the upper castes are in the largest number : 8% Brahmins, 9,2% Rajputs and 7% Banyas. Another significant factor is due to the high proportion of Jats, 9%. The fact that two princely states of Rajputana, Bharatpur and Dholpur were governed by Jat dynasties recognised as Kshatriyas is worth noticing. However, this possibility of elevation of the Shudras was inhibited by the Rajputs' domination. They controlled the overwhelming part of princely states and at a lower level exercised the function of jagirdar or zamindar; hence a cultural as well as a political effect: ...for over a thousand years the people of Rajasthan did not look up to the Brahmans as cultural models, nor did they adopt brahminical customs and life-styles to advance their ritual status. The people of Rajasthan did try to emulate the cultural norms and ritual forms adopted by their respective princes and jagirdars [who were Rajputs]. This imitation of the Rajputs reflects a general rule very little compatible with the rise of lower castes in a social and a political field.

The Shudra castes for instance, may have preferred this 'kshatriyaisation' to the constitution of a separated collective identity. The distribution of castes was almost the same in Madhya Pradesh. In this state the largest princely states (Gwalior, Indore and Dewas) were governed by Maratha dynasties, but the jagirdars and zamindars were often Rajputs. In 1931, the upper castes represented 12,9% (with 5,7% Brahmins, 5,3% Rajputs and 2% Banyas), whereas the Shudras were 42.5%, the Untouchables 14% and the Tribals are exceptionally high 22%5.

On the whole, the Hindi-speaking states display a relative social and political homogeneity, inherited from the structures left by the British regarding land-owning and fiscal levy and related to the influence of the upper castes. The social hierarchy was all the more rigid and oppressive as the upper castes (particularly the Rajputs) were in many regions the dominant castes.In the Hindi-belt the 'twice-born' often meet those three criteria and thus cumulate superiority in terms of status as well as the quality of dominant caste. Generally the

Rajputs hold this position, but there are also exceptions like the Bhumihars in Bihar, the Tyagis (Brahmins who cultivate the land) and even the Jats in western Uttar Pradesh.

In the South, the caste system does not derive so closely from the varna model. The proportion of the Brahmins and even of the twice-born is often low. In Tamil Nadu the Brahmins represented in 1891 only 3% of the population and were concentrated in the Kaveridelta. Correlatively, Tamil society was more fragmented and fluid. If the Vellalas - a caste of Shudra cultivators claiming the statute of Kshatriya - represented 12,42% of the population, no caste, even not this one, extended its domination over more than one district in fact, in most districts the Vellalas shared the dominance with warrior castes, immigrated from Andhra Pradesh between the 15th and the 18th-century and with castes of craftsmen and merchants.

Fragmentation was reinforced because of the division of these castes into many sub-groups, as show the schemes of matrimonial unions in which the endogamous jatis rarely extend than in more than a few neighbouring villages. Ritual purity, except in the extreme ends of the system was less strictly enforced than in the North and the caste-status hindered less than elsewhere the change of professional activities, outside the sphere of those traditionally allowed in the caste.

In Karnataka like in Tamil Nadu, the demographic weight of the upper castes mainly Brahmins was greatly inferior to that of the Hindi-belt, but in addition to that, the 'varnic' scheme was even more deeply affected by the rise of a religious movement - a sect actually -the Lingayats, that was eventually integrated in the caste system as a dominant caste - in some way comparable to that of another land owning, cultivating caste, the Vokkaligas.The domination of these castes, in the villages, has always been less oppressive than in the Hindibelt for two series of reasons. Firstly, they never locally combine superiority in terms of ritual purity (the twice-born status) with a predominant position in the rural economy (as dominant castes) : in the areas where the Vokkaligas are the dominant caste, the Brahmins continue to act as priests ; in the areas where the Lingayats dominate, the dominant castes are part of the Lingayat jatis who till land, whereas the priests are recruited in another jati.

For James Manor, the cohesiveness of society in Karnataka is above all a product of the early presence of an economy of rather small farmer-proprietors. In the former princely state of Mysore - the heart of modern Karnataka - in the 1950s, 65,2% of the farmers made one third of their income with the land they owned. Karnataka, like Tamil Nadu, had an anti-Brahmin movement, led by the Vokkaligas and the Lingayats. But if targeted mainly the arrogant Brahmins living in towns and working in the administrative and the professions. In the villages, where the Brahmins were often poorer and depended on the patronage of the dominant castes, they showed them greater respect.

In Andhra Pradesh too, the balance of demographic power had the effect of putting political power in the hands of the dominant castes at the expense of the Brahmins. In 1921 the latter were only 3% of the state population. Like everywhere else, the Brahmins had been the first to benefit from the modern education system introduced by the British but the castes of cultivators like the Kapu and the Kamma, respectively 15,2 and 4,8% of the population in 1921, fully profited of the modernisation of agriculture, especially in the areas where the ryotwari system prevailed, hence the emergence of middle class people in their midst.Gradually these groups joined Congress and captured its second line of leadership. In Maharashtra, bridge state between the North and the South, the twice-born were in a larger number than in Andhra Pradesh with 3,9% Brahmins, 1% Kshatriyas and 1,69% Vaishyas. Nevertheless, the total number of these varna was lower than in the Hindi-speaking region. The Brahmins took advantage of social change due to colonisation in a dramatic way.

By the late 19century they almost monopolised administrative functions open to Indians as well as the professions. Hence the vigour of the anti-Brahmin movement led by Shudra leaders and then even by Untouchables like B.R. Ambedkar. Actually, Maharashtra had a long history of conflict between Brahmins and Shudra castes, mainly Marathas, who formed a dominant caste. Right from the 17century, Marathas carved out a state for themselves at the expense of the Moghol empire. The dynasty then established by Shivaji claimed the status of Kshatriya. However, Maharashtrian Brahmins - and more particularly the Chitpavans a Brahmin jati acknowledged such a promotion very reluctantly and usurped the throne in the 18century after having served the Maratha kingdom as administrators and generals. This bone of contention served as backdrop to the anti-brahmin movement initiated at the end of the 19century.

The Marathas took an even more active part in this movement as the modernisation of agriculture within the ryotwari system as well as an intense collaboration with the British enabled them to make rapid economic progress. Eventually, Marathas gained control over the Congress which had become a serious contender for power _ and indeed formed the government in 1937. The Brahmins who then run the party, refused to allow them a large space within the governments of 1937 and 1946, but from 1950 onwards, the Congress was gradually dominated by Marathas.

This rapid survey of the North-South contrast suggests that the Hindi-belt remained dominated by an upper-caste élite whose influence derived from numbers, political structures (the continuation of princely states) and the pattern of land ownership as well as tax levy. However, the role of the low caste movements needs to be scrutinised too. While they were very active in South India, they did not succeed in making such a big impact in the North.

The caste system has been traditionally analysed as a 'sacralised social order' based on the notion of ritual purity.

In this view, its holistic character - to use the terminology of Louis Dumont- implies that the dominant values, that of the Brahmins, are regarded by the whole society as providing universal references, role models. Hence the central role played by "Sanskritisation", a practice that M.N. Srinivas has defined as 'the process by which a "low" Hindu caste, or tribal or other group, changes its customs, ritual, ideology and way of life in the direction of a high, and frequently, "twice-born" caste' that is the Brahmins, but also the Kshatriyas or even the Vaishyas.

Low castes may for instance adopt the most prestigious features of the Brahmins' diet and therefore emulate vegetarianism. Such a process reflects a special coherence in society, all the groups admitting the values of the upper castes as the legitimate value system. Such a coherence is not synonymous with cohesion. In fact, sanskritisation itself bears witness of an aspiration to social mobility : low castes constantly try to improve their social status by imitating the high castes and contest the position which has been assigned to them in the system. Moreover, the myths of origin of the low castes are always centred around the idea of an initial decline: even Untouchable castes claim to descend from Brahmin castes and that they have fallen from this rank often because of the malicious intent of some upper caste people.

Robert Deliège points out that through such myths, the Untouchables 'take caste for granted, and by stressing their brotherhood with Brahmans, they acknowledge the superiority of the latter'. This is pure sanskritisation. For Srinivas 'Sanskritisation is generally accompanied by, and often results in, upward mobility for the caste in question but the mobility associated with Sanskritisation results only in positional changes in the system and does not lead to any structural change. That is, a caste moves up above its neighbours and another comes down, but all this takes place in an essentially stable hierarchical order. The system itself does not change'. Indeed, the values sustaining the social system remain the same.

In a way, the caste system, with sanskritisation, incorporates a mechanism of safety valves that enables the upper castes to channel of even defuse the revolt of the plebeians; this is how coherence can be maintained while the system does not display any real cohesion. H. Gould suggests that 'one of the prime motive force motive-forces behind Sanskritization is this factor of repressed hostility which manifests itself not in the form of rejecting the caste system but in the form of its victims trying to seize control of it and thereby expiate their frustrations on the same battlefield where they acquired them. Only then can there be a sense of satisfaction in something achieved that is tangible, concrete, and relevant to past experience'.

Besides sanskritisation, low caste groups have explored avenues for upward mobility through the bhakti movements and the sectarian model. Since the Buddha, gurus have recurrently questioned the caste system on behalf of the fundamental equality of men before god. Their disciples who were initiated into monastic orders forgot about their caste to form new fraternities. Srinivas emphasised that the 'protest sects' in a way 'offered opportunities for mobility to members of the so-called low castes'. However, this equality was other worldly: it did not affect the social order, even if it devalued it as a purely mundane exercise. Ambedkar rightly pointed out that 'from the point of view of the annihilation of caste, the struggle of the saints did not have any effect on society'. The traditional caste system was more directly challenged during the British Raj, when the values propagated through schooling and Christian missionaries and the impact of the State apparatus did not leave it unaltered.

The development of the means of communication led to the opening up of the jati which, till then, was confined to a reduced territory, delimited by matrimonial relations. Hence the emergence of horizontal solidarities and the territorial extension of the frontiers of caste. The members of a same jati were enabled to migrate to find jobs or even obliged to do so, if they were transferred within the British administration for instance. Transfers of bureaucrats out of their native place often generated feelings of anomie and made the finding of the suitable match for endogamous marriages more complicated; hence the idea to create associations which could link members of a same caste.

These institutions were also stirred up by the census, which was a key element in the formation of the colonial state. From 1871 onwards the British enumerated the castes and therefore these 'human groups (castes) [we]re treated to a considerable extent as abstractable from the regional and territorial contexts in which they function[ed]'. This effect reinforced those of the state construction process but the census also raised among several castes the sentiment of having common interests since the British did not content themselves with enumerating them ; they also classified them. In 1901, the Census Commissioner, Herbert Risley, decided to give the ranking of the jatis in their local context and their varna, which was a much more delicate enterprise.

Castes immediately organised themselves and even formed councils to take steps to see that their status was recorded in the way they thought was honourable to them. Caste associations were therefore created also as pressure groups whose aim was to improve their rank in the census. Naturally this process was especially prominent among the low castes and therefore give 'An indication of the widespread desire for mobility among the backward castes...'. Each census provided castes with an opportunity to petition the government for getting a higher place in the order of precedence and for being recorded under new, sanskritised, names. Indeed, this move was in keeping with the logic of sanskritisation since the objective was not to opt out from the system but to rise within it according to its own rules and values.

The Kayasths of North India were probably the first to show the way in that direction. In late XIXth century, Munshi

Kali Prasad, a Lucknow-based rich lawyer from this caste, wrote Kayasthas Ethnology, a book where he showed 'to which of the four great divisions of the Aryans in India [,the Kshatriyas,] the Kayasthas belonged'. Subsequently, the Kayasths claimed that they were the descendants of the Emperor Chandragupta. The Kayastha Conference was founded in 1886 on the basis of the Kayasth Dharma Sabha. One of its resolutions it passed at its first annual meeting in 1887 established a Temperance section and repeatedly - and allegedly successfully - requested the Kayasths to give up drinking.

Moreover, the Kayastha Conference still endeavoured in the 1920s-1930s to sanskritise caste rituals and invited its members to emulate the 'dvijas'. Certainly, this attitude stemmed from modern motives since the main reason for sanskritisation was to standardise the Kayasth culture and to create a homogenous social group, however, sanskritisation remained the key idiom, with its emphasis on positional mobility instead of structural changes.

Caste associations were more successful in promoting the unity of the caste groups and in emancipating themselves from sanskritisation in southern and western India. They have incited the sub-castes to adopt the same name in the Census and to break the barriers of endogamy, even if, within a caste, the members of the upper class still tend to inter-marry - but then it is more economic endogamy than purely caste-based endogamy. This process has been observed by Robert Hardgrave in the case of the Nadars of Tamil Nadu whose caste association, the Nadar Mahajana Sangam was founded in 1910 and promoted what he calls 'caste fusion', as 'the unit of endogamy expanded'. For S. Barnett this kind of fusion tended to transform castes into ethnic groups. His demonstration is based on another Tamil case study, the Kontaikkatti Vellalars who do not represent a large number of people but are influential since many of them are landlords.

From 1920 onwards, the caste association has encouraged them to expand endogamy in new territories and to other Vellallars in order to make up for their numerical weakness. For Barnett these innovations introduced 'qualitative change in the ideological field of caste', since 'blood purity', on which according to him relies ritual purity, has lost its importance. The relevant unit is not the original jati any more, but groups of castes, which represents 'a transition from caste to ethniclike regional caste blocs'. However, this is only the first step towards an ethnicisation of caste which also implies a collective history - at least a golden Age - and a separate, cultural identity. This kind of ethnicisation of castes or caste federations are much more conducive to social change than caste associations or caste fusion pure and simple.

The ethnicisation of caste in western and southern India Maharashtra between sanskritisation and ethnicisation of caste In western India, the ethnicisation process has been started early by the Satyashodak Movement. Developed by Phule in the Bombay Presidency in the late XIXth century, it was more than a caste association since it intended to represent the 'bahujan samaj', the majority of the people, the masses. Yet, this capacity to aggregate low caste people was short lived even though it rested on a rather solid ethnic bedrock.

Jotirao Phulewas a Mali (market gardener), a cultivating caste in close contact with towns where its members sold their products. In one of these towns, Poona, Phule could attend a school of the Scottish Mission. What he learnt about the Blacks in the United States suggested to him a comparison with the lower castes - hence his book, Slavery that he dedicated to the people of America. The writings of Thomas Paine exerted a special influence on Phule who discovered the individualist values of liberty and equality in The Age of Reason and Human Rights. This source of inspiration developed in conjunction with that of Christianity.

For Phule, Jesus-Christ epitomises equality and fraternity. He also regards him as the spokesman for the poor people.

However, Phule did not convert to Christianity and even translated the Christian idiom into a new discourse focused on King Bali, the subterranean god who reigns in the underground world according to Hindu mythology. Phule tried to give the 'bahujan samaj' a new history on the basis of some of the findings of Orientalism. In 1792, William Jones had deduced from the discovery of the Indoeuropean linguistic family the notion of a common, original race whose branches had migrated towards Europe and India. This theory was developed during the nineteenth century by many German philologists. In their writings appear the notions of 'Sanskritic race' or 'Vedic people'. These speculations reached India from the late 1850s onwards through Max Müller, who tended to be somewhat more cautious, and Muir who published in 1860 a study on 'The Trans-Himalayan Origin of the Hindus, and their affinity with the western branches of the Aryan race'.

The first Hindu nationalist ideologues of the late 19th century and early 20th century from Dayananda to Tilak borrowed heavily from the European orientalists. Among other themes, the one they used assiduously related to the common racial origin of the European and Indian people and its corollary, the southward migration which they interpreted to prove that the Hindus were the first race and that they once dominated the whole world. This myth helped the first Hindu revivalists to regain a certain self-esteem by claiming that their ancestors were the first inhabitants of the world.

Phule used the Aryan theory to his own advantage: the fact that upper castes leaders traced their origin from Aryan conquerors could be used to argue that they descended from foreigners and that their culture, including the caste system was alien to India's original people. Phule, therefore, portrayed the Aryans as invaders who had settled in India at a rather late period to subjugate the first inhabitants of India and destroyed their civilisation. For him, the low castes were the descendants of these people. In this reinterpretation of the past, the invaders are identified as Brahmins whereas the indigenous groups are described as descending from the original ruling class, the Kshatriyas. In Phule's ideology, this category does not refer to the second varna but to includes 'all original Indians, from Kunbi-Marathas through Mahars'.

The king of these original Kshatriyas, Bali, was described by Phule as reigning over a rich and prosperous country made of "milk and honey". The extreme fertility of the soil of India, its rich productions, the proverbial wealth of the people, and the other innumerable gifts which this favourable land enjoys, and which have more recently tempted the cupidity of the Western nations, attracted the Aryans [...] The original inhabitants with whom these earth-born gods, the Brahmans, fought, were not inappropriately termed Rakshasas, that is the protectors of the land [...] The cruelties which the European settlers practised on the American Indians on their first settlement in the new world had certainly their parallel in India in the advent of the Aryans and their subjugation of the aborigines [...] They originally settled on the banks of the Ganges whence they spread gradually over the whole of India. In order, however, to keep a better hold on the people they devised that weird system of mythology, the ordination of caste, and the code of crude and inhuman laws to which we can find no parallel among the other nations.

Phule's endeavour had a pioneering dimension since he was probably the first low caste leader who avoided the traps of sanskritisation by endowing the low caste with an alternative value system. For the first time, the low castes were presented as ethnic groups which had inherited the legacy of an antiquarian golden age and whose culture was therefore distinct from that of the wider Hindu society ; secondly, his efforts in favour of the low castes were not confined to his castemen only: he wanted to unite the 'bahujan samaj', e.g. the Shudras and the Atishudras (dalits) and as early as 1853 he opened schools for Untouchables. He projected himself as the spokesman of the non-Brahmins at large and, indeed, kept targeting the Brahmins in vehement pamphlets where he presented them as rapacious money lenders, corrupt priests eager to extort as much as they could from poor and ignorant villagers. He even tried to pressurise the British for reducing the number of Brahmins in the government services.

Phule was also the first low caste organiser. In 1875 he was attracted by the Arya Samaj, but he kept his distance from this movement because he did not trust the upper caste reformerswho pretended to fight against the social system even though they observed its rules. He also remained aloof from the Congress which he regarded as a Brahmin movement. Nationalism, according to him, was an illusion created by upper caste manipulation to conceal the inner divisions of Indian society. He had founded the Satyashodak Samaj in 1873 in order to strengthen the sentiment of unity among the low castes and never diluted this agenda in party politics. He narrated pseudo-historical episodes bearing testimony of the traditional solidarity between the Mahars and Shudrasand protested against the Brahmins' stratagems for dividing the low castes.

In the late 19century and early 20century, the Satyashodak idiom embraced rich peasants as well as agricultural tenants who belonged to very different castes and in some places 'the Sathya Shodhak message seemed to have reached even the untouchable'. A major spokesman of the non-Brahmin movement in Maharashtra in the 1910-1930, Mukundrao Patil, the son of Phule's colleague, Krishnarao Bhalekar, was for instance a radical defender of the Untouchables even though he was a rich peasant. He advocated 'the general Satyashodak ideology, of opposition to Sanskritisation and assertion of the 'non-Aryan' unity of Maharashtrian natives'. By that time, Phule's view of the non-brahmins as non-Aryas had also made an impact on the small dalit intelligentsia. In 1909, Kisan Faguji Bansode, a Mahar from Nagpur, warned the upper castes in the following terms:

The Aryans conquered us and gave us unbearable harassment. At that time we were your conquest, you treated us even worse than slaves and subjected us to any torture you wanted. But now we are no longer your subjects, we have no service relationship with you, we are not your slaves or serfs...The Satyashodak Samaj eventually attracted even Marathas such as the Jedhe family from Poona emerged as the main defender of the caste interests. They realised 'the futility of a purely Maratha politics and the necessity of making the movement more broadbased. From this time on they shifted to a "Satyashodak" orientation, although neither had previously had any connection with the Satyashodak Samaj in Poona'.

The discourse of Keshavrao Jedhe was 'the long-held Satyashodak view of history: Brahmans were outsiders to the country and to the ethnic community of true "Hindus" ; they desired only their own caste superiority and consolidated their power through treachery, through falsification of historical records, and by weaving a web of religious slavery which set up a social hierarchy of superiority and inferiority and divided the masses'.

Maratha princes such as the Maharajah of Baroda strongly approved of Phule's ideological commitments and donated large amounts of money to his movement. A direct descendant of Shivaji, the Maharajah of Kolhapur, Shahu, who reigned between 1894 and 1922 and who was 'intensely proud of his Maratha lineage', was even more supportive.. He recruited Maratha Satya Shodhaks in his administration, reserved 50% of the vacancies in the state administration for 'the members of the backward communities'and patronised the establishment of the Satyashodak Samaj in Kolhapur in 1911. He promoted inter-caste dining and introduced the Inter-caste Marriage Act in 1918.

In 1920 he appointed Maratha priests to circumvent the Brahmins and soon after established the Kshatriya Vedic School to train Maratha priests. However, he remained as much interested in promoting the Marathas as the Bahujan Samaj at large. On the one hand he tried to secure for the

Marathas the status of Kshatriyas and in fact he broke with the local Brahmins in 1900 when they refused to recognise his family's claim to this status and accordingly refused to perform certain rituals. On the other hand, he wanted to 'kshatriyase' also Untouchables to whom he used to symbolically give swords and Maratha names and whom he called 'Suryavaunshi', pretending that way that they could trace their lineage to the sun God, Surya.

Unlike Phule who had described the Kshatriyas as the original people of India, for Shahu they were the warrior castes, a social order to which the Untouchables and the Marathas belonged, and this was in keeping with the logic of the caste system. Shahu made strong efforts to federate the lower castes. In the communal representation scheme that he introduced in 1920 in Kolhapur municipality 85 castes were grouped into 20 'unions of castes'. The Marathas, the Rajputs and the Kunbis formed a constituency in themselves.

Yet, the Sathyashodak Samaj could not become a common platform for all the non-Brahmins on the basis of a non-Aryan identity because of the attitude of Marathas other than Shahu. Most of them refused to mix with lower castes and stuck to the sanskritisation process. For instance, even Bhaskarrao Jadhav, in Marathe ani Tyanci Bhasha, displayed much ambivalence: on the one hand he admits 'the prevalence of Dravidian customs and racial intermixture among Marathas, and on the other asserts, without any qualification, the Marathas are definitely "Aryan Kshatriyas" '. Therefore, even those who had followed Phule's message for some time, eventually joined hands with the Brahmins-dominated Congress, or were co-opted by it.

Congress leaders such as N.V. Gadgil, who was very much aware that the nationalist movement could only acquire a mass-basis if it attracted low caste people, contacted K. Jedhe and made an alliance with him in the early 1930s. A Maratha-dominated Satyashodak Samaj, which had remained aloof from the Congress till then, decided to join the movement. Gradually, the Maratha rose to power within the party. In spite of this ultimate failure, from Phule to Shahu, the low castes movement of Maharashtra was characterised by very distinctive features with long terms implications. For the first time, all non-Brahmin castes were invited to unite on the basis of a common ethnic background - as the original inhabitants of this land - endowed with a Kshatriya ethos and to fight the Brahmin domination. Even though the dominant idiom was imbued with the symbols of kshatriyahood, this movement escaped the sanskritisation process since the upper castes were not seen as role models but as invaders whose culture could be despised. Ambedkar -who regarded Phule as one of his mentors - elaborated on this basis.

Ambedkar was a thinker as much as a political leader, as one could expect from his training since he got degrees - including a Ph. D - in different subjects, ranging from economics to law. He was also most interested in anthropology, so much so that in 1916 he made a presentation entitled 'Castes in India. For Ambedkar caste is not a racial but a social phenomenon that emerged from the strategy of the Brahmins who adopted a strictly endogamous matrimonial regime, leading the other groups to do the same in order to emulate this self-proclaimed élite.

In his subsequent writings, Ambedkar gives a more elaborated and action-oriented interpretation of the caste system. For Ambedkar the varna system establishes a unique social structure since no other society has such 'an official gradation laid down, fixed and permanent, with an ascending scale of reverence and a descending scale of contempt'. The specificity of the system lays in this 'graded inequality' which is a cause for permanent anger for Ambedkar.

Ambedkar is the first low caste politician to offer an elaborated view of the caste system to deplore the division of the lower 'a disunited body [...], infested with the caste system in which they believe as much as does the caste Hindu. This caste system among the untouchables has given rise to mutual rivalry and jealousy and it has made common action impossible'. For Olivier Herrenschmidt the very notion of 'graded inequality' makes a revolution almost impossible in India. Yet, Ambedkar, on the basis of his sociological analysis will endeavour to reshape the identity of the lower castes for enabling them to assert themselves. He first tried to give a new sense of dignity to the Shudras. In Who were the Shudras ? he maintains that they were Aryas, and therefore belonged to the 'twice born' varnas. He argues that in the Laws of Manu (one of the Dharmashastras), that Shudras took part in the coronation ceremonies of the kings, that the Shudras were often presented as rich men in old sanskrit booksand that a Shudra was eligible to the status of a Brahmin after seven generations having married Brahmins. Yet, Ambedkar does not describe the Shudras as former Brahmins but as former Kshatriyas. According to him they formed a very substantial sub-group of the warrior castes to which they even gave some of the most eminent and powerful kings of the solar dynasty. They lost their 'twice-born' status when Brahmins retrograded them to avenge some vexation.

Such a theory contrasts with Ambedkar's usual views in the sense that it is articulated in the framework of sanskritisation or kshatriyaisation: the Shudras are supposed to regain the ethos of the second varna to which they used to belong, not of being proud of their own values and life style. He looks at the Untouchables in a very different way.

In The untouchables. Who were they and why they became untouchables? (1948) he rejects once again the racial theory of some western authors for whom the Untouchables would descend from a group of indigenous people subjugated by the Aryan invaders. He dismisses also the interpretations explaining the low status of the Untouchables because of their professional activities by simply asking: 'The filthy and unclean occupations which the Untouchables perform are common to all human societies [...]why are such people not treated as Untouchables in other parts of the world ? '. His interpretation is much more complicated. He explains that each and every society is subjected to invasions by tribes which appear to be more powerful than the local ones.

Suffering from a process of dislocation, the latter, give birth to new groups that Ambedkar call the 'Broken Men': 'In a tribal war it often happened that a tribe instead of being completely annihilated was defeated and routed. In many cases a defeated tribe became broken into bits. As a consequence of this there always existed in Primitive times a floating population consisting of groups of Broken tribesmen roaming in all directions'. After the conquering tribes became sedentary, they used the services of the Broken Men against the still unsettled tribes to guard the villages. Therefore, they established themselves at the periphery of clusters of habitations, also because the villagers did not want them as neighbours.

These Broken Men became the first and most fervent adepts of Buddha and they remained so when most of the other converts returned to the mainstream of Hinduism. For Ambedkar, 'It explains why the Untouchables regard the Brahmins as inauspicious, do not employ them as their priest and do not even allow them to enter into their quarters. It also explains why the Broken Men came to be regarded as Untouchables. The Broken Men hated the Brahmins because the Brahmins were the enemies of Buddhism and the Brahmins imposed untouchability upon the Broken Men because they would not leave Buddhism'. Yet, Ambedkar does not consider that the Buddhist affiliation of the Broken Men is sufficient for explaining the way the Brahmins have retrograded them. Another reason laid in the fact that the Untouchables refused to become vegetarians and continued to eat beef when the 'Brahmins made the cow a sacred animal'.

In contrast to Ambedkar's interpretation regarding the Shudras, in which one could find remnants of sanskritisation, his - rather complicated - reading of the Untouchable's story reflects his quest for equality. He endows the Untouchables with a separate, prestigious identity deriving from the special status of Buddhism in India. They have a strong ideological basis for questioning their subordinate rank in the caste system, all the more so as Buddhism offer them an egalitarian doctrine. Ambedkar, therefore, did not content himself with elaborating a quasi scientific theory of caste which culminates in the notion of graded inequality, he has also imagined new identities for promoting the emancipation of the Untouchables. Once the latter look at themselves as former Buddhists, they could overcome their divisions and mobilise against the caste hierarchies. However, he did not apply the same line of reasoning to the Shudras who, therefore, appear as depending on the sanskritisation process.

Maharashtra gave to India her first Shudra leader with Phule and her first Untouchable leader with Ambedkar. While the first one insisted on the common pre-Aryan identity of the 'bahujan samaj' he could not really uniting it and while the second endowed the Dalit with a separate identity, he did not do the same with the Shudras and rejected the racial theory on which a pre-Aryan origin could be attributed to the lower castes. While a similar pattern developed in the South with the Dravidian movement, this movement was precisely established on the solid ground of ethnicity.

Dravidian Movement

In Madras Presidency, the Non-Brahmin movement was instrumental in engineering forms of caste fusion and succeeded in endowing the lower castes with an ethnic identity that relied on two grounds: not only its architects presented them as former Buddhists, as Ambedkar was to argue subsequently, but they also claimed that they were the original inhabitants of India, as Phule had already argued, in the wake of the Orientalist vulgate. This twofold argument was first articulated by Iyothee Thass, a Pariah converted to Buddhism who maintained that 'More than 2400 years ago the Buddhist reformation sought to unify all classes but the influence of the varnashrama dharma was too strong'. Thass foreshadowed Ambedkar in his reinterpretation of Indian history since he considered that ancient India had been prosperous and most humanly governed under Buddhist kings who were to be eliminated by Brahmin invaders who imposed the caste system.

The Buddhists were then marginalised and considered as unclean and low. Buddhism had endowed the people with a specific culture that eschewed violence, forbade the taking of alcohol etc.Thass even maintained that in the past India was called Indirar Desam, the land of Indirar, Indirar being the Buddha after he succeeded in controlling his five senses (indiriyams). This original civilisation is none other than the Dravidian civilisation and Thass therefore chose to call its castemates, the Pariahs, 'Dravidas'. As early as the late nineteenth century, the Non-Brahmin movement therefore claimed that the lower castes were the original inhabitants of India.

Again, British Orientalism had prepared the ground for this development. As early as the 19century, the Reverend Caldwell had suggested that Sanskrit had been brought to South India by Aryan Brahmin colonists and that the original inhabitants were Dravidians speaking Tamil, Telugu etc. Gradually, the non-Brahmin South Indian associations adopted the suffix 'Adi' - initial, primordial - in their titles. The Pariah Mahajan Sabha, which had been founded in 1890, became the Adi-Dravida Mahajan Sabha which, in 1918 appealed to the government to replace the pejorative word Pariah by Adi-Dravida, denoting the original inhabitants of Dravida land.

In 1917 an Adi-Andhra Mahajan Sabha had come into existence the same way. In fact, this association was initially called Andhra Panchama Conference but the chairman of its 1917 session, M.V. Bhagya Reddy, in his presidential address, declared that the so-called Panchamas were the original sons of the soil and they were the rulers of the country'. Hence the change of name of the Sabha. Varma was a Mala and in the

1931 census about one third of the Malas and Madhigas gave their identity as Adi-Andhras. One of the most influential proponents of the low caste leaders of South India was M.C. Rajah, a Pariah who became secretary of the Adi-Dravida Mahajan Sabha in 1916 and who presided over the All India Depressed Classes Association since its inception in 1928. As a nominated member of the Madras Legislative Council since 1920, in 1922, Rajah moved a resolution recommending that the terms 'Panchama' and 'Parya' be deleted from the Government records and the terms Adi-Dravida and Adi-Andhra substituted instead.

Such an identity crystallised with Ramaswami Naicker, alias Periyar, a religious mendicant who had been completely disillusioned by the Congress and Gandhi while he was taking part in the Vaikom satyagraha. If Phule had drawn some of his egalitarian inspiration from Thomas Paine, Periyar was much impressed by Robert Ingersoll. Like Phule and Ambedkar, he was egalitarian in a western, individualist vein. He said, for instance, 'A sense of self-respect and fraternity must arise within human society.

Notions of high and low amongst men should disappear'. The notion of self-respect was so central to his thinking that after quitting Congress in the mid-1920s, he launched the Self-Respect Movement which immediately endeavoured to pressurise the Justice Party in order to make it the true advocate of the lower castes. Another of his key words was Samadharma that referred to the general principle of equality. But Periyar regarded it as a Buddhist notion. Like Thass, Periyar presented the lower castes as descending from the first Buddhists and like him he also endowed them with a Dravidian identity, especially after his mobilisation of the late 1930s against the attempt of the Congress government of Madras at promoting Hindi in the schools of the Presidency.

The Dravidar Kazhagam (DK) that he founded in 1944, though its mouthpiece, Viduthalai, considered that the Congress was behind 'the exploitation of of the northern bania and his Aryan [brahmin] mentor'. Thus, 'samardharma came to stand in for a civilizational and cultural alternative: a social order based on radically different principles from the present, which needed to rest on premises derived from a non-Aryan, non-Sanskritic ethos'. Periyar had an explicitly ethnic conception of the low castes' identity since he compared their situation to that of the blacks in South Africa. A direct implication from this viewpoint laid in the unity of the Non-Brahmins who all shared a Dravidian identity. As a result, Periyar advocated the coming together of the Christians, Muslims and low castes Hindus, and, within the latter, of the Untouchables and the Shudras. Such a rapprochement took place indeed since Nadars and Adi Dravidas (Untouchables) were the mainstays of the Self-Respect movement and then of the DK but there were also Vellalas, Mukkulathavar and even Chettis among the lieutenants of Periyar. The scope and strength of this social coalition must not be exaggerated since old lines of cleavages persisted.

As in Maharashtra, the 'non-Aryans' did not form a solid block at all. M.C. Rajah criticised the 'natural animosity' of the Justice Party towards the Untouchables and in 1922-23 his South India Adi-Dravida Congress broke ranks with the party. However, the ethnic ground of the Non-Brahmin discourse which, from Thass to Periyar combined Buddhist and Dravidian references had enabled its leaders to unify low caste people and mobilise them against the 'twice borns'. As early as 1920, 'a non-brahmin constituency with its own distinctive political claims had emerged in Madras' and enabled the Justice Party to win the elections. This ethnicisation process was fostered by the political reforms since the British were much willing to recognise ethnic and/or caste groups as legitimate units for representation in the political arena.

Impacts of Discrimination

The formation of caste federations and the ethnicisation of caste, two inter related processes, were fostered by the British policy of compensatory discrimination based on the reservation of seats in the bureaucracy and in the assemblies. The very decision to grant such or such statutory representation to such and such group in these assemblies contributed to the crystallisation of new groups which resented their non- (or their under-) representation. The State was therefore indirectly reshaping society. Caste groups, often with low status, were prominent among those which mobilised against the state's arbitrary decisions. The Non-Brahmin movement of Madras Presidency was especially active. In April 1920, Lord Chelmsford received a Memorandum protesting against the reservation of only 28 seats out of 65 for the Non-Brahmins in the Legislative Council of Madras.

Interestingly, the signatories emphasised their caste and ethnic differences for justifying their claim: The Brahmins differ from the non-Brahmins in caste, manners, customs and interests and even in personal law in some respects. The former are Aryans and the latter are Dravidians and thus they differ in race. In the past the Brahmins have practically monopolised all or almost all the seats in the Local and Imperial Legislative Councils. The disabilities under which the Non-Brahmins have been suffering were fully set out in the Memorandum which Rai Bahadur K.V. Reddi prepared and submitted to the joint Select Committee on Government of India Bill.

The Non-Brahmins asked for more seats in Madras assembly because they were 'different'. During the 1920 election campaign, they requested 'all non-Brahmins in this presidency to immediately organise, combine and carry on an active propaganda so as to ensure the return to the reformed Council of as many non-Brahmin as possible'. This tactic yielded dividends since the Justice Party came first in the elections. In their plea to the British, the Non-Brahmins also emphasised their marginality in the state services and the 'disabilities' from which they were suffering. This discourse fitted well too in the British approach since the Government regarded also political representation as a means for compensatory discrimination. This policy made a similar impact on the low caste movement in Western India. In Bombay Legislative Council the Marathas showed the way in the 1920s. Their principal patron, the Maharajah of Kolhapur, had circulated a memorandum 'on the necessity of separate Communal electorates for the Marathas, etc., for electing members to the new Councils under the Reforms scheme', where he wrote:

> The Marathas have distinguished themselves in the [first world] war certainly not less, if not more, than the Sikhs or the Mohammedans who have been given separate electorates. They are almost given to agriculture, military service or employment as mil-hands. Being thus not a commercial or educated community, they are poor, and without resources, influence and organisation. In this respect they are even worse of than Telis, Tilaris, Goldsmiths, Sutas, Lohars and even Mahars, Mangs and other Untouchables, to whom many a business line and handicraft are open.
>
> Five great monsters do a lot of mischief to the village agricultural community which mostly consists of the Marathas. The Kulkarni is the biggest of them all. The next to the Kulkarni is the Brahmin Sawkar who has appropriated to himself a very large portion of the village lands. The third in this order is the school-master and his brother the college-professor in big cities. The fourth is the Brahmin bureaucracy watered and nourished by Government themselves. The village priest, securely and permanently installed by Hindu religious puranas invented and developed to maintain the Brahmanic supremacy is the fifth monster.

The Maharajah of Kolhapur demanded separate electorates instead of reserved seats on which, he said, he was 'sure that weak, unprincipled undesirable Marathas will be elected who would be used by Brahmins as cat's paw for them to draw the apples out of the fire', the same kind of argument was used by Ambedkar before the Poona pact. However, the

British were not prepared to grant a separate electorate to the Marathas. Some of them therefore focussed their demand on larger quotas and to pressurise the British more efficiently they tried to appear as representing more than one caste. They held, under the auspices of the People's Union, whose patron was the Maharajah of Kolhapur, a Conference of the Hindu Backward Classes in June 1920. Since the British, so far, designated the Marathas by their caste name, the conference advocated that 'the term "Maratha and allied classes" should include all the Backward communities'.

Maratha leaders obviously aspired to play a pivotal role in the shaping of a caste federation which would adopt the official designation 'Backward classes'. Therefore, the conference made 'an emphatic protest against the misleading statement made in public to the effect that the Marathas, Malis etc. do not belong to the Backward Classes when their percentage of education is very low'. The main demand of the conference was that the 8 seats reserved to the Marathas and allied castes in the Montagu-Chelmsford report should be extended to 15. Simultaneously, the Secretary of the Poonabased All India Maratha Mali Union made a similar representation to the British: The word 'Maratta' [sic] means all the backward classes. As a matter of fact not only the Marattas but all other allied communities have fought in the last world war for the Empire and all such communities are anxious to get the privilege of reserved seats in the council to be hereafter elected.

The Yadav Gavlis then opportunely discovered that they had strong affinities with the Marathas. R.V. Khedekar, the President of the Yadav Gavli Association was an exceptional personality whom we shall meet again in North India. Born in Bombay in 1873, his father had been Private secretary of the Maharajah of Bhavnagar, one of the most progressive states regarding the backward castes. After studying medicine in the United Kingdom, he started practising in 1902 in Bhavnagar and Kolhapur, where he met Shahu Maharaj. The first Yadav association had been founded in 1903 by a relative of his father.

In the early 1920s, Khedekar protested against the fact that the Southborough Committee did not consider the Yadav Gavlis as Marathas : The Yadav Gavli community claims descent from the Great Yadav families to one which Shri Krishna the 8incarnation of Vishnu belonged.

The whole of the North India, Gujarat and Deccan were only ruled by the Kings of the Yadav families. They have kept up their Kshatriya caste traditions, customs and occupations. They have given considerable recruits to the government and have been regarded as Marathas and included in the Maratha regiments. In the end, the Yadav-Gavli association demanded the 'inclusion of this caste in the list of the Marathas and allied communities of the Deccan for franchise purpose'. Access to political power was of course the main reason for this social rapprochement.

Marathas, who had already forged a 'backward' front with the Malis and the Yadavs were striving for shaping an even larger coalition including the Lingayats and the Jains under the all-encompassing label of 'non-Brahmins'. The loose structure of the Marathas lent itself to this kind of aggregative strategy. They have no clear cut sub-castes, they are so 'amorphous' that 'it is hard to tell in some cases, whether a group is Maratha or of another affiliation called Kunbi'. This arrangement naturally 'facilitates incorporation into Maratha caste'of other peasant castes.

In spite of the Marathas' specificity, there is much to learn from this brief case-study on the way state policies can indirectly refashion social groupings. The British approach of political representation - namely their recognition of communities as eligible to a statutory representation - and their sense of compensatory discrimination - through quotas in the assemblies for instance - have accelerated the transformation of castes into interest groups and have fostered a process of amalgamation among the low castes; hence the emergence of groupings such as the Non Brahmins and the Maratha-Kunbis whose aim was purely political.

The rules were those of the game of numbers which, alone could enhance institutional representation in the State. In Maharashtra this strategy was rather successful. Its architects could rely on the legacy of Jyotirao Phule's Satya Shodak Samajwhich had established an idiom - the Bahujan idiom - encompassing all the Non-Brahmins. Another important factor laid in the pivotal situation of the Marathas who represented 20% of the population. They were certainly not able to federate all the Non-Brahmin castes but the mere fact that the British designed a category called 'Marathas and allied' showed that they had been successful to a certain extent. Among these allies were the Kunbis, who have always been regarded as more backward than the Marathasbut who appeared in the same category.

Now, the Kunbis accounted for 10% of the population of Maharashtra and contributed, therefore, to the irresistible rise to power of the Marathas from the late colonial period onwards. In Maharashtra and Tamil Nadu, the ethnicisation of caste and the formation of caste federations, helped the non-Brahmins to get organised and to gradually assert themselves in the political arena. However, the most illustrative caste federations took shape in another state of western India, Gujarat.

Kshatriyas in Gujarat

On the basis of their study of Gujarat politics, Kothari and Maru have defined caste federations in terms which would have suited well the Maharashtrian situation since they emphasise the role of individual caste associations in the shaping of such coalitions and put a stress on political motivations: The concept of caste federation refers to a grouping together of a number of distinct endogamous groups into a single organisation for common objectives, the realisation of which calls for a pooling together of resources or numbers or both. By and large, the objectives pursued are secular and associational, although the employment of traditional symbols for evoking a sense of solidarity and loyalty towards the new form is not uncommon. The traditional distinctions between the federating groups are on the whole retained, but the search for a new organisational identity and the pursuit of political objectives gradually lead to a shift in group orientations.

This definition was evolved in the course of a study of the 'Kshatriyas', a caste federation phenomenon of Gujarat which, indeed exemplified this phenomenon. Right from the 1910s the state Rajput leaders had constituted caste associations for promoting education. In the late 1930s, the descendant of one of its leaders, Natvarsingh Solanki, wanted to extend these associations to other castes which he considered as Kshatriyas. He tried to refashion the social identity of those groups in order to allow others to join hands with the Rajputs and in this way, to acquire more weight.

Gujarat's largest caste was the Kolis. They had been classified by the British as a 'criminal caste' but claimed that they were Kshatriyas and resorted to genealogists for being recognised aristocratic ancestors. In this, they purely imitated the Rajputs. Some Koli clans had been able to establish matrimonial alliances with Rajputs, as those castes practised hypergamyand/or had established small principalities before the British took over. Yet, they had retained some control over land under the Raj as landowners or rather big tenants. Many of them met the necessary conditions for being enfranchised when the British established provincial legislative councils. The right to vote therefore enabled the Kolis to use their main asset, their number : in 1931 they represented about 20% of the population, almost the double of the Patidars (12.16%), the dominant caste, the main rival of the Rajputs, who represented only 4.85% of the population. Solanki opened his caste association to the Kolis for this very reason: for transforming it into a mass organisation.

In 1947, the Kutch, Kathiawar, Gujarat Kshatriya Sabha was created after years of preparatory work. The word

'Kshatriya' was a useful umbrella label to bracket the Rajputs and the Kolis together. The Kshatriya Sabha is a good example of the way castes, with very different ritual status can coalesce - and even merge to a certain extent - for defending common interests. In this case, the Kolis and the Rajputs had the same enemies, viz., the Patidars. Certainly, this alliance has been legitimised in the idiom of 'tradition', by pretending that its components belonged to the same varna, but the use of the word Kshatriya was purely strategic and the original caste identity was seriously diluted. The Ajput leaders of the Kshatriya Sabha emphasised that a Kshatriya is not to be defined by descent but by martial values.

Political calculations had therefore social implications. Several taboos were abolished. Rajputs and Kolis of the Kshatriya Sabha shared mealsand the Kolis elite married their daughters to lower Rajputs - who practised hypergamy anyway - and this process fostered the rajputisation of the upper Kolis. Kshatriyas tended to form a new caste.

The use of terms like Koli Kshatriyas and Ajput Kshatriyas certainly show that the merger was far from complete.But important dimensions of the caste system were eroded by the after-effects of basically socio-economic and political strategies. In fact, the main demands of the Kshatriya Sabha after independence reflected a relative indifference to ritual issues in comparison to material objectives. For instance, the association claimed that the Kshatriyas were part of the 'Backward Classes' and therefore should benefit from reservations in the educational system and in the administration. This claim was the exact opposite of sanskritisation.

The Kolis benefited more than the Rajputs from the Sabha, which created boarding schools, grants, loan systems etc. in favour of the poorest of their community. This development contributed to the emergence of an intelligentsia of Kolis which, even though it remained small gave the Koli masses a new confidence and self-esteem as a caste. The members of this elite 'interact[ed] frequently and chart[ed] out common political strategies'.Right from the 1950s, the Kshatriya Sabha tended to capitalise its electoral support to the Congress in exchange of tickets for a number of its members as party candidates. The party was not fully responsive, especially because of the Patidars who were very influential in the Congress.

The Patidars disapproved of the Kshatriyas demand regarding land reform. The Kshatriya Sabha therefore kept its distance with the Congress before the 1962 elections and the party underwent a setback. Instead, the association gave its support, against large concessions, to the Swatantra Party which became the leading opposition party in the state. This situation persuaded the Congress to change its strategy and to give tickets to Kshatriya candidates before the 1967 elections. The Kshatriya Sabha then supported the Congress which regained a more comfortable majority than in 1962.

Caste federations turned out to be political interest groups with more leverage than caste associations, simply because they represented more people. In Gujarat, after the Congress split of 1969, a majority of the party conservative notables remained with the Congress (O) while a larger number of Kshatriyas joined the Congress. They gradually gained control over the state Congress. Madhavsingh Solanki, a Kshatriya of low birth, became Chief minister in 1976 and appointed a majority of ministers with the same background. During the electoral campaign of 1977 he initiated a new caste alliance regrouping the Kshatriyas, the Harijans (Untouchables), the Adivasis (tribals) and the Muslims (hence the acronym "KHAM"). This KHAM alliance was largely responsible for the Congress success during the 1980 elections.

Between 1957 and 1990 the number of upper caste Congress MLAs decreased from 33 to 6%, while those with a Patidar background remained stable at about one fourth of the total, whereas the Kshatriyas increased from 12 to 25% and the KHAM MLAs at large from 39 to 55%.While the 'Kshatriyas' of Gujarat represent the best example of caste federation, other instances occurred in South India. In the early 1960s, the Kallan, the Maravar and the Agamudiar, three lower castes who had already close ties with each other (especially ritual ones since they claimed that they descended from the same ancestors), decided to adopt the same name, Mukkulator (lit. three castes), in order to merge and to influence local politics.

In North India, none of these processes reached their logical conclusion. Caste associations often followed the sanskritisation path and very few of them prepared the group for an ethnic discourse or developed into caste federations. In North India also British policies had changed the social and political context in such a way as castes could have felt the same strong incentive to get organised. Efforts were made in this direction but they did not bear the same fruits as in the South and in the West. While caste associations took shape at an early date, they did not join hands into federations and they operated within the logic sanskritisation.

For instance, in 1928, the Indian Statutory Commission received an avalanche of petitions and memoranda from caste associations which demanded larger quotas in the assembly. The Government was petitioned by the All India Kushwaha Kshatriya Mahasabha, 'on behalf of the kori, kachchi and murao castes'. The fact that the Kushwaha label stood for three subcastes of castes of market gardeners shows that this caste association promoted the fusion process, but not to a very large extent : this process cannot be compared with caste federations in Gujarat. Secondly, the Kushwahas claimed the rank of Kshatriya, and another association of middle caste of peasants, which sent also a petition, the Kurmi Kshatriya Parishad Sabha, did the same. This is revealing of the fact that sanskritisation continued to play a major role among the low caste associations.

Sankritisation and lack of unity among the Yadavs and the Kurmis The 'Yadav' label covers a great number of castes which, initially, had different names: Ahir in the Hindi belt,

Punjab and Gujarat, Gavli in Maharashtra, Gola in Andhra Pradesh and Karnataka etc. However, traditionally their common function, all over India, was to take care of bovines as herdsmen, cowherds and milksellers.In practice, the Yadavs today spend most of their time tilling land. They are more specially concentrated in the Ganges plain - they represent one of the largest castes in Bihar and Uttar Pradesh with respectively 11 and 8.7% of the population. But the Yadavs are not a dominant caste, as pastoral activity did not go usually hand in hand with land possession. From the ritual as well as the economic point of view, the Yadavs are traditionally regarded as low caste peasants: The very mention of the community invokes, in Bihar, the image of dull, miserly and loud-mouthed people lacking in grace and culture. Besides, the Yadavs are considered as to be unusually prone to casteism and violence.

The Yadavs reportedly descend from immigrants from Central Asia, the Abhiras, who established kingdoms in North India, the most recent of which was built in Rewari, in Haryana in the XVIIth century. And one of the first Yadav associations was founded by the heir of a North Indian ruling family since the scion of the dynasty, Rao Bahadur Balbir Singh, established the Ahir Yadav Kshatriya Mahasabha in 1910. This association claimed that the Ahirs descended from the Yadu dynasty (hence the term Yadav) to which Krishna - the cowherd god - belonged, and that, therefore, they were Kshatriyas. To promote a warrior ethos and the caste's unity, the association leaders could rely on the caste history since Ahirs were easily presented as coming from the same ethnic stock and were known for their martial valour - the prince of Rewari took part in the 1857 Mutiny for instance. This is probably why M.S.A. Rao considers that the 'term Yadava refers to both an ethnic category and an ideology'.

Indeed, the Yadav leaders succeeded in their fusion project since they persuaded their caste fellows to downplay the endogamous units into which they were divided. There have even been some inter-regional marriages. Fusion was made easier from the 1930s onwards when North Indian Yadavs started to migrate from their villages to towns and especially to Delhi. But this project did not incorporate a more ambitious ethnicisation process through which other Kshatriya castes would have been merged. So far as ideology is concerned, it was dominated by sanskritisation, something one can partly attribute to the influence of the Arya Samaj.

The Arya Samaj has been too often regarded as purely Punjabi and confined to the urban middle class. In fact, it made inroads in the adjacent states at a quite early date and attracted then large numbers of low caste people. Dayananda even started his 'campaign against heresy and orthodoxy' - to use the words of an Arya Samajist - in the Kumbha Mela held in Haridwar. Subsequently, he toured in the United Provinces, in particular in the western part of the province. He stayed eight times in Meerut, for instance, between 1866 and 1880 - the Meerut City Arya Samaj was established as early as 1877 and others followed in Farrukabad, Kanpur, Benares, Lucknow. Eventually, the Srimati Arya Pratinidhi Sabha for the United Provinces of Agra and Awadh was founded in 1886. These local branches gradually extended their influence in the countryside. The anti-Brahmin stance of the Arya Samaj was especially appreciated by the low castes of the United Provinces.

In Sathyarth Prakash (The Light of Truth), Dayananda has very strong words against 'the sectarian and selfish Brahmins' who 'often dissuade persons from learning and ensnare them into their evil ways with the result that they lose health, peace of mind and wealth, 'these ignorant, sensual, hypocritical, irresponsible and vicious people'. Dayananda was so critical because he reproached the Brahmans with exploiting the superstition of the Hindus by projecting themselves as the only intermediary between man and god, a monopoly he compares to that of the Catholic Pope and which is evident from the brahminical invention of idol worship: 'These Popes fill their pockets by playing fraud upon you. In the Vedas there is not even a word to sanction idol-worship or invoking invitation and dismissals'.

Dayananda eulogised the Jats for forcefully resisting the Brahmins' 'popish' attitudes. He narrates the story of a Jat whose father was dying and who was asked to give his only cow to the priest as a 'dying gift', allegedly for helping the dying man to cross the river. The Jat had to agree since the priest had already talked to his relatives who put pressure on him. But he went to the priest's house soon after and boldly accused him of being 'a great liar' since he had not taken the cow to the river bank but was milking it.

However, Dayananda's indictment of the Brahmins did not amount to a complete rejection of the caste system. What he condemned was the hereditary caste. He contended that in the initial varna vyavastha children were placed in each varna according to their individual 'merits, actions and temperaments'. He specifically recommended that the 'fixture of the varnas according to merits and actions should take place at the sixteenth year of girls and twenty-fifth year of boys'. Like Gandhi later on, Dayananda was not against caste as such since according to him provided it was not an hereditary system, the castes endowed society with a virtually harmonious structure - which is hierarchical.

In North India, the lower castes really started to get united after the state evolved the notion of Other Backward Classes and promised them quotas in the bureaucracy. The AIBCF and the quotas: an ephemeral low-castes front Even so the report of the first Backward Classes Commission was not taken into consideration by Nehru government - to whom it was submitted in 1953 -, it made an impact on the lower castes because of its method of investigation. In order to determine the needs of the OBCs, the Commission had sent a detailed questionnaire to different representative organisations; it received 3,344 memoranda, in addition to the 5,636 persons interviewedand its chairman concluded from these figures that: the ferment has reached the masses. They have, for the first time in thousands of years, shed their traditional resignation to fate and started hoping that their condition can be improved, that they will be able to take their rightful place in the social structure of to-morrow and that they will have their due share in all schemes of national advancement.

The immediate effect of this ferment was marked in the form of uneasiness and impatience, and some measures of bitterness also, in the minds of the people. These symptoms cannot be ignored because they are indicative of the birth of a new energy which must be canalised into creative effort and constructive activity. There remains no longer any belief in the sanctity of the caste-hierarchy having been established by the will of God.Such comments not only acknowledged the decline of a hierarchical social order but implicitly admits that his Commission has contributed to this development in bringing new hopes to castes which, at once, acquired a new assertiveness. The first Backward Classes Commission thus illustrates how the State not only invented new social categories by mentioning the OBCs in the Constitution, but also, subsequently gave it a concrete shape by soliciting from their ranks representatives who were able to re-design the group's identity.

In 1954 there were 88 organisations 'working for the Backward Classes in 15 states, of which represented individual communities, and 14, Backward Classes in general on a local or state basis'. The UP Backward Classes Federation had been founded in 1929 and the Bihar State Backward Classes Federation in 1947. The All India Backward Classes Federation emerged from these state organisations. The AIBCF was created the same day as the Constitution was proclaimed, on January 26, 1950 in order to protest against the little interest it paid to the OBCs. Its architect, and president, was Punjabrao Deshmukh, a Marashtrian Member of Parliament who had thoroughly supported the backward castes within the Constituent Assembly, even though he was not one of them - he was a Maratha - and even belonged to the establishment.

In the early 1970s, the All India Kurmi Mahasabha abandoning further the Sanskritisation logic, made an alliance with the Koeris and favoured a merger of all the 'backward classes'. At its 1972 session, the main slogan was 'Pichara Jagao Desh Bachao' ("'Backwards', wake-up and rescue the country"). One of the resolutions allowed others than Kurmis to belong to the association and another one asked for the appointment of a Public Service Commission for Backward Classes. However, the trend was short-lived. First of all, other low castes probably resented the Yadav domination over the AIBCF. Jai Narayan Singh Yadav had become its General Secretary in 1959 and when Brahm Prakash Chaudhury took over from Deshmukh, 'the Yadavs gained control of the All India Backward Classes Federation'. Such an influence was all the more problematic as the Yadavs were especially mobilised all over the 1960s.

During the 1962 Indo-China war, Yadav soldiers accomplished heroic deeds in Ladakh and some of them won awards. This episode fostered the Yadavs' Kshatriyahood and their proud in their martial traditions. They immediately asked the Government to established a Yadav regiment in the army, along the same lines as the Ajput or the Sikh regiments. Pant rejected this claim but in 1965 the Yadavs again 'exhibited their bravery on several occasions'.

So far as the comparison with western and southern India is concerned, the career of the low caste movement in the Hindi belt before the 1980s reconfirms that it suffered from two specific weaknesses: first, the resilience of sanskritisation, a sociological pattern which inhibited the egalitarian agenda to a large extent and second, a (partly correlative) inability to coalesce within caste federations or even caste fronts, as the loose and ephemere crystallisation of the OBC coalition testified in the 1950s-1960s. Interestingly, the Dalit movement was affected by similar shortcomings in the larger state of the Hindi belt, that is Uttar Pradesh.

Untouchables in Uttar Pradesh

Like the low castes, the Untouchables first mobilised in U.P. in reaction to the State's reservation policy. The way the British classified castes was in itself a factor of mobilisation. It was especially evident from the impact of the 1935 Government of India Act, in which there was a lot at stake since it enfranchised a larger number of Untouchables and granted quotas for the Scheduled Castes. In the United Provinces some castes had strong objections to their classifications as Scheduled Castes. The Bundelkhand Prantia Kori Sabha, which claimed 20,000 members passed a resolution in 1936 to support the view that 'the Koris of India have always been classified amongst the touchable castes with the right to Samskaras' and that in the Manusmriti they are 'held to be born of a Kshatriya in a Vaishya mother'.

Worshipping Kabir and Ravidas then became widespread among urban untouchables migrants in U.P, and ceased to be practised only by insular religious orders: new temples and statues were built, festivals and pilgrimages organised. However, such a promotion of what was after all a form of Hinduism was not likely to imbue the Untouchables with a separate identity like the Dravidians in South India. If 'bhakti was resurrected as a caste-based religious expression solely of the untouchables', how can it be practised 'as a form of denial of caste distinctions'?

Indeed, N. Gooptu admits that 'the criticism of the caste system by the Adi Hindu leaders was rather limited and had a narrow focus on the lack of rights or opportunities for the untouchables. The leaders did jettison the notions of 'low' or 'impure', but concentrated on proving that such stigma and disabilities should not be attached to them due to caste status. Nor did they attempt to question the concept that work was inherited. Instead they claimed that 'low' work was not the true inheritance of the Untouchables. It was largely to buttress this claim that they asserted their pre-Aryan ancestry as the original rulers of India, for it enabled them to argue that they should re-inherit the ancient rights of which they had been deprived'.

Far from establishing a separate identity that would situate the Untouchables out of the caste system, the Adi Hindu movement used their so-called original identity as a means for promoting their status within the system. And correlatively, the bhakti resurgence did not imply a radical questioning of their belonging to Hinduism. Certainly, they opposed Brahminism by adhering to a rather popular tradition, but their practise of this religious cult recalls the modus operandi of the Hindfu sects-which precisely derived from bhakti whose egalitarian impact has always been otherworldly. While in Pundjab the Ad-Dharm movement was projected as a quaum, or independent community, rather than a panth, or religious path, in the Hindi belt-the Adi Hindu movement could not achieve so much. The movement also suffered from organisational weaknesses. While the 'informal nature of links between apex Adi Hindu organisations in the towns and local caste groups in neighbourhoods contributed to the strength and breadth of the movement', by 1924 local Adi Hindu Sabhas had been set up in only four cities of U.P..

In fact the Adi-Hindu movement remained chiefly confined to Agra and Kanpur. Out of the 23 main Dalit leaders of the United Provinces in the first half of the century, almost 50% were from these two cities (eight from Agra and two from Kanpur). In both places, the social reform work had been prepared by sectarian movements such as the Radha Soami Satsang established by Radha Soami (1818-1878) in Agra and the Dev Samaj, founded in 1887 by Siva Narayan Agnihotri of Kanpur.

In addition to these limitations, the movement also failed to overcome the traditional cleavages opposing the untouchable caste groups. Its leaders tried to organise interdining ceremonies but did not meet very enthusiastic responses. All these shortcomings were precisely in evidence in the case of one of these individual castes, that of the

Chamars and more especially of the Jatavs who got organised around the same time as the Adi-Hindu movement.

The Jatavs are the descendants of Yadu, the founder of Jadav [sic] tribe, from which the great Hero of Maha Bharat, Lord Krishna, came. But this position of superiority could not remain intact. Our community fell down from that great height to this degraded status in the Hindu fold our present position is the outcome of the age-long inhumane oppressions of Brahminism or the Kshatriyas. We, Kshatriyas of the past, are labouring under various sorts of disabilities, restrictions and religious injunctions imposed on us by the Orthodox Hindus [...] But we are at loss to understand the exclusion of our (Yadav) Jatav community from the list of the Scheduled Castes given in the White Paper. The result of this horrible negligence would, no doubt, be the sacrifice of the interests of our community. Such a discourse suggests that the Jatav movement was still under the influence of sanskritisation in the mid-1930s. Owen Lynch points out that 'The Jatavs were not attempting to destroy the caste system; rather they were attempting to rise within it in a valid, though not licit, way'.

The influence of Ambedkar made a strong impact on the Jatav movement in the 1940s so much so that the Maharashtrian scenario with Dalit acquiring a separate Buddhist identity could be used to avoid the trap of sanskritisation. Even those who did not convert themselves to Buddhism regarded the Untouchables as descending from the original Buddhists and, therefore, prided themselves of being the original Indians: O. Lynch could then conclude that 'Buddhist identity has replaced Sanskritic Kshatriya identity'. The Jatav movement could therefore rely on the same solid - ethnic - ground as the Bahujan movement in Maharashtra and the Dravidian movement in Tamil Nadu.

Also, for the Jatavs, 'political participation' became a 'functional alternative' to sanskritisation, in the sense that they tried to achieve social mobility through access to power. This empowerment process was fostered by the British policies of positive discrimination and gradual democratisation since they both incited the caste to transform itself into a pressure group and to assert itself as a collective body. However, such a change was rather exceptional in Northern India. It was almost confined to the Jatavs of Agra. Even though the president of the Scheduled Caste Federation of the United Provinces, Piarelall Kureel was a Kureel from Unnao district, most of the supporters of Ambedkar were confined in the Agra Jatav movement.

Sanskritisation - on the basis of arya samajist influences or not - continued to prevail in many other Untouchable castes. In the 1911 and 1921 censuses, some 26 low castes claimed the status of the twice-born castes. Certainly, sanskritisation and social mobility were not mutually exclusive but the former reflected the domination of the value of the caste system anyway. In 1935, the All India Dhobi [washermen, launder] Association protested against the exclusion their caste from the Scheduled Castes which had been decided under pressures from other associations such as the Arya Samaj oriented United Provinces Razak (Dhobi) Association which pursued the sanskritisation path. The President of the latter organisation, for whom Dhobis were Kshatriyas, considered that giving his caste fellows the status of Untouchables would be 'a stigma on character and ability, an obstruction to selfadvancement and improvement'. Similar conflicts happened in the case of the Khatiks, an Untouchable caste of meat cutters. The Dusadh Mahasabha also claimed that Dusadhs were Kshatriyas.

In contrast to the Untouchables' movements which developed in the Presidencies of Madras and Bombay, those of U. P. did not articulate a vigorous ethnic discourse. The Adi-Hindu movement certainly presented the Untouchables as the original habitants of India but as Hindus and the proponents of sanskritisation remained quite strong. The Dalit movement therefore faced the same difficulty as the OBCs in the Hindi belt, whereas things appeared to be easier in southern India and even in the West - though the differences must not be exaggerated.

6

Geopolitical Characteristics of South Asia

Geopolitics is not static and unchanging; far from it, it is extremely dynamic. In 1971, when the last full scale war in South Asia was fought and Bangladesh was carved out of the-then Pakistan, the geopolitics of South Asia presented itself within the context of the bipolar division of the world. Today, geopolitics presents itself in a very different way, in the context of the unipolar world of the US and the multipolar world desired by other big powers. But if we begin from the premise that the 21st century must belong to the people who will take the centre-stage and defeat the big powers and their dreams to dominate the world, we have to examine the geopolitics in a radically different way.

India is home to nearly 1 billion people. To that large number, if you add 140 million people of Pakistan, 125 million people of Bangladesh and another 75 million from the other five countries, we have nearly a quarter of the world's population living in this region at this time. The role of Canada or more precisely the role of Canadian people in the world in the 21st century, is also the question being posed for the peoples of South Asia. What role do they play today and what role they must play in the world in the future are the two issues to be analysed and discussed if we have to address ourselves to the solution of how the marginalisation of people from affairs of the society and the globe can be ended.

South Asians are posing the question within their conditions - how they can end the marginalisation of South Asia from world affairs and the marginalisation of the peoples from the affairs of their own countries, societies and collectives. It is in this common struggle to end the marginalisation of the peoples from the affairs of the countries and the world which unites us all, from opposite faces of the globe.

India was a colony of the British Empire until 1947 and when it gained formal independence, it was partitioned into India and Pakistan. That was the time when the British Empire was collapsing and the US was on the rise. The USSR had vast influence in every corner of the globe. India and Pakistan were created on the basis of religion, after organising the bloodiest massacre that the region had ever seen before. This manipulation of religion to effect division occurred at a scale unheard of before. The use of religion in the division of Ireland had been tried in a limited way until that time. The consequence of the division of India on the basis of religion was bound to have consequence beyond the geopolitics of South Asia. Its effect was global.

Since 1950, India played one role in the world and Pakistan played another role in the global context. Nehru, the first prime Minister of India is on record after partition for saying that the boundaries of India's aspirations extended from Tashkent to Cape Comorin. This was a presentation of India in geo-political terms - i. e. India had interest beyond its borders. Before 1950, the British had introduced electoral franchise on the basis of religion. That franchise laid the foundation for the two biggest nations of South Asia, Punjab and Bengal, to be partitioned to East and West Punjab and East and West Bengal respectively.

East Bengal was known as East Pakistan until 1971 and became Bangladesh which is an independent country following a war between India and Pakistan. The government of Bangladesh today does not discuss the division of Bengal, both past and present, and nor does it pose the question of the reunification of the nation of Bengal. Instead, Bangladesh wants to discuss matters such as water-sharing with India, which is done on the basis of accepting the division of Bengal. Bangladesh has even gone further to sign agreements allowing the US navy to use its ports, has plans to buy jet fighters from the US and even to provide facilities for the US marines to land there if they make a request. The case with divided Punjab is similar within the context of Pakistan where West Punjab is the most dominant nationality that steers the politics of Pakistan but never poses the question of why this nation is divided.

Similarly, if one examines the way the Indian government views the world, you will not get a sense that there is any problem of division, or that India has any enemies in this world who are perpetuating the divisions. But the same considerations that existed in 1947 still exist. The US and Europe are very active with respect to keeping the divisions alive in South Asia. United Europe has historically sought to conquer Asia, and although the Germans, French, and British have different aims, there is much consanguinity of interest with respect to Asia if you examine their positions, for example with respect to the Comprehensive Test Ban Treaty (CTBT), which India has refused to sign.

During the entire debate on the CTBT, India did not say anything against NATO, which is a military organisation in Europe and the biggest nuclear power in the world. India did not say anything when NATO started expanding eastward. India considers itself as a regional power in the Indian Ocean region. India wants to be recognised as a power, if not for any other reason, but for the size of its population. By 2010, India will have first-rate consumers. Who does not want to conquer India and South Asia? With the push for a market oriented economy in the countries of South Asia - from Bangladesh to Pakistan, from Nepal to Sri Lanka, this region is a giant big market, a giant reservoir of labour force, a giant source of raw materials and so on.

In the 1940's, South Asia, the Middle East, etc., were places of extreme tension where people were rising up against colonial rule for national liberation. The US policy of containment was formulated in that period on the basis of the theory that any country which had national liberation would go towards communism. The US welcomed the creation of Pakistan and went on to make Pakistan its centre for containing communism in South Asia at that time. India began the 1950's by developing its relations with China on the basis of panchsheel in the hope that the India-China axis would be a deterrent for the US to realise the kinds of interventions that it was organising everywhere else with military coups, fascist regimes, the Suez crisis and so on. That policy ended when China and India fought a border war in 1962.

The linkage between India and the Soviet Union under Khrushchev and Brezhnev were formulated under the leadership of Nehru and Indira Gandhi. The policy of "non-alignment" was created by India, Yugoslavia and Egypt in that period, a nomenclature which effectively ended up facilitating the linkage of countries like India with both Moscow and Washington under the pretext of being equidistant from both. For example, in 1991, when Iraq was attacked during the Gulf War, the Indian government permitted American planes from the Philippines to fly over its airspace. Iraq was a non-aligned country and so was India. But Iraq had been made a "rogue state" after it had served American interests in the decade long war with Iran following the overthrow of the Shah. In the 1980's the US used Pakistan to wage war in Afghanistan. Again, India was a partner in that war. The US has called various Asian states such as Iran and China as rogue states. Just within last few months, the US has labelled India a "responsible power" and has called on the Pakistani army generals not to overthrow the Nawaz Sharif government.

In July, the US ordered the Pakistani government to withdraw its troops from Kashmir. What these developments show is that just as Iraq had become expendable and a war with Iraq facilitated the US to militarily move into the Middle

East, Pakistan seems to have become dispensable and if the US can move in there, it can have a direct eye on not just India, but China and Russia besides Iran and Central Asia with its rich resources.

Another factor increasing in importance is that the big Indian business houses are closely linked to the American and European powers. Military budgets are rising at a rate of 20 to 25 percent annually because it is most lucrative sector of economy. The Germans used this in the 1930's, the Americans did in the post Second World War period and Brezhnev followed it in the USSR. Through the arms race, massive expenditures were made in all these countries. In 1974, when Indira Gandhi tested the first nuclear bomb, India warded off the US by pointing to India's alliance with the USSR and to the newly opened nuclear option. All governments - India, Pakistan, Bangladesh and even Sri Lanka - want the arms race. Under it, billions of rupees are handed out to very lucrative private contractors and the growing domestic private-sector defence industry, who benefit from the continuation of tension.

When India tested the nuclear devices last year, it was a statement that with the end of Cold War, India was willing to assert its independent nuclear power status. India developed and tested the Agni missile and a number of medium and short-range missiles. This missile, as a military weapon has no place internationally. India has no possibility to command the air and sea, but it can invade its neighbours and the development of these missiles is a statement that that is what India intends to use them for. India is a late-comer in terms of the economic and military prowess of Asia. It wants economic links with Iran, Central Asia and East Asia beside the countries of South Asia.

South Asia has remained on fire for the whole of 20th century. There are uprisings in Kashmir and the north east of India while Afghanistan continues to be devastated. Can the Kashmir problem really not be solved, or is it that there are vested interests in preserving the status quo, to generate chauvinism, deploy force, and justify defence expenditures? In Sri Lanka, can a small population sustain the war without support from India, the US and so on? In Punjab, it is said that the insurgency was ended because Narasimha Rao used overwhelming force to crush it. But it is known that the US supported the movement there as long as they had differences with the central government in Delhi.

In the official positions of the Indian government or in the programs of the political parties in India who want to form the next government, it is characteristic that they do not even admit that there are any problems in South Asia and the world. The only reason that can be given is that India is a partner in these conflicts. India's geopolitics is to keep South Asia divided, become the most important power and come to terms with other powers - possibly China, the US, Russia. It is keeping its options open towards the United Europe. The next war for the re-division of the world will inevitably have India as an active player. Within that, all the big powers are very keen to see that India does not renew itself. That is the reason why the Queen of England went to India to celebrate the 50th anniversary of the loss of her possession. That is the reason, the US President is going to India in the year 2000 - to assure the Indians that they must noot renew any institutions there.

In the last few years, all the predators of the world have praised India's democratic credentials. Canada is in the forefront of this praise because they are as much a partner in the conflicts going on today and those that are being hatched. None of the powers want the people of India to look any other way. The British in particular are the most active because they view that India is their territory, its institutions as their institutions. They will ally with the US to ensure that when South Asia is destabilised, they become the main beneficiaries to move in.

Nuclear Geopolitics

There are three different factors which shaped the South Asian strategic environment. First one is, antagonism between India and Pakistan resulted from the partition of British-ruled India in 1947 and has continued since. The second factor is India's determination to be a regional and even international power, and Pakistan's efforts to defend itself against India. This factor has led both countries to develop nuclear weapons and missiles. They are likely to become more dangerous as new nuclear weapons are developed and India's conventional military advantage grows. This could lead to a "hair trigger" mentality, if both believe that they must strike first in a crisis. The third factor has been economic development and domestic politics in South Asia.

Domestic politics in both countries has often been a source of instability, particularly since corruption is a major problem. India's economic prospects are hopeful and will continue to outstrip those of Pakistan, whose social and economic underdevelopment exacerbates public dissatisfaction with politics and domestic crime and violence, and increases support for Islamic groups. America's ability to influence both countries, especially Pakistan, has diminished. This partly reflects the importance the United States places on nonproliferation, including its use of sanctions.

Political agitation, Indian independence movements, and demands for a Moslem homeland led to British India being partitioned into two new democratic states. The first became the Republic of India with an overwhelmingly Hindu population. The second became Pakistan with an overwhelmingly Muslim population. This partition was bitterly resented by many in India. Even after partition, more Muslims remained in India than Pakistan. Minority communities became widely dispersed throughout India.

Nearly a thousand miles of Indian territory lay between East Pakistan, with its Bengali-speaking, Muslim majority, and West Pakistan, with its Urdu-Punjabi, Sindi, Baluch, and Pathanspeaking population. The result was Pakistan's cultural, political, and economic division. This negatively affected national unity and led to civil war two decades later. Feelings over partition became further embittered when some 12 million refugees fled across borders, and one-half to one million deaths resulted from related political violence. There were also sharp differences over the distribution of British assets between the two states. Most of all, differences arose over India's establishment of Hindu rule over the predominantly Muslim state of Jammu and Kashmir. Events surrounding India's accession of Jammu and Kashmir have been intensely debated in India and Pakistan and in international forums, including the UN Security Council.

Jammu and Kashmir has a complex mixture of minorities, including Buddhists and Hindus. It is also strategically located in the Himalayas, bordered by India, Pakistan, Afghanistan, Tibet, and China. Pakistan resisted India's takeover of the state in a short but bitter conflict in 1947-48. Jammu and Kashmir was divided in half between the two countries. For Pakistan, this conflict came to represent its national and Islamic obligation to Muslims. Pakistanis believed the latter were unjustly denied membership in their new state. For India, Jammu and Kashmir became an integral part of its state, something Pakistan has never accepted. Tensions from partition led to wars in 1965 and 1971.

Indian forces were dominant in both. An uneasy line of control (LOC) was established in December 1971. This was guarded by forces on both sides and observed by a small UN force (UNMOGIP) that is still in place. It is an alternative to an international border. Both sides have alerted their forces and exchanged artillery fire across the LOC regularly since 1972. They intensified in 1998, with a Pakistani incursion in 1999. However, both sides have avoided escalation into major confrontations. Each side regularly accuses the other of overtly and covertly undermining the internal stability and the integrity of the other. They also periodically accuse each other of preparing for war. The situation has been exacerbated by political tensions within both Pakistan and India. Consequently, the hostility and resentment over the initial partition have never lapsed.

Pakistan was further angered by India's open support for the Bengali revolt against West Pakistani dominance in 1971. This led to brief but bloody fighting in Kashmir and East Bengal, and ultimately defeat of the Pakistani Army. India provided Bangladesh its independence when Pakistan reluctantly accepted the Simla Agreement in 1972. Although the agreement included steps aimed at improving relations, few were implemented. Neithei side ever really accepted steps that would ease tensions, increase trade, prevent mutual attacks through state-controlled media, expand communications, or increase tourism and business travel. Since 1972, tensions have waxed and waned. For example, based on strong evidence, India believed Pakistan was training and equipping militant Sikhs seeking independence or greater autonomy for the Indian State of Punjab. After years of violence, civil disorder was eliminated in Punjab by the early 1990s.

In 1989, widespread armed resistance broke out against Indian rule and corruption in Jammu and Kashmir. This began a prolonged and costly confrontation in Indo-Pakistani relations. Kashmiris in the key Kashmir valley demanded independence. Some sought association with Pakistan, while others demanded at least greater autonomy. Civil disorder and kidnappings of prominent individuals increased. India strengthened its civil and paramilitary presence, and casualties mounted rapidly. Pakistan insisted it had a "moral and political" obligation to support several of the groups by providing funds, arms, and training for young Kashmiris in Pakistancontrolled areas. It also helped raise radical Islamic resistance groups modeled after the Afghan resistance.

Islamic "volunteers" from Afghanistan, Pakistan, and other Moslem states joined these groups. India strengthened its military, paramilitary, and police presence even more and increased military activity, including shelling of villages along the LOC, to which Pakistan responded. Every aspect of this continuing low-level conflict has been a matter of intense controversy. Pakistan charges that over 700,000 Indian forces are in Jammu and Kashmir. India acknowledges less than half that number. The Pakistanis claim over 60,000 Kashmiris have died, while Indians acknowledge less than half that number. Pakistanis accuse India of grossly violating human rights, a claim international human rights groups support to some degree. India denies these allegations.

Pakistan seeks international mediation of the dispute and insists that the Kashmiris must agree to any settlement through such means as a plebiscite. India argues that the two countries must resolve this issue bilaterally, and international intervention is unacceptable. It further argues that Kashmiris can have free elections but cannot demand separation. India maintains this position, despite recommendations from five permanent members of the Security Council, other major states, and even Nelson Mandela, who convened the 1998 session of the Non- Aligned Movement.

A negotiated resolution that goes beyond just reducing tensions along the LOC is unlikely. Forces on both sides occupy long-held positions on the Siachen glacier, where more troops die from cold than enemy fire. The military on each side acknowledge that these positions have little strategic meaning. Yet, negotiations founder because each country fears that withdrawal would be regarded as a sign of weakness by the military and political opposition. Prolonged discussions, backed by high-level political support on both sides, may be the only practical option. They could focus on the permanent status of Jammu and Kashmir and on avoiding a dangerous escalation of tensions.

They could also seek to resolve other less volatile disputes and to begin to increase economic, social, and political exchange. Privately, many Indians and Pakistanis acknowledge the need for such discussions. Publicly, the prime ministers of both countries met in Lahore, Pakistan, on February 20, 1999, and issued a joint statement pledging mutual work toward better relations. Concerning Kashmir, they said, "We will negotiate sincerely on this and on all other issues." Serious talks could evolve over the next few years if new violence, terrorism, or political shocks do not occur. However, Pakistan's involvement will require political will and leadership, which has been absent. The Pakistani-backed incursion along the LOC in May 1999 shattered faith in the Lahore agreement. It will also require India's commitment to political, economic, and social reforms in Jammu and Kashmir and giving Kashmiris a stronger voice in any eventual agreement. However, these seem unlikely in eitherIndia or Pakistan.

India's efforts to gain recognition as a major international power, and Pakistan's search for security vis-a-vis India, strongly influence South Asia's strategic environment. These motivations are unlikely to change in the near future. For the last 50 years, India has sought international recognition as a political and moral leader. Mahatma Gandhi was widely admired for his moral leadership that enabled British India to gain independence without violence. Jawaharlal Nehru, India's first Prime Minister and preeminent political leader until the early 1960s, largely ensured Indian democracy's stability and led the Non-Aligned Movement, which he hoped would be a counterweight to East-West tensions.

The world's largest democracy, with the world's second-largest population, India has never felt it receives the international respect it deserves from the major powers, particularly the United States. The United States has been perceived as regarding South Asia as a region of secondary importance, except when military threats were posed by China's border war in 1962 and the Soviet occupation of Afghanistan between 1979 and 1989. During the Cold War, the United States saw India and the Non-Aligned Movement loosely linked with the Soviet Union, but not as a Communist ally. Indian criticism of U.S. policies toward China and Vietnam were a constant source of friction-at least until India's own war with China. Pakistan was a link in such U.S. alliances as the Southeast Asia Treaty Organization and the Central Treaty Organization. Except for its value in intelligence collection, the United States never saw Pakistan as the vital security interest Pakistan hoped it would be.

India's national security policies have focused on Pakistan since partition. This focus has shaped the structure and deployment of India's armed forces. However, India's defeat in the 1962 border war with China raised concern about long-term relations between the two countries. The Chinese nuclear test in 1965 caused India to rapidly develop a nuclear capability. Moreover, as a permanent member of the UN Security Council, China could influence international affairs in ways that were unavailable to India. Additionally, implementation of the Non-Proliferation Treaty (NPT) in 1970 meant China's inclusion as a nuclear power and India's exclusion from any prospect of becoming a "nuclear weapon state"-unless it defied the NPT regime. Indian policymakers saw this as a matter of national security and pride.

China was courted by world leaders, who rarely visited India, including those from the United States. China was allowed to cooperate with the United States on nuclear and space activities that were off limits to India. At some point in the 21st century, many Indians concluded, the two largest Asian powers, India and China, would become rivals not just in Asia but elsewhere. There is little evidence that China shared this perception of future rivalry. However, some Southeast Asian states, particularly Singapore, were privately responsive to Indian concerns. Today, India's relations with China remain a long-term concern.

Nuclear Capabilities

India's test of a "peaceful" nuclear device in 1974 was not followed by further tests, although research intensified. By the early 1990s, India seemed to have the fissile material and technology for a limited nuclear-weapon capability. It had also developed missiles with ranges from 75 to 1,500 miles. India's decision to test warheads in May 1998, debated by successive Indian governments for nearly a decade, had been almost conducted 3 years earlier. Pakistan quickly followed with its own tests. The size and number of Indian and Pakistani tests are disputed. Officially India claims that one of five tests was thermonuclear; this is questioned by analysts, who collected international seismic data. Two Indian tests appear to have been no more than 15 kilotons. Two other tests produced no seismic data that could be identified by international monitors. The Indian Government stated they tested very small weapons. The four Pakistani devices appear to be 4 to 12 kilotons.

Public opinion in both countries strongly supported the tests, but enthusiasm dropped afterwards. However, public support was sustained in both countries despite the negative world reaction. Both governments knew they would face strong international opposition and sanctions. India estimated the economic cost at one percent of gross domestic product (GDP) growth, but assumed sanctions would not last more than a year and that India could weather the cost. The damage to Pakistan's economy caused by sanctions is more serious. It has exacerbated other economic problems and civil disorders.

India's official rationale for the tests was to provide a minimum nuclear deterrent against Pakistan and China. It believed that this had to be achieved before India was internationally confronted with joining or killing the Comprehensive Test Ban Treaty (CTBT). India's quest for international status and recognition was a major factor in its decision to test. The United States offered Pakistan substantial economic and military assistance if it did not follow India's lead. However, domestic political pressures and concerns over its security compelled Pakistan to demonstrate it had the same capability.

Both governments declared that no further tests were planned. Both will almost certainly sign the CTBT, although they argue strongly that sanctions should be lifted in exchange.

Both agreed not to export nuclear or missile technology and to work with the United States to strengthen existing export control systems. They also agreed to negotiations on an international cutoff treaty for fissile material. However, they will clearly insist on increasing their own stockpiles until such a treaty is completed, or until an interim multicountry agreement exists that includes China, Russia, and the United States. Neither will roll back its capabilities and join the NPT, as South Africa, Argentina, and Brazil did. They will probably eschew limits on weaponizing or deploying weapons.

Pakistan will watch India, while India watches China and Pakistan. Both countries know they face complex and potentially costly problems regarding nuclear weapons. These include ensuring weapons security, command, and control, integration of nuclear weapons into military doctrine, early warning intelligence requirements, and other considerations. How either country will deal with these issues is uncertain. Both claim they seek only a "minimum credible deterrent." Neither country appears to regard nuclear weapons as employable in conflict. This is reflected in India's "no first use" policy. However, Pakistan's military officers and politicians are reluctant to commit to "no first use," fearing India's conventional military power. They have considered nuclear weapons as an "Armageddon" threat in a conventional war that could break up Pakistan.

Has the risk of nuclear war increased? Those arguing against it say a semblance of peace has existed for over 25 years. During this time, India and Pakistan have seemingly assumed each has a limited nuclear capability. Moreover, international attention is now focused on India and Pakistan. International powers will likely act swiftly and decisively to prevent war, if it seems likely. The contrary argument points, first, to the current availability to Pakistan of ballistic missiles and to tested warheads in India for aircraft delivery. Further acquisition of nuclear weapons capability by both sides is inevitable. Second, in both countries there are great political frailties, short response times if conflict occurs, and ambiguities regarding capabilities of delivery systems. Third, the military balance between both countries has steadily deteriorated, leaving Pakistan increasingly dependent upon nuclear weapons and missiles. Additionally, terrorism in either country could jeopardize nuclear stockpiles, particularly in unstable domestic environments.

The risk of nuclear conflict has increased, even though it may be by a small degree. This danger could increase over the next decade, if both countries continue to develop and deploy nuclear-capable missiles and aircraft. The greatest danger of nuclear conflict comes from vulnerable forces and the two countries' close proximity. Little warning time is available. This engenders a "use them or lose them" mentality. The risk of accidental conflict, along with rapid, preemptive use of nuclear weapons, is aggravated by the uncertain capabilities of Indian and Pakistani intelligence agencies. Both have been prone to distortion, exaggeration, and other mistakes. The fact that both countries also have inadequate early-warning systems further compounds intelligence problems. Their relative lack of sophistication can contribute to accidents.

On the other hand, Pakistan and India have avoided conflict for almost three decades, despite considerable violence, mutual provocation, and some close calls. They may ameliorate nuclear danger by developing effective command and control systems, mutual early warning, and other confidence-building measures. They may accomplish this bilaterally, or with other governments' assistance. The United States leads an international effort to stabilize the nuclear equation, prevent or at least minimize development and deployment of missiles, curtail further production of fissile Has the risk of nuclear war increased? Those arguing against it say a semblance of peace has existed for over 25 years. During this time, India and Pakistan have seemingly assumed each has a limited nuclear capability.

Moreover, international attention is now focused on India and Pakistan. International powers will likely act swiftly and decisively to prevent war, if it seems likely. The contrary argument points, first, to the current availability to Pakistan of ballistic missiles and to tested warheads in India for aircraft delivery. Further acquisition of nuclear weapons capability by both sides is inevitable. Second, in both countries there are great political frailties, short response times if conflict occurs, and ambiguities regarding capabilities of delivery systems. Third, the military balance between both countries has steadily deteriorated, leaving Pakistan increasingly dependent upon nuclear weapons and missiles. Additionally, terrorism in either country could jeopardize nuclear stockpiles, particularly in unstable domestic environments.

The risk of nuclear conflict has increased, even though it may be by a small degree. This danger could increase over the next decade, if both countries continue to develop and deploy nuclear-capable missiles and aircraft. The greatest danger of nuclear conflict comes from vulnerable forces and the two countries' close proximity. Little warning time is available. This engenders a "use them or lose them" mentality. The risk of accidental conflict, along with rapid, preemptive use of nuclear weapons, is aggravated by the uncertain capabilities of Indian and Pakistani intelligence agencies. Both have been prone to distortion, exaggeration, and other mistakes. The fact that both countries also have inadequate early-warning systems further compounds intelligence problems. Their relative lack of sophistication can contribute to accidents.

On the other hand, Pakistan and India have avoided conflict for almost three decades, despite considerable violence, mutual provocation, and some close calls. They may ameliorate nuclear danger by developing effective command and control systems, mutual early warning, and other confidence-building measures. They may accomplish this bilaterally, or with other governments' assistance. The United States leads an international effort to stabilize the nuclear equation, prevent or at least minimize development and deployment of missiles, curtail further production of fissile has explored procuring military and dual-use technologies from the United States, but nuclear tests set this initiative back. Constraints on some American exports may be gradually relaxed over the next decade, but the United States is unlikely to become a major source of military equipment or technology for India in the future.

Pakistan's military equipment comes from several sources-American, French, Eastern European, Chinese, and British. Pakistan's capabilities are less than half those of India's. The U.S. Congress passed the Pressler Amendment sanctions in 1990 which seriously set back modern conventional capabilities for Pakistan. Aside from small equipment, Pakistan's own weapons production is limited and unlikely to improve. Its ability to modernize is constrained by increasing budgetary pressures. Today, India's active military forces number 1.2 million troops and include 39 division-equivalents and 840 combat aircraft. Pakistan has 587,000 troops, to include 25 divisions and 410 combat aircraft. Both countries are well armed. Together, they could wage a major conventional war in which WMD systems could affect the outcome.

Some in India have always viewed the entire subcontinent as an Indian sphere of influence. Ethnic, religious, and cultural interaction between the populations of Nepal, Sri Lanka, Bangladesh, and India have often led to tensions. India did not hesitate to use military force to help dissidents separate Bangladesh from Pakistan. It also unsuccessfully tried to assist the Sri Lankan Government to suppress a Tamil separatist movement which Indian intelligence services had earlier helped to create. India has primarily used economic and political pressure to resolve these issues, to include dissuading Sri Lanka and Nepal from purchasing military equipment. Relations have improved in recent years, and Indian policymakers are increasingly discreet in their regional diplomacy. India's prospects for good political and economic relations among South Asian states are probably better than ever.

In terms of strategic interests, Pakistan has consistently sought support from more powerful states to balance India and to develop a nuclear capability to deter India. Pakistan has been disappointed in bilateral security relations with the United States, in membership in three U.S.-sponsored regional security instruments in the 1950s and 1960s (the Southeast Asian Treaty Organization, in the Baghdad Pact, and the Central Treaty Organization), and in its close involvement with the United States during the Soviet-Afghan War in the 1980s. Pakistan provided valuable intelligence bases for the United States in the Cold War and received military assistance and substantial economic aid. However, Pakistan felt it never was treated as a reliable partner or received the help it desired.

Pakistan shared U.S. concerns about Soviet expansionism, but its primary adversary was India. Despite ambiguous hints to the contrary, the United States never provided credible security assurances. Moreover, U.S. military assistance was often suddenly interrupted. It was cut off during the 1965 and 1971 wars with India. During the Afghan war, the United States turned a blind eye to Pakistan's nuclear program. However, in 1990, U.S. legislation barred all economic and military assistance, because the Bush administration could no longer certify Pakistan's inability to produce a nuclear device. The delivery of 71 F-16s was halted after Pakistan had paid some $658 million. Subsequent U.S. efforts to resolve the issue by selling the planes to another country came to naught in 1998. This badly limited Pakistan's conventional capabilities vis-a-vis India, along with cancellation of such advanced U.S. weapons systems as helicopters and P-3s and the inability to acquire replacements from other countries.

Pakistan was forced to turn increasingly to ballistic missiles and nuclear weapon development for deterrence and defense. In the early 1990s, China supplied M-11 missiles and technology which have a 300-kilometer range. In the late 1990s, North Korea supplied the 1,500-kilometer range No Dong, which Pakistan named the Taliban Ghauri. These missiles are capable of delivering nuclear warheads that Pakistan seemingly can produce.

In the early 1960s, Pakistan turned to China for political and technological support. China's tensions with the Soviet Union and India and concern over its southwest borders made Pakistan an attractive geopolitical balance. China provided Pakistan with low-cost conventional arms. More importantly, China became a source of technology for Pakistan's nuclear and missile programs. By the 1990s, these bonds had weakened. Sino-U.S. relations had improved. The Soviet threat had ended. U.S. pressures to halt missile and nuclear technology transfers overcame China's interests in helping Pakistan, although mutual friendship and defense cooperation continued. China also sought to minimize tensions with India.

Chinese technology assistance to Pakistan increasingly lagged behind that which India obtained from Russia and France. North Korea replaced China in providing Pakistan with longer range, more modern missiles. This relationship will likely continue, so long as India pursues its own longer range and solid-fuel missiles. Pakistan's relations with the Muslim world are driven partly by common religious bonds, but also by a need for political and economic support. Pakistani laborers working throughout the Persian Gulf have sent remittances home for years; this has become a major source of income, equal to or exceeding Pakistan's cotton and textile exports.

Islamic support for Pakistan was critical during Zia al Haq's military rule, when relations with the United States were strained, and especially after the USSR invaded Afghanistan. Pakistan feared being caught between India and the Soviets in Afghanistan. Pakistan also relies on Islamic support when the issue of Kashmir arises in international forums. Pakistan has reciprocated by supporting Arab causes, particularly against Israel. However, support from Islamic countries was more rhetorical than real, except during confrontations with the Soviets in Afghanistan.

India's Democratic Politics

Democratic politics are India's great strength and weakness. India's constitution is modeled after that of the United States. However, it is nearly 300 pages long and has been amended 75 times. During India's first 30 years, the Congress Party was dominant. The last 20 years have seen an explosion of parties reflecting the complexity of India's nearly one billion people, dozens of languages and dialects, and hundreds of social caste and community divisions. Government by coalition in New Delhi and state governments is routine. This has complicated consensus building and slowed decisionmaking at every level.

In the February 1998 national elections, the Bharatiya Janata Party (BJP) became the largest single Indian party, with 25 percent of the electorate and 179 legislative seats. The Congress Party received almost the same number of votes. Political parties with mostly local constituencies won enough seats to force a coalition with the BJP. The BJP, the political wing of a social and religious group linked to several institutions, is deeply committed to a Hindu national and religious heartland in India. It is rallying many Indians seeking a strong India. It is also potentially dividing India's religious groups. The coalition formed by the BJP in March 1998 had a relatively small majority. The BJP is also divided within its ranks and among coalition partners on many economic, social, and political issues. However, the party platform demanded nuclear testing, which was widely supported. The BJP, therefore, moved quickly to demonstrate a willingness and ability to act. The party also seeks to modernize and strengthen India's conventional forces. Its economic policies focus on supporting Indian business, but are ambiguous about foreign capital's role and the spread of consumerism in India.

The BJP government coalition collapsed in spring 1999 and continues in caretaker status. The Congress Party, however, has taken full advantage of BJP difficulties. In the last few decades, the number of Indians living below the poverty level has gradually declined, but Indian studies differ widely over the degree of improvement. Clearly, the gap between rich and poor has grown and likely will continue growing. The rapid spread of communications is making Indians aware of modernization and the gap between them and the West. Inadequate law and order has been a growing problem for years seriously affecting every Indian state. This problem is a consequence of poverty, corruption, tensions between castes competing for political power and jobs, and tribal groups separatist demands in India's border areas. The problem is exasperated by a growing awareness of the gap between India's "haves" and "have-nots."

Growing law and order problems have led to an increase in lightly equipped Central Government paramilitary forces. They number 1.5 million, nearly 60 percent larger than the regular army. They deal with major insurrections and prolonged challenges like those in Jammu and Kashmir, or in northeastern India's tribal areas. This paramilitary force does not include local or state police. This internal security focus will likely continue even with increasing expenditures for conventional and missile programs.

Domestiuc Uncertainty of Pakistan

Pakistan's domestic political stability is fragile and has often been disrupted. Its 1971-72 civil war led to East Pakistan's break-away and the establishment of Bangladesh. While Karachi became Pakistan's largest city and its financial center over the last two decades, it had the world's highest crime in 1998. This is largely the result of tensions between postpartition immigrants, the native population, and sectarian gangs with powerful political backing. Small Shia and Sunni Muslim groups violently clash in the Punjab. Bandits and young Islamic fanatics increasingly threaten ordinary citizens, even in Islamabad, the capital. Tribal chiefs largely control Baluchistan and the Northwest Frontier, where a very strong Islamist, pro-Taliban presence is also felt. Government rule greatly depends on the consent of these tribal chiefs.

While Pakistan is considered a democracy, political power lies in the hands of a few clans and families that dominate the political structure. The Bhuttos and Sharifs, for example, control the two major political parties. Challengers to these parties come from similar social-political backgrounds. Corruption has been high in most Pakistani governments, including the Pakistan People's Party (PPP) and the Pakistan Muslim League (PML) administrations. They have been in power for the last 30 years, except when the army was in control from 1977 to 1985. Feeble attempts to punish corrupt individuals are unlikely to change soon.

Pakistan's political system is unlikely to change fundamentally. The army is not inclined to return to power but influences politics behindthe-scenes. Military rule would be a possibility, although an unlikely one, if economic and social unrest could not be controlled by ordinary means. Violence in Karachi reached this level in October 1998. Prime Minister Sharif dismissed the elected government and imposed governor's rule. However, martial law was avoided, based on army and civilian preferences. Islamic political parties have never been successful in elections, failing to produce strong candidates. Additionally, most Pakistanis do not want the mullahs to rule and have consistently rejected candidates from the Islamic political parties. However, Islamists have been able to mobilize street demonstrations and provoke extensive sectarian violence.

The Taliban experience in Afghanistan could change public attitudes. Many Pakistanis are frustrated with the existing political structure. By comparison, the Taliban has reduced crime, ended corruption, collected weapons, and protected the "common man." Islamist appeal is such that even Osama Bin Laden enjoys strong public support, even though government officials decry his links to sectarian violence in Pakistan as well as to international terrorism. Some think this experience might cause a surge in support for an Islamic party, particularly if it produces a charismatic leader. While it may be unlikely, the emergence of a more Islamic government in Pakistan opposite a more ideological Hindu government in India could generate greater tensions than South Asia has seen in half a century.

Economic development, trade, and investment are shaping the strategic environment in South Asia. India's prospects are better than Pakistan's in the long term. India's development strategy has emphasized government planning for the economy. This has meant tight control of the private sector. Pakistan started with a more pro-business approach. However, within 10 years, Pakistan turned to a more planned economy. Neither India nor Pakistan has received significant U.S. investments. The United States provided economic and technical assistance to both countries and strongly encouraged private business with India. However, economic relations have been negligible: they represent less than 0.5 percent of U.S. trade, and investment is even lower.

In the 1980s, Pakistan initiated economic reforms designed to reduce government control over investment. Faced with a growing financial crisis in 1991, India announced its own plans for economic reform that were intended to reduce government controls and encourage foreign investment. The Indian market's potential attracted the attention of the United States and other nations. The GDP rose from 4 to 5 percent in the preceding decade to 6 to 7 percent during the 1993-96 period. International corporations initiated investments, and over $12 billion in foreign capital flowed into India in the mid-1990s.

U.S. oil companies considered building pipelines and refineries in Pakistan. This would enable Central Asian oil and gas to reach the Arabian Sea and potentially the Indian market without going through Iran or the Gulf. Infrastructure development promised tens of billions of dollars in new investment for both India and Pakistan. These plans were derailed by continuing civil war, growth of heroin trafficking, the Taliban's socio-religious policies, and tensions between

Afghanistan and its neighbors. Pakistan's vision of being the commercial corridor between Central Asia and the outside world faded.

The Clinton administration saw India as one of the new emerging markets that would transform U.S. international economic relations. Hundreds of U.S. corporations that had never been connected with the region opened offices, factories, and joint ventures. By 1998, India had become a key software provider for thousands of U.S. companies. However, India lags significantly in developing a diversified economy. Its economy ranks at the bottom of international assessments.

India has major deficiencies in its infrastructure, particularly electrical power, ports, telecommunications, and transportation. These are major constraints, yet they provide opportunities for the United States to resume major economic relations with India. At the same time, such growth faces some major challenges. These include systemic problems in mobilizing domestic capital, unresolved issues in government decision-making, and major differences over foreign capital's role. Moreover, it will be difficult to overcome many of India's cultural and social constraints, such as reliance on family and caste connections in business management, employment restrictions, expectations that government will resolve problems and meet needs, and suspicion of foreign influence. U.S. involvement remains small for these reasons.

Demand for change is growing. It is being facilitated by the flood of information reaching every corner of India. In principle, India's democratic institutions provide a framework for change, but it may not always happen in ways that the United States likes. India's long-term economic prospects are essentially good. In the 21st century, India is likely to become an increasingly important economic partner for the United States and other developed countries. Prospects in Pakistan are less promising.

Weaknesses in the entire political-economic system have undercut reforms intended to reduce the role of state-owned enterprises and promote a free market. Debt payment and defense expenditures are 80 percent of the budget and have been for over a decade. Under 3 percent goes for education, health, and social programs combined. The quality of services is low and often does not reach the poorest sectors. Agriculture generally stagnant. Investment and savings have declined. Inflation remains in double digits. Foreign investment is moribund, discouraged by violence in such areas as Karachi. The banking system has been damaged by bad loans often made for political reasons. Finally, foreign debt has left the country on the verge of default.

Infrastructure development has been undercut by corrupt managing agencies, poor project choices, bitter political infighting, and disillusionment after plans for oil and gas pipelines were cancelled. The economy remains heavily dependent on cotton and cotton cloth exports and lacks significant diversification. In the agricultural sector, large landowners are often indifferent to long-term consequences of land use. Pakistan does not have a strong industrial base. Its literacy rate is below 40 percent. The overwhelming majority of women are excluded from all but the most menial work. Pakistan's infrastructure is weak, particularly in the areas of railroads, roads, ports, and telecommunications.

The 1998 census indicates that population growth has begun to slow. Pakistan's 130 million population was six million lower than anticipated. However, few resources will be available to correct developmental weakness in the foreseeable future. Pakistan's society is more conservative than India's. In a decade, social change is unlikely to have progressed much beyond today's levels, particularly in rural areas. Unless there is a breakthrough in the oil and gas sector, there is a low likelihood of improvements in Pakistan's economy, as well as in economic relations with the United States.

During the 1990s, the United States has had four interests in South Asia. First, it seeks to reduce the risk of conventional and nuclear conflict between India and Pakistan. Second, it seeks to encourage better relations between the two. Third, it wants to engage India and Pakistan in international regimes on nonproliferation, environmental protection, antiterrorism, and other global issues. Fourth, it has an interest in strengthening both countries' economic and political structures and broadening economic relationships through investment and trade. Nonproliferation has been the paramount U.S. concern, pursued at the cost of the others. This was especially the case after India and Pakistan conducted nuclear tests.

Recently, U.S. interests in South Asia have been growing, because nuclear proliferation could not only destabilize the region but also have larger damaging consequences. Regional tensions are deep-rooted in geopolitical and historical issues. Yet, dialogues exist among all regional countries. These need to be encouraged by all parties, including the United States. These dialogues are the means of discussing and resolving these issues. U.S. influence in the region is limited. It is difficult for the United States to influence one country without adversely affecting relations with others. At some time, the United States may be more able directly to ease tensions caused by these issues, but such circumstances are unlikely to develop soon.

India seeks primarily to enhance its regional and global status. Pakistan's predominant concern is its security with respect to India and its internal stability. This latter concern is affected by Pakistan's socioeconomic structure and by developments in Afghanistan. The Taliban which, ironically, was created by Pakistan, now threatens its economic interests, as well as its domestic political stability. In the past, both India and Pakistan have opposed specific U.S. policies. Additionally, Pakistan has close ties with some Muslim states the United States regards as rogues. However, neither is likely to join a coalition hostile to the United States or to pursue national policies explicitly threatening the United States.

Over the next 5 years, several trends are likely in South Asia. Political tension is likely to continue just short of major conflict. Moderate economic growth can be expected, approximately 6 percent annually for India and less for Pakistan. While both countries have weak governments, Pakistan has a greater risk of political instability than does India. Neither country is likely to risk large-scale conventional war or allow escalation to nuclear confrontation. Nevertheless, a "hair trigger" situation could develop. Both might conclude that they do not have assured second-strike capability; this would be further aggravated by the perception that the other side was about to attack first. Even short of nuclear war, accelerating WMD proliferation in South Asia and elsewhere endangers U.S. strategic interests.

After Indian and Pakistani nuclear testing, the most important U.S. interests in South Asia are: preventing the dissemination of nuclear weapons and technology to rogue states and terrorists; reducing the nuclear arms race and chances of a nuclear conflict; and suppressing radical groups which might possess nuclear weapons. Inherent in preserving these interests is the continuation of a relative peace between India and Pakistan. They also imply that the United States will persuade India and Pakistan not to weaponize and deploy their nuclear capability. Another war would endanger the region. However, it would not directly affect vital U.S. national interests, unless India or Pakistan lost control of their nuclear weapons, or such a war led to nuclear conflict; this would dangerously affect the global environment as well as the regional strategic balance.

The United States has an interest in halting the flow of weapons of mass destruction (WMD) technology to the region. This includes China's provision of nuclear-related technology as well North Korea's delivery of missile technology to Pakistan. It also means controlling Russia's supply of missile-related technology and advanced conventional weaponry to India and minimizing Chinese and North Korean involvement in the region. This includes reducing Sino-Indian tensions and halting delivery of nuclear weapon-related supplies or missiles to Pakistan. India's development of a navy with nuclear submarines and ballistic missiles, along with aggressive claims to the Indian Ocean, would negatively affect U.S. interests.

Indian support for dissidents in Tibet, or expansion of Chinese military involvement in Burma, could significantly increase Sino-Indian tensions. Chinese initiation of a long-envisaged railroad to Lhasa would also arouse Indian concerns about the potential for enhancing Chinese military capabilities and represent a major destabilizing factor. If immediate U.S. concerns ease regarding regional conflict and nuclear weapons control, then substantial longer term objectives could be pursued. One goal is to reconcile Indian and Pakistani nuclear regimes with the NPT, removing this obstacle to better U.S. relations.

The United States has an interest in both countries viewing themselves in a much broader, regional context, rather than focusing on the last 50 years of bilateral tension. Both countries would benefit from Central Asia's energy reserves. A cooperative effort to gain access would reduce friction and forge a common approach to stabilizing Afghanistan and working with Iran. Opening Central Asia would also serve U.S. interests. Other long-term U.S. interests are furthering Indian economic reform and development and encouraging U.S. trade and investment. These have been hampered by preoccupation with nuclear issues and regional tensions. Achieving these interests will depend on India's access to U.S. technology and removing impediments to it. Aiding Pakistan's economy is also a U.S. interest, provided Pakistan seeks cooperation with the West.

The United States has only intermittently viewed India and Pakistan as a high priority in its overall foreign policy. This high priority was the result of such Cold War events as the Sino-Indian War and the Soviet occupation of Afghanistan, rather than an inherent interest in the subcontinent. Previously, the United States has sought even-handed dealings with both India and Pakistan. However, the United States has made clear a greater interest in India than Pakistan, based on its continued sanctions against Pakistan and its determination that India is a new, emerging market. In the long term, India's political and military potential is greater. This could create an asymmetry in U.S. interests with Pakistan and India, which should be recognized. However, both India and the United States would be seriously affected if Pakistan were to be destabilized or succumb to Islamist pressure.

In 1998, a close dialogue developed over nuclear policy between Deputy Secretary of State Strobe Talbott, special Indian representative Jaswant Singh, and Pakistan Foreign Secretary Shamshad Ahmed Khan. It is a model for future dialogues between these nations even though it is probably too narrowly focused on nonproliferation. This dialogue was private, strongly supported at the highest political levels, focused on important issues, and conducted by individuals able to establish a strong personal rapport and trust. Such dialogue is not unique in U.S. foreign relations, but it has been less common in subcontinent relations. It will take time and continued effort to succeed.

Following the imposition of bilateral and multilateral sanctions, political pressure and persuasion, along with this dialogue, have caused both countries to move closer to CTBT adherence and negotiating a global cutoff of fissile material production. This pressure and persuasion have come from the UN Security Council, G-7 countries, the European Union, China, Australia, South Africa, Argentina, and Brazil. Neither country has rushed to weaponize or deploy more missiles. Both seem to be seriously concerned about nuclear dangers. This concern has led to a series of bilateral talks on such issues as Kashmir, nuclear and missile restraint regimes, confidence-building measures, and easing trade and travel restrictions.

The meeting of the two prime ministers in Lahore on February 21-22, 1999, is an unprecedented effort to move the process forward. However, the outcome will depend on the sustained political will of leadership in New Delhi and Islamabad, public reactions, and sustained interest by other countries. Above all, it will depend on continued, active U.S. involvement.

India and Pakistan are likely to weaponize and deploy their nuclear capabilities, but on a limited scale. These weapons will be difficult to monitor, no matter what restraint regime might be negotiated. Some estimate that over the next decade India could produce as many as 500 weapons and that Pakistan could produce about 100 weapons. However, neither country is likely to produce and deploy such large numbers of weapons in the next 5 to 10 years or engage in a nuclear arms race. They also will not abandon their nuclear and missile capabilities or join the NPT unless it is amended.

This outlook sets the stage for developing U.S. policy that can live with India's and Pakistan's nuclear capabilities, provided they behave responsibly regarding their deployment and nonproliferation. It means gradually moving away from rigid sanctions and nonproliferation as the dominant U.S. policy issue. This would allow the United States to improve its relations with both countries, and better help them exercise restraint and reduce tensions. It would also enable economic cooperation and development to be placed ahead of politico-military priorities, especially in Pakistan, and encourage both countries to adopt a regional, rather than bilateral approach.

The United States has no regional infrastructure for major military operations in South Asia. Should such operations be required, U.S. air forces could operate from distant bases in Diego Garcia, Guam, or the continental United States Additionally, U.S. Navy and Marine Expeditionary Forces in the Arabian Sea and Indian Ocean might be deployed to indicate willingness to protect U.S. interests. U.S. carriers would probably be available with sufficient notice, but global requirements are a constraint on deploying U.S. forces to the region for extended periods. It is unlikely that U.S. force deployments could effectively forestall a nuclear crisis, although some technologies might be made available that could contribute to this objective.

Nuclear War

If a South Asian nuclear war occurs, who uses nuclear weapons first makes little difference to U.S. policy. The other side's retaliation would almost be certain. The only question is whether the targets would be military or civilian. U.S. nuclear authorities estimate that a single 12-kiloton weapon detonated over any major South Asian population center would immediately cause over half-a-million casualties, and eventually up to 12 million casualties. Intervention by other nuclear powers in an Indo-Pakistani war, with or without nuclear weapons, is remote but cannot be discounted. Certainly U.S. relief efforts would be requested and would involve significant U.S. air and naval deployments.

The United States would press other states to limit the damage to the rest of the region and the global environment. Once international pressures from nuclear tests have ebbed, a U.S. dialogue with India and Pakistan will be critical. While previous dialogues focused on nuclear testing consequences, they should be broadened to include regular and systematic exchanges on regional security issues and the U.S. role regarding them. The U.S. Government approved the restoration of military training and exchange programs in February 1999. They should be implemented rapidly. Regional conferences organized by the United States, with senior Indian and Pakistani military officers participating, should also be revived. Ultimately, the key issues to be resolved are those affecting Indo-Pakistani relations and perceptions of mutual security.

7

SAARC and Sub-regional Cooperation

Regional Trade Agreements (RTAs)

Where do the nation states derive motivation from to establish an RTA? This will help one comprehend the motivation behind the establishment of a FTA and eventual establishment of an economic union in the South Asia Region.

Most of the RTAs take European integration as the template for regional integration, little realising the uniqueness with which Europe was (and is still) blessed. Europe's overriding objective, which was brilliantly achieved, was political and military: to use economic integration to overcome the historic animosities of its chief protagonists and thus render future wars impossible. Indeed, the preamble to the 1951 treaty establishing the European Coal and Steel Community, out of which EU grew, states its aim as follows: "To create, by establishing an economic community, the basis for broader and deeper community among peoples long divided by bloody conflicts. "A second driving force in Europe was the common enemy embodied by the Soviet Union.

The United States (US), driven by its own strategic priorities of deterring the Soviet Union and avoiding another fratricidal war in Europe itself, was willing to accept some negative economic effects from the European unity and even the build-up of a potential future rival. Despite US support for European integration, a subtext of the latter has been Europe's own quest for independence from the pervasive influence of the US. All participants in the European integration process have been democracies. Indeed, several countries in the region - notably Spain and Portugal - were deliberately shunned until they shed their dictatorial regimes. Security also played an important role in initiating regional integration in the Southern Cone.

The Argentine and Brazilian militaries had long perceived each other as potential threats. Economic agreements covering steel and automobiles were signed in the mid-1980s as part of an attempt to reduce tensions, and the creation of Southern Common Market (MERCOSUR) in 1991 reinforced this process. The political impetus to European and Southern Cone integration was thus based on the belief that increasing trade would reduce the risk of intra-regional conflict. Similar motives, inter alia, were found in the creation of the ASEAN - to reduce tension between Indonesia and Malaysia. Unfortunately, the assertion that regional economic integration reduces political tension between the participating countries is not a rule of thumb.

Some economic integration arrangement could result in political conflict after regional integration, mainly as a result of huge income transfers from the poorer countries to the richer ones. Conflict within regional integration agreements can be illustrated, among others, by the example of the East African Common Market. In this case, Kenya was receiving more than proportionate income transfers from Uganda and Tanzania, which induced a fear that there would be increasing agglomeration of manufacturing in Nairobi, which had a head start on industrialisation compared with the smaller industrial centres of Tanzania at Dar es Salaam and of Uganda at Jinga.

Arguments about compensation for the income trans fers contributed to the collapse of the Common Market, the closing of borders, and the confiscation of Community assets in 1978.

Sometimes political impetus for intra regional cooperation can also be provided by a common extra-regional threat. For example, two subtle motives for the formation of European Economic Community (EEC) were: a) to counter the potential spread of communism in Western Europe coming from Eastern Europe; b) to counter the hegemony of the US in global economic and political spheres.

ASEAN also had as one of its goals to prevent Communism spreading from China to East Asia. Another good example was the formation of the Southern African Development Coordination Conference in 1980 to provide a united front among the small countries of the region against the apartheid regime in South Africa. Part of the strategy was to reduce economic dependence on South Africa both as a trading partner and to use the Southern African Development Coordination Conference as a conduit to trade with the outside world.

"United we stand", as the saying goes, and by joining hands together weak countries can become stronger. Just as workers unite by forming trade unions to have better bargaining power, smaller countries too, in theory, have a greater bargaining power in international negotiations when they negotiate as a group. It is a lot easier for the smaller countries to get noticed and be able to cut deals with the major economic power when they act in a unified manner.

However, in practice this has really not been the case. Barring the European Union and a few exceptions under some circumstances, other regional groupings have failed to make a concerted and unified position in international negotiations. For example, ASEAN does not act as a group in the WTO negotiations, which became clear during the run up to Doha Ministerial Conference. While countries like Singapore and Thailand were in favour of launching a new round of multilateral trade negotiations, Malaysia remained singularly opposed to this issue till the last moment. Similarly, many

African regional groupings did not have the same positions during the various stages of negotiations at the WTO.

Caribbean Community and Common Market (CARICOM), the alliance of smaller Caribbean island states, is an exception among the developing countries groupings inasmuch as it negotiates in most of the international fora, including the WTO, in a unified manner. CARICOM is not only focused on achieving regional integration - rather its objective is common action. Without solidarity, it would be quixotic for any single island to spend resources on international negotiations, and so it was evident that there were gains from pooling the costs of negotiations. CARICOM has been strikingly successful in getting its members noticed. For example, they have taken the lead in formulating and articulating the position of the African, Caribbean, and Pacific (ACP) countries group in negotiating the Lome Convention.

Economic effect

The economic effects of regional agreements are of two main types. The first are "scale and competition" effects. Removal of trade barriers is like a market enlargement -separate national markets move toward integration in a regional market. This allows firms to benefit from greater scale and attract investment projects, mainly in the form of Foreign Direct Investment (FDI) for which market size is important. Removing barriers also forces firms from different member countries into closer competition with each other, possibly inducing them to make efficiency improvements. Although these are major sources of benefit, they are not always achieved.

The effects depend on design and implementation of the agreement. Some of these benefits may be achievable with unilateral trade liberalisation, although the same may not always be politically feasible. The second source of economic change is "trade and location" effects. The preferential reduction in tariffs within a regional agreement will induce purchasers to switch demand toward supply from partner countries, at the expense of both domestic production and imports from non-members. This is trade creation and trade diversion. Governments will lose tariff revenue, and the overall effect on national income may be positive or negative, depending on the costs of alternative sources of supply and on trade policy toward non-member countries.

Changes in trade flows induce changes in the location of production between member countries of a regional agreement. These relocations are determined by the comparative advantage of member countries, by agglomeration or clustering effects, and by possible technology transfer between countries. In some circumstances, relocations can be a force for convergence of income levels between countries. Labour-intensive production activities may move toward lower-wage countries, raising wages in those countries. In other circumstances, relocations can be a force for divergence. Industry may be pulled toward a country with a head start or with some natural advantage, driving up incomes ahead of other countries leading to income divergence. It is more likely that the North-North or North-South RTAs lead to income convergence.

However, South-South RTAs are likely to result in income divergence. An emerging economic view is that RTAs can increase world income and abet multilateralism so long as they remain open to new members, avoid raising external trade barriers, enhance intra-bloc growth through scale economies, stimulate competition, reduce transport costs, avoid protectionist rules of origin or anti-dumping regimes and generally force recalcitrant interventionist members to liberalise more rapidly than they would otherwise do.

South-South regional integration arrangements are formed with much enthusiasm, but they tend to break up fairly quickly. Several factors are responsible for this. Some of them are below:

Low intra-regional trade: Most South-South PTAs (Preferential trading arrangements) have a low level of intra-regional trade. For example, in 1996, intra-EU exports were 62 percent and intra-NAFTA exports were 47 percent. In the middle income PTAs, MERCOSUR had 23 percent, ASEAN 20 percent, dropping still further for low income PTAs, at 9 percent for Economic Community of Western African States (ECOWAS), and 1. 9 percent for Union Economique et Monaitaire de l'Afrique Occidentale (UEMOA). Table 1 compares export trade among, three Nort h dominated PTAs/ RTAs and three South-South PTA/RTAs. It is obvious that where the intra PTA trade is very low, it cannot create the required impact and stimulate economic growth thereby ensuring prosperity. With low volume of intra-regional trade, there is hardly any incentive for the member countries to fully implement the agreement on preferential tariffs.

Table 1. Export trade in regional coorperations(as % of total exports)

	1970	1990	1995	1999
APEC	57. 8	68. 3	71. 9	71. 9
EU	59. 5	65. 9	62. 4	62. 6
NAFTA	36. 0	41. 4	46. 2	54. 6
MERCOSUR	9. 4	8. 9	20. 3	20. 5
ASEAN	22. 9	19. 8	25. 4	22. 2
SAARC	3. 2	3. 2	4. 4	4. 7

Competing for the same market: Major countries of the South export the same or similar products to the same markets - mainly Organisation for Economic Cooperation and Development (OECD) countries. This leads to mutual distrust among the members of the FTA that one country might outmaneuver the other. One can take the example of South Asia where readymade garment is the major export of five out of seven countries - Bangladesh, India, Nepal, Pakistan and Sri Lanka. All of them export their garments to either the EU or the US market. Entering into an FTA like SAFTA will entail loss of market for the lower income countries because their industries will either go bankrupt or will be bought over by the larger and more efficient companies from bigger countries. In such a situation, small countries may have an incentive not to cooperate.

Heterogeneity: Most Sout hern countries are politically and economically a heterogeneous group. Let us take the example of ASEAN (or ASEAN Free Trade Area, AFTA) where members vary greatly in the composition of their exports (for instance, industrial versus agricultural goods) and their current level of protection. Consequently, going to zero tariff on substantially all goods will entail very asymmetric - and therefore - politically difficult - 'concessions' in terms of both tariff cutting and 'winning the losing' sectors. This is very much the case with SAARC as well.

High coordination cost: Implementing FTA is a costly exercise; it requires high coordination cost to administer strict rules of origin requirement and implementation of reform process. This does not only demand financial resources, but also human resources, technical expertise and skills. Since these resources are lacking in the Southern countries, FTAs formed exclusively within and among them tend to suffer a setback.

Loss of government revenue: For the North, which hardly relies on tariff as a source of revenuethere is only negligible loss in government revenue even after the implementation of an FTA. However, for many countries in the South - which most often run high budget deficits - trade taxes are an important source of government revenue, and membership of an FTA leads to loss of tariff revenue. This arises directly - as tariffs on intra- FTA trade are reduced - and also indirectly, when trade diversion occurs, such as when importers switch away from external imports subject to tariffs.

Fear is ripe that such rivalry is likely to slow the implementation of SAFTA, even after its eventual signing.

Signing an FTA is not a difficult task, all it requires is the willingness among the politicians of the founding members to ask their bureaucrats and experts to calculate the cost and benefits and prepare an agreement to be signed. The main challenge lies in implementing the same. The economic, political and social costs of sustaining an FTA are very high and all the Southern countries are not necessarily capable of incurring them. The problem is further compounded by multiple memberships thus creating 'spaghetti bowl'like phenomenon. Das, therefore, rightly comments "Not all the RTAs were negotiated with the sincere trade-expansion and economic integration intentions. To be sure, some had mere vague aspirations". The majority of South-South RTAs fall into this category.

One cannot, however, reproach the draftspersons for being bad economists; it was not until 1950s that, under the stimulus of a few pages book by Jacob Viner,professional economists began to give serious thought to the conditions under which the allocation of world resources is improved by regional trade arrangement. That is the theory of trade creation and trade diversion.

Cross-country evidence shows that four pre-conditions are required for successful regional trading arrangement: first, pre- FTA tariffs should be high; second, the members of the FTA should be important trading partners before entering into an arrangement; third, there should be complementarity in demand, i.e., countries would need to have difference in economic structures; fourth, the countries should have different factor endowments. If such preconditions are not valid, the potential gains from regional trading arrangements will not be very significant for most of the countries. However, this view has been criticised on grounds of being under a static framework. A dynamic perspective would take into account the trade creating opportunities opened up by PTAs and FTAs.

Recent evidence suggests that when participating countries actively promote policies geared towards overcoming of initial difficulties through carefully sequenced cooperation agendas, put in place regional division of labour, jointly exploit natural resources, take cognizance of locational advantage and promote intra- regional investment, the net outcome from trade creation and trade diversion is usually positive.

Regionalism and Globalism

At the turn of the 20Century, both globalism and regionalism are coexisting in the global trading system. If anything, regionalism is burgeoning. These developments raise important questions for the global trading system. During the 1990s, it was widely assumed that building complementary between regional and multilateral institutions was the only way to grapple with the complexities of the fast changing global economic and trade realities. However, it has become necessary to take a good look at this stand and to question this easy assumption. Does regionalism have a direct, effective, and systemic link with trade liberalisation? The opposite can also be true, i.e., regionalism could be fragmenting global trade, and in the process creating a new global disorder characterised by growing rivalries and marginalisation.

Economists, political scientists and policy makers are still working very hard to find out what RTAs really mean to the global economy in general and participating countries in particular. However, the picture is becoming increasingly complex as RTAs proliferate, change their goals, produce overlapping blocs, and take on a so-called 'hub and spoke'pattern with one major counry at the centre of several blocs. The assumption that regionalism would lead to globalisation need not be correct. Cogent arguments exist on both the sides.

As per Larry Summers, any "ism" (bilateralism, regionalism and multilateralism) is good as long as its ultimate objective is trade liberalisation. Regional arrangements promote freer trade and multilateralism in at least two sense: that trade creation has generally exceeded trade diversion, and that the RTAs contribute to both internal and international dynamics that enhance rather than reduce the prospects for global liberalisation. The internal dynamic is particularly important for developing countries: regional commitments, which can be negotiated much faster than global pacts, lock in domestic reforms against the risk that successive governments will try to reverse them. Internationally, the RTAs often pioneer new liberalisation ideas that can subsequently be generalised in the multilateral system. Moreover, regional liberalisation creates incentives for other regions and individual countries to follow suit and thus to 'ratchet up' the global process.

Regionalism, by allowing stronger internalisation of the gains from trade de-restriction, seems likely to be able to facilitate freer trade in highly restrictive circumstances or sector. The proponents of regionalism assert that it often has important demonstration effects. Regional initiatives can accustom officials, governments, and nations to the liberalisation process and thus increase the probability that they will subsequently move on to similar multilateral actions. "Learning by doing" applies to trade liberalisation as well as to economic development itself, and can often be experienced both more easily and more extensively in the regional context with far fewer negotiating partners.

They further contend that it has had positive rather than negative political effects. Trade and broader economic integration has created EU in which another war between Germany and France is literally impossible. Argentina and Brazil have used MERCOSUR to end their historic rivalry, which had taken on nuclear overtones in recent decades. Central goals of Asia Pacific Economic Cooperation (APEC) include anchoring the United States as a stabilising force in Asia and forging institutional links between such previous antagonists as Japan, China and the rest of East Asia.

Even if the argument that RTAs can potentially result in reducing global trade and, therefore, global welfare is correct, one must know the counterfactual. If an RTA is reducing global welfare, it is doing so in comparison to what? To be sure, in comparison to complete free trade, RTAs are clearly the second best. But compared to the global trading system in which tariffs and NTBs were rampant, the case against RTAs is generally far from clear. Formation of an RTA is sure to have some trade diversion, but while forming or joining an RTA countries expect trade diversion losses to outweigh the trade creation gains.

RTAs are able to achieve a deeper degree of economic integration than the multilateral trading system. This is well within the realm of feasibility because RTAs usually entail neighbouring like-minded countries. A smaller forum [with homogenous or semi-homogenous membership] makes it possible to establish the necessary centralised institutions or federalising policy-making and enforcement institutions. However, economists also argue that it will be difficult to conclude negotiations between a group as diverse as the Free Trade Areas of Americas (FTAA), which is being joined by 35 countries and where the socio- political as well as economic realities of the countries are as diverse as the WTO membership.

A group of trade economists follow the logic that expansion of RTAs could have positive effects on the global economy provided the emerging RTAs are "open" to trade from outside. One key benefit to the global economy comes from the impact of RTA in stimulating domestic growth, which in turn increases the demand for extra-regional exports. A major analytical contribution dealing with this issue is of Baldwin. Focusing exclusively on the incentive to seek entry on the part of outsiders, Baldwin identifies a "domino" effect, which may yield global free trade through PTA expansion. Using a variant of what have come to be known as models of economic geography, Baldwin shows that under the "domino" effect, more and more outside countries have an incentive to become insiders as PTA expands.

The countries are assumed to differ in a way that the PTA is not equally attractive to them. Initially, it attracts one member who finds the entry worthwhile. The addition of this member enlarges the internal market and makes it more attractive to yet another outside country at the margin. Once this country joins, yet another country finds accession profitable, and so on until the PTA becomes global. Consequent to expansion of membership in a PTA, trade diversion obviously gets minimised. In the words of Baldwin:

> "Idiosyncratic incidents of regionalism triggered a multiplier effect that knocked down bilateral import barriers. Forming a preferential trade area, deepening an existing one, produces trade and investment diversion. This diversion generates new political economy in non-participating nations, i.e., pressure for inclusion. The pressure increases with the size of the trade bloc, yet bloc size depends upon how many nations join. Clearly, a single incidence of regionalism may trigger several rounds of membership requests from nations that were previously happy as non-members. If the trade bloc is open to expansion, regionalism may spread like wildfire. If the enlargement burn-path is barred, the new political economy flames may find vent in preferential arrangements among excluded nations. "

As per Baldwin, this domino theory is derived from the expansion of the EU. He then goes on to explain the American dominos. Indeed, the possibility of facing exclusion due to US-Mexico trade, when the trade talks were going on between the US and Mexico, Canada requested the parties to trilateralise talks which led to the birth of NAFTA. Similarly, when other Latin American countries, which were interested to join NAFTA only received lukewarm response from President George Bush (Senior), four of them decided to form MERCOSUR. The pressure for inclusion was so much that Bolivia and Chile joined MERCOUSR as its associate members.

Now that FTAA has been announced, covering the entire Western Hemisphere, virtually every country in the Americas is looking forward to joining the same. Asian dominos have not fallen so much because ASEAN has only expanded its membership to 10. However, the first ever FTA, which Japan entered into with Singapore and the one Korea is planning with Chile are likely to knock down dominos of a greater magnitude. ASEAN plus three is another example of this.

The concept represents an effort to achieve the best of both worlds: the benefits of regional liberalisation, which even the critics acknowledge, without jeopardising the continued vitality of the multilateral system. Indeed, proponents of open regionalism view it as a device through which regionalism can be employed to accelerate the progress toward global liberalisation and rule-making. APEC was modelled on this concept based on the suggestions of the Eminent Persons Group (EPG), which was chaired by Bergesten himself. As per EPG, in order to achieve the goal of "open" regionalism, following alternative approaches have been suggested:

— the maximum possible extent of unilateral liberalisation;

— a commitment to continue reducing its barriers to nonmember countries while it liberalises internally on a most favoured nations (MFN) basis;

— a willingness to extend its regional liberalisation to nonmembers on a mutually reciprocal basis; and

— recognition that any individual APEC member can unilaterally extend its APEC liberalisation to non-members on a conditional or unconditional basis.

Prof. T. N. Srinivasan has very correctly noted: "if regional liberalisation is to be extended on the same time table 'in practice and in law' to non-member countries on an MFN basis, it would be multilateral and not regional. If that is the case, why should any group initiate it on a regional basis in the first place?" He goes on to call 'open regionalism' as an oxymoron. The practical problems of this concept have been highlighted by the current status of the APEC and the Indian

Ocean Rim Association for Regional Cooperation (IOR-ARC) where the progress has been far from satisfactory.

As early as in 1992, Prof. Jagadish Bhagwati, who claims himself to be a multilateralist and a critique of regionalism, posed the following question: is regionalism truly a building, rather than a stumbling, bloc towards multilateral free trade for all: in other words, will it fragment, or integrate, the world economy? Bhagwati calls "the revival of regionalism" as "unfortunate". He emphasises the need "to contain and shape it in ways that it becomes maximally useful and minimally damaging, and consonant with the objectives of arriving at multilateral free trade for all. "Expanding on these arguments, Panagariya uses two different analyses, through formal model as well as informal arguments to prove that regionalism is a stumbling block to multilateral trading system. He takes two formal models by Levy and Krishna.

As per Levy's model, if the voters in two different countries, which are the members of both FTA and multilateral trading system were given a choice to vote, they felt that FTA cannot make previously infeasible multilateral liberalisation feasible. Krishna uses a three-country, partialequilibrium, oligopoly model in which trade policy is chosen to maximise national firms' profits. He shows that more trade diverting the FTA between two countries in this set up, the greater the backing it receives and the more it reduces the incentive to eventually liberalise with the third country. With sufficiently large trade diversion, an initially feasible multilateral liberalisation can be rendered infeasible by the FTA option.

Similarly, using a three-country, two-goods general equilibrium model, Lipsey demonstrated that, after the union is formed, the gain in consumption due to the reduction in the prices of the imported good by a union member could more than outweigh the loss from switching imported goods from the low-cost outside country to the high-cost union partner. He then analyses the informal arguments in the following sequence. Firstly, it has been suggested by Summers and others that multilateral negotiations will move more rapidly if the number of negotiators is reduced to approximately three via bloc formation. This argument gained some popularity at the time the Uruguay Round (UR) negotiations were stalled but has lost force since the successful completion of the Round.

The argument is that due to a large number of members involved at the WTO and the associated "free rider problem", negotiations at the WTO are slow and difficult. If the world is first divided into a handful of blocs, multilateral negotiations will become easier. Secondly, PTAs may serve as a threat to force unwilling parties to negotiate in earnest at the multilateral level. As per this argument, the EU was dragging its feet too long for the conclusion of the UR, but when President Clinton called for the formation of a free trade with APEC, the EU decided to conclude the negotiations during the UR.

Thirdly, it is argued that due to their high visibility, PTAs can energise and unify protectionist lobbies, turning them into effective obstacles against multilateral liberalisation. Finally, there is the related issue of attention diversion and scarce negotiating resources. If the US President and his Trade Representative are preoccupied with cutting deals in Latin America, they will have less time and motivation of multilateral negotiations.

Successful trade negotiations also require political will and administrative effort. Reserves of administrative skill, political capital, or imagination are finite; if they are devoted to a Regional Integration Arrangement (RIA) they are not available for multilateral objectives. These arguments were advanced to explain both EU and US behaviour during the Uruguay Round, but they must be several times more important for developing countries. Negotiating a RIA, especially with the major power that has its own objectives, will absorb a huge portion of policymaking skills of a developing country. Perhaps one of the opportunity-costs of

RIAs is that less negotiating and political capital are available for multilateral negotiations.

However, this argument can be easily refuted now because the US has recently concluded the negotiations of FTAA, but still has the energy, resources and commitment to make WTO a powerful institution and both the present President and United States Trade Representative (USTR) have reassured the international community of their commitments to strengthen multilateral trade liberalisation. It can also be argued that the learning curve of being able to cut deals at the multilateral forum become steeper because of the successful conclusion of the RTAs resulting from accumulation of negotiating skills. Das argues that growth in regionalism does not necessarily have to lead to a short cut to free trade or a liberalised trading regime.

It is difficult to claim that the target of free or a liberalised trade is easier to reach in large regional agreements like the FTAA and the APEC forum with memberships as large as 35 and 21, respectively. These two and other large regional groupings contain economies as different in size, outlook and level of development as any in the WTO. Panaghariya crticises "open regionalism". According to him, the open-membership criterion has three important limitations, which give critics reason to be sceptical of open regionalism. His arguments can be summarised in the following manner:

— Discrimination against non-members at any point in time remains in place by definition as long as the regionalism is of Article XXIV variety.

— Openness is not as innocuous as it sounds - the admission price can include several unpleasant "side payments" that are essentially unrelated to trade.

— Open membership does not necessarily translate into speedy membership.

Further, Ben Zissimos and David Vines assert: "If the benefits from membership of an exclusive club are derived partly by making outsiders worse off, then the club will not throw open its doors to all comers. Facilitating trade between bloc members has exactly this effect. The purchasing power of bloc currencies increases, whilst that of outsiders declines. Consequently, trade blocs do not have an incentive to allow all applicants to join, because some of the benefits of membership come from being able to purchase the products of outsiders more cheaply on world markets. So there is a limit to the expansion that can be expected from existing blocs, and free trade between all countries will not arise."

Open membership also raises the issue of broadening versus deepening. Broadening the membership of any regional grouping inherently complicates the process of deepening its integration. Too many new members can make decision making more time consuming and cumbersome. APEC realised this and imposed a moratorium in expanding membership in early 1998. On the whole, there seems to be four major arguments in support of the claim that RTAs are stumbling blocks to multilateral trade liberalisation.

Firstly, open regionalism may be a myth in the sense that when a new member accedes to an RTA, the preferences enjoyed by existing members are eroded, thus creating an incentive to limit the membership. Secondly, as many RTAs are strongly emphasising investment liberalisation, this may create a vested interest against trade liberalisation amongst mobile firms once they establish costly plants and marketing systems in other member countries. Thirdly, governments and officials often suffer from 'negotiation exhaustion' which could cause long delays in taking further steps, if not indefinite postponement. Fourthly, closer integration may generate a backlash against erosion of national sovereignty.

According to Winters, "Regionalism vs. Multilateralism" switches the focus of research from the immediate consequences of regionalism for the economic welfare of the integrating parts, to the question of whether it sets up forces, which encourage or discourage evolution towards globally freer trade. The answer is "we don't know yet. " One can build models that suggest either conclusion but to date these are sufficiently abstract that they should be viewed as parables rather than sources of testable predictions.

A comprehensive study done by the World Bank on the debate relating to regional integration, titled Trade Blocs finds out that regionalism is generally a building bloc to multilateral trade liberalisation. It goes on to explain how benefits of trade creation resulting from an RTA outweigh the costs of trade diversion. This study is of the view that North-North regional integration agreements can produce beneficial effects for all the participating countries because it results in income convergence among the participating countries. Citing the example of EU before the accession of relatively poorer countries, it maintains that they were the clear gainers from RIAs.

The study further points out that even North-South RIAs are beneficial in as much as poorer countries catch up with richer countries in a short time span. The income convergence in the EU after the entry of Greece, Portugal and Spain, and the success story of Mexico after joining NAFTA are provided as examples to prove this point. The study, however, sounds a strong note of caution on the formation of South- South RTAs. It cites the example of East African Common Market in which income divergence did actually take place.

As per the study, South-South RTA causes income divergence among the participating nations. However, the study considers MERCOSUR as an exception, which has set an example as a successful South-South RTA. It is worth noting that ASEAN countries too have been growing very fast, barring a temporary period of slackness due to the East Asian crisis. However, they did not grow because of regional integration per se but due to a number of other favourable factors. As per the study, emergence and/or solidification of regionalism is unstoppable - all one should look at is the choice of design. There are two economic effects of regionalism, namely, competition and scale effect and trade and location effect.

Complementarity between regionalism and multilateralism is also stressed by Ethier, who argues that "the new regionalism is in good part a direct result of the success of multilateral liberalisation, as well as being the means by which new countries trying to enter the multilateral system compete among themselves for direct investment". He also suggests that regionalism - by internalising an important externality - plays a key role in expanding and preserving the liberal trading order.

Commenting on complementarity of regional liberalisation on services with multilateral liberalisation, Hoekman suggests that both conceptual considerations and the available data on trade and investment flows suggest that RTAs in the area of services should be easier to negotiate and be more far-reaching than a multilateral agreement. However, he admits that the two approaches are substitutes. Reviewing existing agreements, he concludes that sectors that are excluded from RTAs are also excluded from multilateral liberalisation. This suggests that "the GATS is likely to be seen as complementary to the regional arrangements by major service industries in OECD countries."

There is absolutely no doubt concerning the fact that multilateral trade liberalisation is clearly superior to RTAs in terms of welfare effects. However, if multilateral liberalisation is not possible, either due to heterogeneity of members or due to acrimonious nature of negotiations, the alternate way to move forward is to form or strengthen RTAs. It is more so because of the mercantilist stand taken by many countries towards trade liberalisation where reciprocity of concessions as opposed to unilateral liberalisation, is the name of the game. In multilateral, MFN based trade liberalisation there is always a problem of free riding and foot dragging.

One should not also forget the fact that successive milestones in European integration, from creation of the common market to the coming of the single market, did much to stimulate the three big postwar multilateral trade negotiations. The creation of NAFTA and APEC helped persuade Europe to conclude the UR. When EU was dragging its feet and impeded the process of conclusion of UR of multilateral trade liberalisation, the USA went ahead towards forming NAFTA, which contributed to bringing EU back to the negotiation to conclude the UR.

We are of the view that the increase in intra-regional trade between the regional partners shows that benefits of trade creation outweigh costs associated with trade diversion. Regional economic integration has served the useful purpose of creating a thread for multilateral trade liberalisation on several counts. If that were not the case, the size and number of RTAs would not have grown with leaps and bounds as is happening, especially after the formation of the WTO. Indeed, RTA is the favourite of all the countries of the world - whether they are members of the WTO or not.

South Asian regional integration and the WTO SAARC Preferential Trade Agreement (SAPTA), the precursor to SAFTA has already been notified to the WTO. However, it has been notified under what is technically known as "Enabling Clause"which, inter alia, allows a group of developing countries to form an RTA among them. One can consider SAPTA to be compliant with the relevant WTO provisions. It is just because of the fundamental flaw in the present examination/decision making process of the Committee on Regional Trade Agreements (CRTA),that the WTO has not given a 'certificate of approval' to SAPTA. It is not surprising because economic groupings such as EU and the NAFTA too have not received the approval from the CRTA so far.

However, notifying an RTA under the Enabling Clause could limit the possibility of trade expansion within the region and may in turn become counterproductive for the region as a whole. Since all the serious RTAs are notified under the Article XXIV of the GATT and/or Article V of the GATS, South

Asian countries should also strive to fulfill the conditions outlined in these two relevant provisions so as to ensure greater degree of policy lock-in on the one hand, and providing security and predictability to the RTA on the other. Moreover, if and when South Asia becomes a major global player in international trade, developed countries would not allow it to continue taking shelter under the Enabling Clause.

Principle of non-discrimination is the cornerstone of the GATT, which has been carried forward as it is, in the WTO Agreements. Article I of the GATT establishes the central requirement that signatory governments are required to extend unconditionally to all other contracting parties any advantage, favour, privileges or immunity affecting customs duties, charges, rules and procedures, that they give to products originating in or destined for any other country. This is referred to as the much-vaunted MFN principle. The Article reads thus: "With respect to customs duties and charges of any kind...any advantage, favour, privileges or immunity granted by any contracting party to any product originating in or destined for any other country shall be accorded immediately and unconditionally to the like product originating in or destined for the territories of all other Contracting Parties. "

Considering the fact that MFN provision relating to border measures may not be sufficient to make the contracting parties to firmly institute a system of non-discrimination in letter as well as in spirit due to some possibility of them discriminating goods of foreign origin vis-à-vis national ones, the Article III of GATT clearly mentions that once the foreign goods have cleared the border they should be provided the same treatment as domestic goods. As per this Article, foreign goods should be provided treatment "no less favourable than domestic like products". This treatment, which is another form of non-discrimination, is referred to as "national treatment. "

However, RTAs, comprising FTAs and CUs as contained in the Article XXIV of the original GATT Agreement, are the single major derogation from the MFN principle whereby the

Members of an RTA can agree to provide concessional treatment to goods or services in a discriminatory manner, i.e., without having to extend the same treatment to other WTO Members on an MFN basis. The question as to why the drafters of the GATT did permit the contracting parties to form an RTA is a genuine one and the reason for this is still far from clear. Some assume that the belief that the conditions inserted into Article XXIV would ensure that RTAs would become complementary to the multilateral trading system, could be the single major motivation.

Regional Integration

South Asia has a common destiny in the 21century. Though comprising only three percent of the world's total area, it houses 21 percent of the world's population. The irreversible process of globalisation is throwing up many daunting challenges for developing countries in general and the SAARC countries in particular. One of the ways of meeting these challenges is to overcome regional apprehensions and constraints and irreversibly and speedily move towards regional cooperation and integration. Like other RTAs, SAARC is aiming to reap the benefits of regional cooperation. For example, economic integration in South Asia may lead to realisation of potential economic benefits from: lower intra-regional transport and transactions costs; more favourable terms of trade; economies of scale in investment, production and distribution; and possibly higher efficiencies due to increased intra-regional competition and cooperation from increased external and intra-regional trade creation.

Despite these apparent benefits, progress in achieving regional cooperation has been, at the best, very modest. The SAARC, comprising seven South Asian countries: Bangladesh, Bhutan, India, the Maldives, Nepal, Pakistan and Sri Lanka, formally came into existence in 1985 with the adoption of its Charter at the first Summit in Dhaka (7- 8 December 1985). The idea of regional cooperation was first proposed through 'a regional forum' by Bangladesh in 1980, with a view to holding periodic, regional-level consultations among countries in South Asia on matters of mutual interest and possible cooperation in economic, social, cultural and other fields. The rationale was primarily predicated on the premise that regional experiences elsewhere in the globe had been highly successful and that the countries in the South Asia region would benefit enormously from such cooperation as it would strengthen their competitive position, both individually and as a group.

The Bangladesh proposal argued that inherent logic strongly justified regional cooperation, particularly among South Asian countries, because the countries in the region enjoy geographical contiguity, historical, social, cultural and ethnic affinities which would act as centripetal forces and thus, contribute substantively to facilitate coordination and reducing transaction costs. Despite the obvious rationale for regional cooperation in the area of trade and investment, progress has been glacially slow. The cost of non-cooperation in a static framework is high. Further, although there is substantial informal trading, official trading among SAARC countries accounts for less than 4 percent of their total trade volumes. The corresponding figure for EC is 66 per cent, 37 per cent for NAFTA and 21 per cent for ASEAN.

Despite the fact that the idea for economic cooperation was mooted in 1986 at the first Ministerial Meeting on International Economic Issues 31 March - 3 April, Islamabad), the formal initiative towards regional economic cooperation was realised in 1995, when the framework agreement on SAPTA formally came into operation. The Agreement reflected the desire of the SAARC countries to promote and sustain mutual trade and economic cooperation within the SAARC region through exchange of concessions. Regional free trade was not in the agenda of SAARC in the beginning.

According to the agreement, the PTA is based on the following four principles:

— Overall reciprocity and mutuality of advantages among contracting parties.

— Step-by-Step negotiations to be improved and extended in successive stages with periodic reviews.

— Inclusive of all manufactured products and commodities in their raw, semi processed, and processed forms.

— Special and favourable treatment to LDCs.

The objectives of SAPTA as stated in the preamble of the Agreement are as follows:

— To promote regional cooperation for the benefit of their peoples, in a spirit of mutual accommodation, with full respect for the principles of sovereign equality, independence and territorial integrity of all States.

— Expansion of trade which could act as a powerful stimulus to the development for their national economies by expanding investment and production, and help securing higher living standards for their population.

— To establish and promote regional preferential trading arrangements for strengthening intra regional economic cocperation and the development of national economies.

— To promote the intra-regional trade which presently constitutes a negligible share in the total volume of the South Asian trade.

SAARC has taken important steps to expand cooperation among member countries in the core economic areas. In December 1988, the fourth SAARC summit held in Islamabad gave direction to all member states to identify immediately the specific areas where economic cooperation might be feasible. When the sixth SAARC Summit was held in Colombo in December 1991, the then heads of states of the member countries declared liberalisation of trade in the region through a step-by -step approach in such a manner that countries in the region share the benefits of trade expansion equitably. In fact, the completion of the regional study on Trade, Manufactures and Services (TMS) in 1991 was the first significant step, which paved the way for SAARC to move forward in strengthening cooperation in trade and investment. The study also outlined a number of recommendations for promoting regional cooperation in other core economic areas.

As per the mandate given by the sixth SAARC Summit in Colombo, a high level Committee on Economic Cooperation (CEC) comprising the Commerce Secretaries of member states was established in July 1991 to act as the forum to address trade and investment issues. The committee was charged with the responsibility of, inter alia, monitoring the progress in the implementation of decisions relating to expansion of trade and economic cooperation under the framework of SAARC. It considered the reports of Inter Governmental Group (IGG) on trade liberalisation, Inter Governmental Expert Group (IGEG) on transition to SAFTA and Committee of Participants (COP). The Committee was also responsible for reviewing the progress in the implementation of the decisions of meetings of SAARC Commerce Ministers.

The Colombo Summit in December 1991 approved the establishment of IGG to seek agreement on an institutional framework. The IGG was requested to recommend measures for trade liberalisation within SAPTA. This was proposed by Sri Lanka. Subsequently the SAPTA agreement was signed by the Council of Ministers in Dhaka on 11 April, 1993 during the Seventh SAARC Summit. After completion of all the formalities by all SAARC member countries and subsequent to a notification issued by the Secretariat to this effect, the SAPTA Agreement entered into force on 7 December 1995.

However, the first round of trade negotiations covered only 226 products, largely of little relevance to the actual trade that was taking place amongst the member countries. Indeed, it has been estimated that the value of intra-regional import coverage in respect of the 226 tariff lines, which were subjected to tariff concession, amounted to a mere 6 percent of the intra-regional imports. After the operation of SAPTA, the IGG on trade liberalisation started the second round of negotiations in 1996. This was successfully concluded after four meetings of the group in Colombo, Islamabad, New Delhi, and Kathmandu in March, September, October, and November, respectively. Up to the second round, the number of products enjoying preferential treatment had increased to more than 2000.

The NTBs in the way of expansion of intra SAARC trade were also identified and listed in order to make the process more transparent. The third round of trade negotiations under SAPTA was also concluded in 1998 and after this round, the number of products enjoying preferential treatment increased to more than 5,000 commodities. During this round, tariff concessions were offered on 3,456 tariff lines. However, most member countries, despite serious limitation of productby-product approach for tariff concessions (an array of concerns were voiced against this approach during the second round), chose to follow the same approach during the third round.

India had bilateral FTAs with Nepal and Bhutan at the time of the third round of SAPTA negotiations. Therefore, additional offers to these smaller countries were not granted by India. Since Nepal and Bhutan had reciprocated concessions to India (to the extent possible) under the bilateral FTAs, they also did not provide any concession to India during the third round of negotiations. However, an analysis of the SAPTA negotiations underlines the constraints that South Asia faces in attempting to integrate as a regional entity. With the conclusion of the third round of negotiations in November 1998, over 5,000 tariff lines of a total of 6,500 have been covered by preference to member countries. However, one should not be swayed by the argument that PTA in South Asia is an effective building block towards the FTA within the region.

On the contrary, there are inherent problems of using preferential trade concessions as a means of increasing trade volume within any given regional framework. Countries can appear very generous simply on the basis of the number of concessions given, but what is more relevant is the actual trade coverage of those preferences. Similarly, the depth of tariff cuts offered under a preferential agreement can again be limiting. The SAPTA suffers from both these factors.

Following the ratification of SAPTA by all member states, the sixteenth session of the Council of Ministers agreed that member states should strive towards the realisation of SAFTA. For this purpose an IGEG on transition to SAFTA comprising experts from the member countries was set up to identify the necessary steps towards moving into a FTA. The IGEG has met and held in-depth discussions and agreed on the draft terms of reference for the group and has also drawn up a broad framework of Plan of Action for achieving SAFTA. This chronology of official developments related to SAPTA clearly brings out that:

— the SAARC has gone about entering into the politico-economically sensitive area of trade liberalisation in a cautious and mutually acceptable manner;

— despite its cautious and sensitive approach, the SAARC countries were able to commence the implementation of SAPTA on schedule; and

— the SAARC countries did not see the liberalisation of intra-regional trade as an end in itself, but as a means towards improving the economic welfare of the people of South Asia.

SAPTA was envisaged primarily as the first step towards the transition to a SAFTA, leading subsequently, towards a Customs Union, Common Market and Economic Union. The Agreement on SAPTA has identified four types of trade-restrictive measures for progressive elimination. They include:

— tariffs;

— paratariffs;

— non-tariff measures (NTMs); and
— direct trade measures.

The three Rounds held so far have addressed the first two trade restrictive measures to a large extent. There was not much progress, however, on the third one, which relates to removal of NTMs, including QRs. The Tenth SAARC Summit held in Colombo in July 1998 took note of the need to remove NTMs and to deepen the tariff concessions already exchanged. It directed that these should be addressed in the next round of trade negotiations. Since the WTO rules (Article XI of the GATT) prohibit the use of QRs (barring under certain exceptional circumstances), QRs among the SAARC member countries are not expected to continue for long. The two countries, which have not yet become members of the WTO, in any case, maintain negligible QRs.

The fourth round, which was intended to implement the Summit directive, was delayed due to the postponement of the SAARC Summit. The Eleventh SAARC Summit, which finally concluded in Kathmandu on January 6, 2002, however, instructed to conclude the meeting of the IGG on trade liberalisation for the fourth round of negotiations under SAPTA as early as possible as per the decision of the Tenth SAARC Summit in Colombo. Therefore, much hope can now be placed on this round of negotiations, especially in the area of reducing NTBs. Meanwhile, the Government of India, which had maintained a higher number of QRs, decided to unilaterally remove all NTBs within SAARC countries in August 1998. This amounted to over 2,000 items.

Then again, India moved forward to unilaterally dismantle most of the QRs on a global scale from 1999. It is interesting to note that this change in the trade policy of the government of India was brought upon by a decision of the WTO Panel under the Dispute Settlement Procedure. As per the decision, India is required to phase out its QRs within the period of four years from the date of decision of the Dispute

Settlement Body. This left the Government of India with little option. The outcome was a trade policy re-orientation in India aimed at dismantling QRs, which to date continues. On 01 April 2001, India removed many QRs that were applicable in its trade regime.

However, other NTMs are proving hurdles to the smooth flow of regional trade and commerce. These measures are not only non-transparent and difficult to comply with, but are at times arbitrary and could act as disguised restriction to regional trade. This problem becomes more severe while dealing with countries with a federal political structure where different states have different rules and regulations and they are not harmonised at the sub-national level.

Rules of Origin (ROO)

Rules of origin (ROO) requirement is another area which proved to be much contentious within SAPTA since its inception. In theory, ROO not only prevent 'trade deflection' in a regional grouping but also contributes to the development process of member countries through different trade and value addition effect. However, in practice, it puts countries with inadequate domestic capacity at a disadvantageous position. Therefore, Jayasekera argues, "SAARC should explore the possibility of further relaxing its ROO in order to assist the least developed and smaller developing countries in the region. Recognising these difficulties, the SAPTA Agreement provides for differentiated ROO criteria for a developing country member and a least developed country member.

The local content requirement necessary for tariff preference on an LDC product was set down to be 40 percent in case its components are sourced from within the region and 50 per cent in case they are from non-members at the commencement of SAPTA in late 1995. For a developing country member, however, the requirement was set down at 50 per cent and 60 per cent, respectively. Bangladesh, which maintains no bilateral trade treaty with any of the SAARC countries, particularly with India, felt that the local content requirement was too high. Sri Lanka, a developing country member with no substantial industrial base compared to India and Pakistan, felt that the higher local content requirement particularly discriminated against it. It was argued that there was not much of formal trade between India and Pakistan for the trade effect of this requirement to be tested as between them.

Since Sri Lanka was the only other developing country left, its grievance had a basis. The matter was referred to the COP in 1998, which suggested a reduction of 10 per cent in the local content requirement of both LDC members and developing country members. The Commerce Ministers who met in Dhaka in January 1999 recommended the revision of the ROO of the SAPTA Agreement to give effect to a new local content requirement. The SAARC Council of Ministers, which convened subsequently, endorsed this recommendation for implementation. The Agreement on SAPTA was modified to accommodate the change in the ROO accordingly. Now member states are in the process of giving effect to the revised ROO.

Simultaneous with the SAPTA process, a number of trade facilitation measures have also been addressed. These measures can be broadly divided under the following sub-headings:

a) *Customs*: A Group on Customs Cooperation was set up in 1996 and so far has held three meetings. It was, inter alia, decided to harmonise Harmonised System (HS) lines and customs rules and regulations; simplify procedure for intra-regional exports; upgrade infrastructure facilities and provide training facilities. A Custom Action Plan was drawn up in Islamabad and agreed to by all member states.

b) *Transportation*: The need to improve transportation infrastructure and transit facilities in the region was recognised and the 11Session of the SAARC Council of

Ministers in Colombo directed the CEC to take appropriate steps in this regard. Accordingly, a study was commissioned to assess the existing transport infrastructure and transit facilities, including procedural and documental issues in the region in relation to volume and composition of the existing trade in the region and to make recommendations for their improvement, with a view to enhancing trade within and outside the region. The study was completed in 1994 and has made far-reaching recommendations.

c) *Standards*: Recognising the importance of standards and measurement, institutions involved in standards, testing and certification in the member states met in New Delhi in June 1999 to identify how national standards may be harmonised and a regional standard agreed upon. It was agreed that product standards, control and certification measures applied in the region needed to be converged.

d) *Taxation*: A Meeting on Avoidance of Double Taxation was convened in Islamabad in 2000, which endorsed the need for a common format of double tax avoidance measures.

Classic examples of trade remedies include: balance of payment, antidumping, safeguards, countervailing measures. While most of the RTAs make use of all these measures even within the member countries, some make use of only selective measures. For example, while NAFTA still has anti-dumping provisions, EU has done away with it. However, in the context of SAPTA there are only two types of trade remedies that are available for member countries, which are discussed below:

a) *Balance of payments measures*: As per Article 13 of SAPTA, any Contracting State facing serious economic problems including balance of payments difficulties may suspend provisionally the concessions as to the quantity and value of merchandise permitted to be imported under the Agreement. When such action has taken place, the

Contracting State, which initiates such action, shall simultaneously notify the other Contracting States and the Committee.

b) *Safeguard measures*: As per Article 14 of SAPTA, if any product, which is a subject of a concession with respect to a preference under this Agreement, is imported into the territory of a Contracting State in such a manner or in such quantities as to cause or threaten to cause, serious injury in the importing Contracting State, the importing Contracting State concerned may, with prior consultations, except in critical circumstances, suspend provisionally without discrimination, the concession accorded under the Agreement. When such action has taken place, the Contracting State which initiates such action shall simultaneously notify the other Contracting State (s) concerned and the Committee shall enter into consultations with the concerned Contracting State and endeavour to reach mutually acceptable agreement to remedy the situation.

Special treatment for Least developed countries

As per Article 1 of SAPTA, "Least Developed Country" means a country designated as such by the United Nations. As per this definition, Bangladesh, Bhutan, Maldives and Nepal fall under the category of LDCs among the contracting states. As per Article 10 of SAPTA, in addition to other provisions of this Agreement, all contracting states shall provide, wherever possible special and more favourable treatment exclusively to the least developed states. Such treatments as set out in the Agreement are as follows:

(a) Duty free access, exclusive tariff preferences or deeper tariff preferences for the exportable products;

(b) The removal of NTBs;

(c) Removal, where appropriate, of para tariff barriers;

(d) The negotiations of long term contracts with a view to assisting least developed contracting states to achieve reasonable levels of sustainable exports of their products;

(e) Special consideration of exports from LDC Contracting States in the application of Safeguard measures.

(f) Greater flexibility in the introduction and continuance of quantitative or other restrictions provisionally and without discrimination in critical circumstances by the least developed contracting states on imports from other states.

(g) There are some special and additional concessions and favours provided to the LDCs as per Article 6. According to this Article, technical assistance and cooperation arrangements have been designed to assist them (LDCs) in expanding their trade with other contracting states and taking advantage of the potential benefits of SAPTA. This agreement has also listed some of the potential areas, which are mainly industrial, agricultural, export maximisation, export marketing, joint venture, etc.

The Ninth SAARC Summit held in Male in 1997, constituted a Group of Eminent Persons (GEP), which was mandated to undertake a comprehensive appraisal of SAARC and to "identify measures, including mechanisms to further vitalise and enhance the effectiveness of the association in achieving its objectives." Though a decision was to be taken on the basis of this report - that was submitted just prior to the Tenth Summit in 1998 - it was postponed since member states needed more time to study it. The report, however, did form the basis for the decisions made, especially in the areas of trade and economic cooperation, during the Eleventh SAARC Summit concluded in Kathmandu in early 2002. A central piece in the Report of the GEP is the proposal for moving from an Association to Community. The GEP proposes the following stages:

— The establishment of SAFTA by the year 2010 by the least developed member states and by 2008 by other member states.

— Establishment of a South Asian Custom's Union (SACU) by 2015

— Commencement from the beginning of 2016 of the process of implementing the remaining measures for moving towards South Asian Economic Union (SAEU) by the year 2020.

Based on the political and economic realities of the region, the GEP report has been criticised for being too ambitious. Jayasekera remarks: "Given the considerable backtracking that has taken place over the years, to expect SAFTA to be in place by 2008 [for developing countries] is not practicable. The GEP recommends an across the board reductions of tariffs by 12. 5 percent annually to achieve their objective of eliminating restrictions on substantially all trade. This is a laudable strategy, but given the protracted product-by-product negotiations, which took place under SAPTA, this may not be acceptable to all member states. "

While Jayasekera feels that the target of phasing out all the NTBs by the year 2010 is attainable, he is skeptical about the creation of a CU by 2015. There are many skeptics who feel that it is not possible for South Asia to become an EU within such a short period of time, especially when one considers the fact that it took nearly 50 years for the EU to become what they are now. However, the issue is not that South Asia should take as much time as the Europeans given the fact that there are number of lessons available from the European model, but the level of preparedness and the commitment among the South Asian countries to enter into such an arrangement within a reasonable period of time. Added to that are other socio-political problems, which must be resolved before an Economic Union is created.

There are reasons to be skeptical about the creation of an Economic Union by 2020. Economic Union would have been a utopia had EU not become a reality. This is the deepest level of economic integration, which does not look feasible in any other RTA at this point in time. Despite the commitments made at the political levels, it will take a while even for the established regional groupings like MERCOSUR or AFTA to be converted into the Economic Unions in a practical sense. The first step towards Economic Union would be a single market, where it is presumed that the transport, telecommunications and energy infrastructure would be substantially integrated. Then come the issues of monetary union (another thorny issue), harmonisation and/or mutual recognition of standards, harmonisation of tariff procedures, free movement of capital and labour, adoption of common competition policy, among others.

Given the difficulties that SAARC member countries are likely to encounter in the process, the target seems virtually impossible to attain. One of the related means to attain greater coherence in the regional policy making in the areas of trade and investment as proposed by the GEP was for SAARC countries to take a common position on emerging global economic issues. In fact, the former Secretary General of SAARC stated: "The analytical capacity of SAARC has been developed and we take collective positions at international negotiations such as the WTO. "

Accordingly, SAARC Commerce Ministers prepared their common positions in the Bandos Island, Maldives, in 1999 prior to the Seattle Ministerial Conference of the WTO. A second such meeting was organised in New Delhi in August 2001 to form a common position for the WTO Doha Ministerial Conference. However, despite these efforts, the Ministers could not maintain a common position during the Doha Ministerial Conference. While it is clearly stated on the common position that the SAARC countries would oppose any new round, unless and until implementation issues were fully addressed, during the Ministerial Conference, Sri Lanka pointed out that it could be flexible on environment and Pakistan mentioned that it could be flexible on investment. Such deviation from the agreed framework weakens the common position and reduces SAARC's credibility. Therefore, it is advisable not to prepare a common position at all, if the Ministers cannot stick to the same.

Reliance on a preferential trade regime has proven to be of little help for the South Asian trade liberalisation process. Failure of SAPTA to provide meaningful trade liberalisation has led to the largest economy in the region, viz., India, to sign three consecutive bilateral FTAs with its smaller neighbours (Bhutan, Nepal and Sri Lanka) with the possibility of having a similar agreement with Bangladesh. While such initiatives have helped to open up protected markets of the smaller countries, they have created tremendous confusion to the exporters and investors alike.

Any potential benefits of bilateral agreements have to be weighed against the political fallout in a wider South Asian context. Not only is there the real danger that bilateral agreements may undermine commitment to a greater South Asian Economic Area, but there is a far greater danger of alienating key players even further. SAFTA, however, will be completely different inasmuch as members are required to show greater degree of commitment towards free trade now, thanks to WTO rules governing RTAs.

Framework for a SAFTA treaty is supposed to be decided by the end of 2002, and there are a number of challenges drafters are likely to encounter. The first challenge before the drafters is to ensure that the agreement is going to be compatible with the relevant provisions of the WTO. Secondly, as is the general practice, LDCs should be provided with longer transition period to implement trade liberalisation, with even longer transition period for landlocked LDCs (LLDCs) so that they do not lose out disproportionately compared to relatively better off countries.

Reflecting the deep-seated concerns of the LLDCs, the CASAC has taken an extreme position as described below: As experience of other regional organisations have shown that an equitable sharing of benefits of cooperation is the key to success of regionalism, special care must be taken to ensure that the least developed countries can take full advantage of the freeing of trade by other countries. As a means of compensating the cost incurred by them in moving to a free trade regime, it is important to have special elements in their favour. These include:

i) a longer time period for freeing trade in general and staggering the process of freeing trade in particular sectors;

ii) resort to safeguard measures for a longer period of time;

iii) establishment of a special fund for compensating for the loss of revenue suffered as a result of reducing or eliminating tariffs;

iv) creation of a reasonably large sized fund for the development of their infrastructure, human resources, export production and diversification of capacity; and

v) facilitating freer movement of private capital to the least developed countries from other member states.

While CASAC's position may not be acceptable to the relatively more developed countries of the SAARC, it is a good idea to devise some type of 'transitional' mechanism to address the fears of the relatively weaker countries in the region. Here, the emphasis on the word 'transitional' is important because an eternal compensation mechanism is neither sustainable nor desirable. Thirdly, the dispute settlement process should not only be fair and transparent, but also provide option to the member countries to either resort to the regional dispute settlement mechanism or resort to the WTO dispute settlement mechanism, as in the case of NAFTA.

Political Economy and Issues

South Asia is at cross roads; the regional cooperation umbrella promoted by respective states, i.e., SAARC, has progressed very little while regional cooperation espoused by the South Asian civil society, although well meaning, has not been effective. There is a shrinking sense of purpose in the SAARC member countries. SAARC has become weak because member states assign a low status to it. The Indo-Pak relationship is a core issue in South Asian cooperation. Underlying this core issue is a core structural problem, i.e., the difficulty in portraying and building of South Asia as a region in a world that is rapidly organizing into regional blocs. It may be useful to look at SAARC from the perspective of some elements of the economic cooperation framework.

Frequently, in the SAARC debate the following five issues have been raised:

(i) the trade deficit of the smaller members with that of the larger members,

(ii) geographical asymmetry of the region that could be more favourable to the largest country,

(iii) India's attitude towards SAARC,

(iv) Pakistan's attitude towards SAARC, and the most talked about

(v) security situation in the region.

Simple economic arguments show that (i) cannot be considered as an issue in the modern day world and it is not dwelt with here. The asymmetry, however, may be an issue if it is related to the political economy of regional cooperation. Attitude of major players of the region towards the region is equally important, for the small nations alone cannot carry the entire region with themselves. The security issue is important because it cuts across economic, cultural, and social relations and thus can undermine them effectively.

In the SAARC, India is not only the physically largest, but also the economic and military powerhouse unlike in the EU and ASEAN. Thus, the hegemonic suspicions among the other SAARC members run strong. For India, there is the suspicion that the smaller nations will gang up against her at an institutional forum. Moreover, any external power can always cultivate a smaller nation to gain a foothold in the region, and India in particular. These suspicions, whether we like it or not, exist in South Asia and it is the reality.

That asymmetry is an issue can be demonstrated in the area of economic cooperation. Das, for instance, argues that Islamabad suspected that India gained relatively more advantages from SAPTA II. He argues that the "discrepancy should be rectified in future SAPTA deliberations". Clearly this type of thinking defeats the broad concept of "cost of non-cooperation". After all, when deciding whether to cooperate or not, it is the gain over non-cooperation that counts, not the amount that the partners will obtain. But such thinking does not prevail in some nations. Be that as it may, even if the problems related to asymmetry are fully addressed by the proposed SAFTA treaty and other measures, there are issues related to the perception of SAARC by India and Pakistan that act as impediments to regional cooperation.

India and SAARC

Bargava argues that due recognition should be made by all other SAARC members of India's pivotal role in regional cooperation. But does India really have a desire to play this pivotal role?Muni, for example, argues: "For India, though SAARC is a preferred channel of integrating South Asia through cooperative interdependence, it does not promise high economic incentives. India's regional trade in South Asia is around 1 per cent of its total foreign trade. Even in a strengthened SAARC when this trade increases substantially, it cannot fulfil the needs of the growing Indian economy.

India also feels frustrated in its failure to induce Bangladesh in forging comprehensive economic cooperation ties and to induce Pakistan in establishing normal trade and economic relations at the bilateral level, not to mention the irritations arising out of the communal question in these relations. Therefore, India has to look towards other economically dynamic regions for its investments, technology and trade. Hence, its moves towards ASEAN, APEC and the Indian Ocean Rim". ASEAN emerged as the third largest foreign direct investor in India after US and EU. There has been a doubling of trade between India and ASEAN in the 1990s. India already has two channels to ASEAN, viz., (1) Dialogue Partner status with ASEAN since 1993, and (2) membership of BIMSTEC since 1997.

India's "Look East" policy is served well by these two arrangements. The IOR-ARC also gives India access to Thailand, Malaysia, Indonesia, and Singapore to discuss economic issues. Why should India bother too much with SAARC when it already has bilateral free trade agreements with two important partners in South Asian nations and can achieve much more from cooperating with ASEAN? So from an economic cooperation point of view SAARC has little meaning for India.

India now considers itself as a global player and the US officials accept this fact. Pakistan has refused to accept the pivotal role of India in South Asia and received encouragement from several external forces for challenging India's role. It is because of these factors that India has been reluctant to give leadership to the SAARC process. The leadership that Suharto gave to ASEAN played a major role in keeping ASEAN together. Regional groupings without political leadership have fallen apart like the Bangkok Agreement. During a limited period, SAARC received the Indian leadership of Prime Minister Gujral with the "Gujral Doctrine" coming into place. But thereafter, SAARC is back to square one with no leadership. For an Association that is still in its early stages of development, lack of political leadership is an issue.

However, Indian leadership not going to be accepted by every country of the region (even if one does not take into account Pakistan's animosity with India). At present, India is acting the Big Brother towards its neighbours. Its size overawes them. It has to introspect its policies. Former Foreign Minister Yashwant Sinha did well to start his stint with visits to countries like Nepal and Bangladesh. But then there was no follow-up. There have been such spurts in the past with no long-term strategy.

Pakistan and SAARC

For Pakistan integration of South Asian economies that has India as the dominant partner can threaten its political and strategic identity and thus may not be fully acceptable. Pakistan's attitude to SAARC is summarised in following terms by an Indian author: "Pakistan is a split personality; she has not been able to completely identify herself with West Asia; in South Asia she feels odd." The author goes on to argue that while geography, common history and socio-cultural traditions pull Pakistan towards South Asia - factors like ideology, economy, and serious differences on a number of regional and international issues with India push Pakistan outside South Asia and accordingly help it to determine its policy and attitude towards South Asia.

From the last 17 years of SAARC it could be stated that Pakistan views SAARC as a harmless organisation and is not terribly excited by it. However, Pakistani Delegation argues, "The imperatives of economic survival must persuade Pakistan, like other South Asian states, to increase its faith in regional cooperation, especially in view of the shifts in the priorities of the traditional aid-givers. "There is a new dimension that shapes Pakistan's attitude towards SAARC. Following the September 11, 2001 event, Pakistan has become key player in Washington-determined politics. Consequently, USA has dropped sanctions related to Pakistan's nuclear test in 1998.

Moreover, penalties imposed on Pakistan discarding democracy are also no longer applicable. Pakistan wanted more open market from the West and is now getting it. In fact, Pakistan has been rewarded by the West with aid, loans from the IMF, and possibility of obtaining trading arrangements, similar to those granted to Sub-Saharan Africa, Central America, the Caribbean, Israel, and Jordan by the USA. After the decision of Pakistan to postpone Twelfth SAARC Summit to be held in Islamabad, there has been cross firing of opinions from Indian and Pakistani media alike blaming each other for the scuttling of the Summit.

Problems in security

Despite all the rhetoric on economic cooperation, as long as Pakistan and India remain locked up in adversarial relationship, security issues will dominate over all other issues. This is the reality in South Asia. South Asia is more vulnerable to instability from within than from outside. The development of security issues has not received as much attention as it deserves, probably because it is embedded in a nation state. The Kashmir issue with enormous security implications for regional peace and stability has never featured on the SAARC agenda, since the SAARC Charter excludes bilateral and contentious issues from the deliberations of the Association.

Can bilateral issues that cut across all cooperation efforts be left out of the SAARC agenda any longer? Some commentators have argued that it would be appropriate to define a new concept of security, which encompasses not only military security but also broader issues such as poverty reduction, environment conservation, energy and food security. It is argued that such an approach will: (a) contribute to a shift from state-centric security perception to individual security, and (b) will encourage countries to jointly address the issue of "Common Enemy". However, while such theorising remains good sounding, the experience of SAARC so far shows that this approach is not practical. Recall that the

Independent South Asian Commission for Poverty Alleviation (ISACPA) came up with a report titled "Meeting the Challenge" in 1992 and up to this date there has hardly been any follow up on the recommendations.

Instead, at the Eleventh SAARC Summit in Kathmandu, SAARC decided to have a reconstituted Commission to once again look at the poverty situation in South Asia. Furthermore, as the GEP Report stated the SAARC Food Security Reserve has never been utilised despite the need for urgent food imports by member states. From these examples it is clear that until the main state-centric security problem is solved no other alternative conceptualisation of security issues is going to be of much use. Security cooperation in the region is inconceivable in the absence of mutual trust between the two old South Asian adversaries - India and Pakistan. A US delegation called Kashmir the "most dangerous nuclear flashpoint in the world today".

The cold war nuclear confrontation was between two stable superpowers that were secure, not given to volatility, with back channels for communications. They also shared a great degree of rationality because deep down their philosophical paradigms and world outlook had common roots. The two cold war rivalries did not have an ancient history, no civilisation burden of partition, and no old scores to settle. They never shared the same landmass or the same borders and never fought a land war. Indo-Pak antagonism has an atavistic dimension due to its historical and civilisation roots. Thus, the relations between the two are far more 'envenomed' than that of the two super powers.

The event of September 11th has added a new dimension for Indo-Pak relations. Pakistan has been forced to the forefront of the war against the Taliban regime in Afghanistan, and the Al Quaeda movement. As the Afghan war radicalise Islamic communities worldwide how will the hard-line Hindus react to the rise of Islamic fundamentalism? The small countries in the SAARC are living under this sub- continental volcano. Can they be further burdened with this problem? Optimists such as Das have argued that enormous scope exists for mutually beneficial cooperation between India and Pakistan. The question here is not the scope and good intentions of the civil society in both countries but deeply embedded political divisions, which ultimately decide on cooperation.

Given the problems of military and economic asymmetry, perceptions of the SAARC by the two major countries in South Asia, and the dangerous security situation, regional cooperation in the SAARC is faced with a major political problem. In such an environment economic cooperation becomes difficult, as it cannot stand on its own. But as the ensuing section shows, even if economic cooperation stands on its own, it has its own problems.

Many studies have looked at regional integration in South Asia to determine potential economic gains. Srinivasan using a gravity model concluded that, at the time, most of the pre-conditions needed to enhance the probability of a successful FTA were not present in South Asia. South Asia would be better off liberalizing unilaterally and trying to tie up with an established group such as NAFTA or the European Union. One may have some reservations about the first conclusion in regard to the degree of unilateral liberalisation, but at least the second conclusion is strongly supported by the existing trading patterns of the region.

Srinivasan et al also found that removing all tariffs in South Asia will lead to a 3 per cent of GDP increase of trade for India, 59 percent of GDP increase for Nepal and in-between for other countries. A 50 per cent reduction in tariffs would increase trade by about 1 per cent of GDP for India and 9 per cent of GDP for Nepal. However, these estimates have been challenged by Karmacharya where he argues that the theoretical foundation of the gravity model estimated by Srinivasan appears to be weak because the model does not capture the major determinants of inter-and intra-industry trade.

RIS (Research and Information Systems for the Non-Aligned and Other Developing Countries) also states that from preferential trading in the region it will be the small countries that would gain more. Weerakoon and Wijayasiri after making a comprehensive survey of the existing studies conclude: "...the empirical results appear to be mixed and offer different interpretations of the cost and benefits (of both trade and welfare) that South Asia may experience at deeper level of economic integration. While some studies appear to suggest that the smaller countries will benefit, this is found not to be the case in other studies". The point made here is that there is no consensus that small countries would gain more from preferential trading than the larger nations.

The perceived gain is an issue that needs to be addressed in the context of economic cooperation. And this can be done using an appropriate regulatory framework. It was argued elsewhere that the issue of asymmetry in South Asia could be to some extent accommodated by a clearly defined negative (or reserved) list, differentiated ROO, and the implementation of the Gujral doctrine in India. But work in the area of a regulatory framework for the functioning of an FTA - SAFTA Treaty - is still on-going and is expected by end 2002.

The other argument that is put forward in favour of moving to a FTA is the cost of non-cooperation. RIS, for instance, has estimated that the cost of non-cooperation amounts to US $ 266 million for Sri Lanka on account of Sri Lanka's imports from outside the region despite the fact that those items were available in the South Asian region, in particular, India. In fact, it is this realisation that led Sri Lanka to go into the Indo-Lanka Bilateral Free Trade Agreement ILBFTA). So far, there have been only limited gains from the three rounds of SAPTA and Weerakoon and Wijayasiri show that the gains for Sri Lanka have been insignificant.

SAPTA dialogues have been completely unproductive due to various differences among countries that emerge from time to time. Should so much of finance and time of the officials be spent for meetings/negotiations when the gains are limited? It took more than one year for Sri Lanka and India to agree on the negative list after the ILBFTA was signed. In multiplying this process to include all seven SAARC countries, the task for agreeing on a negative list is going to be an extremely cumbersome exercise. Then there are questions such as will the negative list come before or after the SAFTA agreement is signed? These are crucial questions that cannot be brushed aside in any dialogue on the cost of non-cooperation in the region under the SAARC umbrella.

The cost of non-cooperation is in any case not a significant issue because the tariff and non-tariff barriers of South Asian nations are gradually coming down under WTO regulations and IMF/World bank led liberalisation programmes. So the gains of liberal trading are in any case on the way. Some have even argued that there is a large amount of illegal trade between South Asian countries and the intra-regional trade will be boosted by the illegal trade coming into the formal net via SAFTA. There are doubts whether all the illegal trade will come into the formal net with SAFTA coming into operation. Leaving this fact aside, by a PTA what we expect is new trade or trade creation, not intra-regional trade getting a boost from an existing component of trade coming into the formal net. So the crucial question is trade creation via SAFTA. There are a number of doubts on this area too. Despite the evidence received from the Latin American experience, why SAARC followed the slow product-by-product approach in all three Rounds of SAPTA negotiations remains very much questionable. Was it deliberately done for the purpose of confidence building? This is unlikely.

Countries can appear very generous simply on the basis of the number of concessions offered with hardly any trade coverage. This precisely happens to be the case with all three SAPTA Rounds. Weerakoon and Wijayasiri show the irrelevance of much of the goods for which concessions have been offered to stimulate trading, and goes on to show that the percentage of imports into Sri Lanka falling into SAPTA concessions has declined marginally over the 1997-1999 period. Why are bilateral agreements and other arrangements spreading in South Asia? Pakistan has so far not extended MFN status to India. A SAFTA cannot become a realistic proposition until bilateral issues are addressed. The non-existence of MFN status to India means that Pakistan is in effect constrained from granting tariff concessions to other member countries of SAARC due to the fact that those same concessions have to be offered to India as well....

Pakistan, for example, was reluctant to grant concessions on tea to Sri Lanka under SAPTA negotiations since the same concessions would have to be extended to India. As a result, Sri Lanka and Pakistan are in the process of negotiating their own bilateral free trade agreement. "Clearly the key explanatory factor is the slow progress of SAPTA and the political problems. In figure 1 we can see the current pattern of regional cooperation. There have hardly been similar trends in other regional groupings. Subregional cooperation in ASEAN was based on the concepts of "natural economic territories/zones", "transnational economic zones", "transborder economic neighbourhood", and "geoeconomic development zones" which are nothing but sectoral cooperation arrangements with limited objectives to achieve and did not involve preferential tariffs.

Proponents of such tariff-based subregional groupings in South Asia argue that they will eventually be building blocks for the SAFTA, but this argument does not hold much water. First, a country like Sri Lanka enthusiastically supported SAFTA to gain access to the large Indian market and perhaps to gain access to the Pakistan market for particular products. Now the former has been achieved and the latter is almost about to become a reality. Given this fact, Sri Lanka's enthusiasm for SAFTA has tapered away. It is likely to be the case with other South Asian nations that sign bilateral free trade agreements (FTA) with India and Pakistan. Second, how

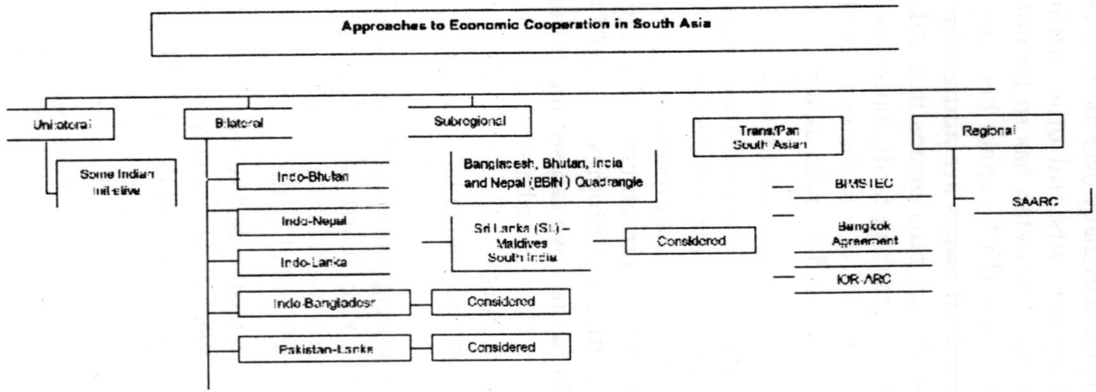

Figure 1. Current pattern of regional cooperation

are bilateral agreements going to be integrated to SAFTA negotiations? If they are to be integrated then they will have to be the starting points for negotiations. If not they will exist as parallel trade agreements, generating a "spaghetti bowl" phenomenon and lead to confusion among traders and investors.

Regionalism (especially economic cooperation) was seen as a means of facing the challenges of globalisation in the early 1990s and the argument was that South Asia was lagging far behind other regions and that the region has to leap frog. It was on this thinking that, in the Male Summit of SAARC in 1997, the SAFTA timetable was expedited for 2001. The EPG Report, however, stated that this accelerated timetable was unrealistic in the background of the nuclear explosions in the subcontinent in 1998 and the problems of the SAARC least developed countries, and extended it to 2008. Taking stock of the overall situation the EPG went on to state: "that the next phase of evolution of SAARC should be one of consolidation and concentration on the one hand, and new major thrusts' on the other.

Instead of further expanding SAARC scooperation horizontally, activities already undertaken should be consolidated and there should be a concentration of effort in areas that have greater potential of making a visible impact on the life of the common man in the region" (37-38). Time and again it has been said that the SAARC institutional framework is inadequate for promoting rapid regional economic cooperation. Here again, the point needs to be made that there are already a number of institutions that contributes to enhance cooperation in the region. For economic cooperation too, a number of institutions are in place or either emerging. But the existing institutions have failed to deliver.

The GEP suggests the streamlining of existing institutional structures and rationalising Technical Committees under the Integrated Programme of Action (IPA). As the EPG suggests steps that are taken should make a visible impact on the common people, if not the demand for institutions suggested by the EPG [(a) Common Investment Area, (b) South Asia Development Bank, and so on] will emerge only when economic cooperation is at a higher level and the civil society in SAARC has tasted the benefits of economic cooperation under the SAARC umbrella, not before that. The problem with SAARC is that there is a tendency to push aside the major problem and go in for ambitious projects. Leap frogging is not going to be easy for SAARC.

In ASEAN, the role of Japan in stimulating economic cooperation is well known. There are a number of external agencies and countries that are interested in supporting cooperation in South Asia such as Japan, EU, Germany (Friedrich Ebert Stiftung), etc. But they too have taken a cautious approach realizing the limitation of the role that they can play given the current major problem of the SAARC, i.e., Indo-Pakistan relations. It has been argued by some commentators that if economic cooperation takes off quickly in SAARC, the political issues could be sidelined and could lay the foundation for solving them. This argument is not really valid in South Asia although it was to some extent valid for ASEAN.

Critics have pointed out that SARRC is very much 'summit centred', that the nitty gritties need to await the approval of the highest body in the absence of which, every pre-determined agenda comes to an untimely halt. For example, the 4Round of SAPTA negotiations and the drafting of the SAFTA Treaty have been stalled for more than three years now. Muni, for instance, has argued that SAARC "cannot therefore remain as an Association of governments and needs to be pulled-out from the hallways of foreign office". But is this realistic? Which regional association worked outside the state framework and achieved results? There are number of channels outside the state where regional cooperation in South Asia is discussed. A study was conducted on the existing non-governmental dialogues in South Asia and what contribution they are making to promote regional cooperation. The study found that there are more than 40 dialogue channels in South Asia and about 12 outside South Asia.

Regular interactions among groups of scholars, experts, retired diplomats and military officials have been going on between India and Pakistan for the last 10 years. The report argues that most non-official dialogues are at an early stage of development, and points out the obstacles for these dialogues producing concrete results. These include:

1. the prevailing atmosphere of mistrust in the region, especially between India and Pakistan, not only between government officials but also among civil society organisations,
2. geopolitical asymmetry of the region,
3. political fragility in South Asia which makes it difficult for governments to take the initiative on issues where opposition parties can exploit,
4. dialogue organisers often not conducting sufficient preparatory research and consultation or post-dialogue follow-up activities.

Rarely have they found ways to communicate their results effectively to the broader public. The challenge in South Asia is to overcome these and find new ways to cooperate. But what is this new way? Behera et al broadly categorise seven methods of conducting dialogue, which include "track two", 'track three' and so on. But what can the outcome of these be? This is particularly pertinent in the context of the outcome of a prominent Track II activity, i. e., the Citizens Commission of South Asia that was headed by the former Prime Minister of India, Inder Kumar Gujral. The high-standing Commission met in Kathmandu in December 2000 and prepared a statement for reviving the SAARC process to all Heads of States. The outcome of it was far from satisfactory. If this was the fate of a high profile Track II activity what could we expect from other tracks?

The South Asian People's Summit which could be categorised as a Track III activity commenced in December 2000 in Colombo and had its second summit in Kathmandu in early January 2002. What was the outcome of this summit - nothing but high sounding statements and declarations to the effect that people's rights have to be safeguarded and so on. It is pertinent to pose the question whether statements and declarations of the SAARC official process (Track I) have had any impact. The Convention on Suppression of Terrorism, Narcotic Drugs and Psychotropic Substances has had no impact on controlling terrorism or drug trafficking through regional cooperation in South Asia.

Some of the countries have still not even enacted enabling legislation to give effect to these conventions. When high sounding declarations of the SAARC official process have had no impact how could Track III have an impact? SAARC's Confidence Building Measures (CBMs) at whatever level - Nuclear CBMs, Non-Nuclear Military CBMs or Economic CBMs - are all very vulnerable to Indo-Pakistani relations, and this has been the experience so far in SAARC. Track II and Track III have hardly been significant in making a major impact at the official level. SAARC civil society has not found a device to insulate itself from the unending political problems of the region.

Bibliography

Mahbub ul Haq, Human Development Centre, Human Development in South Asia 2001, Oxford University Press, Oxford, 2002.

Maskay, Nephil Matangi, "South Asian Monetary Integration in Light of the Optimum Currency Area, Criteria," South *Asia Economic Journal,* 2 (2), 2001.

Mattli, Walter, *The Logic of Regional Integration: Europe and Beyond,* Cambridge University Press, Cambridge, 2000.

Millet, Kate, Sexual Politics. London, 1972.

Mies, Maria, *Indian Women and Patriarchy.* New Delhi: Kali for Women, 1980.

M.S.S. Pandian, "Jayalalitha: 'Desire' and Political Legitimation", Seminar 401, January 1993, pp. 31-34.

Mukerji, I.N., 'The Report of the SAARC Group of Eminent Persons', *South Asia Economic Journal,* Vol.2, No. 2, 2001.

Mukherji, I.N, *South Asian Preferential Trading Arrangement: Assessing Trade Flows in the First Round of Trade Negotiations,* Friedrich Naumann Stiftung, New Delhi, 1996.

Mumtaz, Khawar, "Political Participation: Women in National Legislatures in Pakistan". In Shaheed, Farida, Sohail Akbar Warraich, Cassandra Balchin and Aisha Gazdar. Ed. Shaping Women's Lives: Laws, Practices and Strategies in Pakistan, 1989.

Muni, S.D., "Regionalism Beyond the Regions: South Asia Outside SAARC" in Gonsalves, E. and N. Jetly (eds.), *The*

Dynamics of South Asia: Regional Cooperation and SAARC, Sage, New Delhi, 1999.

Plage, Policy Leadership and Advocacy for Gender Equality. Dhaka: Ministry of Women and Children Affairs, Government of Bangladesh, 1999.

Rahaman, Z and A. Kamal, "Accountable Administration and Sustainable Democracy in R. Sobhan". Ed. *The Decade of Stagnation*. Dhaka: UPL, 1991.

Winer, Myson and Dilara Chowdhury, "Women's Participation in the Formal Structure and Decision Making Bodies in Bangladesh". Dhaka: Women for Women, 1995.

Index